Notes from a Low Singer

Michael Langdon with Richard Fawkes

Notes from a Low Singer

 Julia MacRae

A DIVISION OF FRANKLIN WATTS

First published in 1982 by
Julia MacRae Books,
a division of Franklin Watts
8 Cork Street, London W1X 2HA
and 387 Park Avenue South, New York, N.Y. 10016

Typeset by Computape (Pickering) Ltd
Printed and bound in Great Britain at
The Camelot Press Ltd, Southampton

British Library Cataloguing in Publication Data

Langdon, Michael
Notes from a low singer.
1. Langdon, Michael   2. Singers – Biography
I. Title   II. Fawkes, Richard
782. 1'092'4   ML420.L/

UK ISBN 0-86203-106-0
US edition – ISBN: 0-531-09877-x

Contents

List of Illustrations

15. The same production almost ten years later, with Derek Hammond-Stroud as Faninal, Gwynneth Price as the duenna and Edith Mathis as Sophie. This was to be my last appearance as Ochs at Covent Garden. (*Donald Southern*)
16. As Don Basilio in *The Barber of Seville*, with Fernando Corena as Dr Bartolo, Covent Garden, 1969. (*Donald Southern*)
17. As Baron Zeta in the 1981 Chicago Lyric production of *The Merry Widow* – a post-retirement appearance. With Alan Wilder as Kromow and Victoria Vergara as Valencienne.
18. (*and on front of jacket*) Baron Ochs. (*Mike Evans*)
19. As Pistol in the Zeffirelli/Giulini production of *Falstaff*, Covent Garden, 1961. (*Houston Rogers*)
20. As Osmin, *Entführung*, Aix-en-Provence, 1962. Luigi Alva as Belmonte. (*Serge Lido*)

(between pages 168 and 169)
21. On stage at Covent Garden during a Friends of Covent Garden Christmas Evening, 1972. (*Anthony Crickmay*)
22. Gazing over the Danube at Budapest during my engagement at the State Opera in 1964.
23. The cast of *The Magic Flute* at the Budapest State Opera, 1964. I was Sarastro, György Melis (front) sang Papageno.
24. Celebrating the birth of Solti's daughter in a Berlin restaurant while on tour with the Covent Garden company in 1970. Also at the table are Donald McIntyre and Ava June. (*Ludwig Binder*)
25. Members of the cast of Strauss's *The Silent Woman*, Covent Garden, 1961. Left to right, David Ward, me, Joseph Ward, David Kelly, Ronald Lewis.
26. Meeting the Queen Mother after a gala performance of *Die Fledermaus* in which I played Colonel Frank. Sir John Tooley watches. This was to be my final appearance at Covent Garden before my retirement from singing. (*Donald Southern*)
27. With Sir Geraint Evans at a Savoy luncheon given in his honour by the Friends of Covent Garden to celebrate his 25th anniversary with the company, 14 February 1973. (*Donald Southern*)
28. The cartoon by Coia which Scottish Opera presented to me to mark my retirement, 4 January 1979. Also in the picture, left to right, Sir Alexander Gibson, Sir Patrick Thomas (the then Chairman of Scottish Opera) and Peter Ebert. (*Scottish Opera/Lewis Segal*)
29. Vera with the girls, Christine (left) and Diane (right).
30. Outside Buckingham Palace with (l to r) Diane, Vera and Christine, after receiving my CBE in 1973. (*Herald Photography*)

Acknowledgements

I would like to take this opportunity to thank my many friends and professional colleagues over the years without whom I would not have had a story to tell, especially those of them who have helped to refresh my memory or put me right on what actually took place.

For their help in checking dates and performance details I would like to thank Francesca Franchi of Covent Garden Archives, Shelagh Nelson and Muriel Pointon of Welsh National Opera, Richard Telfer of Scottish Opera, Helen O'Neill of Glyndebourne Festival Opera, and Harold Rosenthal, editor of *Opera* magazine.

Six other people must be mentioned here: Richard Fawkes, whose untiring research, expert advice and practical help in the writing of this book have proved so invaluable; Graham Garton, who first introduced us; Deanne Edwards, who typed the final manuscript twice after the first one had been drowned in coffee; Paul Hirschman, for his help with the proofs; Claire Lister; and last, but by no means least, Julia MacRae, whose advice, encouragement and constant enthusiasm for this book have made working on it such a great pleasure.

FOR VERA

Chapter 1 First Notes

'Mr. Langdon, isn't it?' the producer asked. 'You know the Revolution Scene, don't you? I want you to be a cripple. Can you crawl on, using perhaps your left elbow and your right knee?' With that, the producer, Peter Brook, left me and turned his attention to another member of the Company. We were on stage at Covent Garden rehearsing the revival of the controversial production of *Boris Godunov* with which he had opened his reign as the Royal Opera's Director of Productions some four months earlier, and I and four other new choristers were being fitted in.

If you have ever tried to crawl on your left elbow and your right knee, you will know how difficult it is, but I tried, how I tried. I began to crawl slowly across the stage, past the stamping feet of the other choristers, with the dust blowing up into my eyes and throat. By the time I reached the centre of the stage, Brook had disappeared and I had no idea what I was supposed to do next. Standing on a rock, however, looking very regal and singing, 'Death to Boris!' was a contralto lady. She'll tell me what to do, I thought, and so I tugged at her skirt. She turned round and promptly hit me on the head, very hard, with a big stick. That was my first experience of opera.

The year was 1948 and, at 27, I had just become a member of the Covent Garden chorus. It was no more than a job as far as I was concerned, a way to pay the rent and support my wife and baby daughter. I had no ambition to be an opera singer. And yet that crawl was to be the start of a career that was to keep me at Covent Garden for the next thirty-two years, and take me to many of the great opera houses of the world.

So what was I doing crawling around in *Boris*? To explain that means going back to the beginning.

I was born in Wolverhampton on the 12th November 1920. My father, who kept a public house called 'The Traveller's Rest', already had six children – four girls and two boys – by a previous marriage. My mother was his second wife and I was their first and only child. If I came rather late into my father's life, I came extremely late into my mother's,

11

for she was just short of her fortieth birthday when I was born.

My father never saw me, nor, indeed, any of his children, for he was blind. When he was fourteen during a bout of horseplay with his elder brother, a pitchfork had entered one eye, infection had set in and the eye had had to be removed. I doubt whether even today's opthalmic specialists could have saved it, but this happened in 1880, when doctors still used leeches. Worse was to follow, for his remaining eye had also been affected by the infection and he began to lose the sight of that one, too. By the time he was twenty the lights had gone out for him forever. Perhaps that is not strictly true, for in his mid-thirties, something monstrous took place. My sister Ida, who was then a very small child, was sitting in the kitchen with him when he suddenly called out to her to keep still. She froze in surprise while my father looked fixedly in her direction. After a moment he turned his head away, got up and left the room. For the first time since attaining manhood, so he told my mother many years later, he wept bitterly because of his blindness, for his sight had returned suddenly for some five or six seconds, and then, just as suddenly, gone away.

Despite his disability my father succeeded in carving out a very successful business career. Apart from being the landlord of 'The Traveller's Rest' – as a tenant, buying and selling for his own profit, not as a salaried manager – he kept pigs in a yard across the road from the pub, and cows and horses on a few acres of land he owned on the edge of the town. He also bought a number of small houses in the street opposite the pub, and let them out to augment what was in those days a very healthy income. In what was a very working-class district he was known to everyone as Squire, or The Guv'nor.

Even more remarkable was the fact that he surveyed his own property and judged his own animals before buying them. Although I never saw him weigh up the value of a house, I heard many descriptions of him pacing out rooms, reaching for the ceiling with his stick and using his considerable weight to test the strength of the floors and joists. As far as I know, he rarely, if ever, made a bad buy.

I did, however, see him buying cattle. I went with him to Penkridge Cattle Market, near Stafford, on the day he selected six heifers to start what he intended would become a farm for me to take over when I was old enough. He handed me his stick, climbed over the fence into the pen, and shouldered his way into the middle of a mass of lowing cattle. He went to a beast, felt it, pressed it and patted it, and then, if he was satisfied with its condition, called out for it to be set aside. And so he selected the six he wanted. Such was his prowess that many other prospective buyers would ask his advice before closing a deal.

It was probably because of his heightened sense of hearing that my father loved music so much, and music, in an amateur sense, was an important part of our upbringing. As soon as I was old enough, he insisted that I should learn to play the piano. My tuition began when I was seven, by which time my father had retired from the pub to a house in the country some six miles from Wolverhampton.

I went to a local teacher, a Mrs. Till, for weekly lessons and my father would sit in the room with me while I went through my scales over and over again. Although I resented this enforced study – like any small boy I wanted to be out playing football – I have lost count of the number of times since that I have blessed every moment I spent at that piano. Although I never became an accomplished pianist, I did learn to read music and to play straightforward accompaniments.

As a young boy, however, I rarely sang. I didn't have a particularly good voice, and although I became a treble in the local church choir when I was seven or eight, I only lasted a couple of Sundays: a friend and I were spotted by the organist in his mirror, doing a jig in time to a hymn, and were unceremoniously kicked out.

It was my mother's brother, Uncle Ernest, who first introduced me to the sound of some of the great voices of the day. He was fanatically keen on opera and possessed a fine collection of old 78 records. My cousins, Doris and Marjorie, also had a collection that included Gilbert and Sullivan, grand opera and popular songs, and between them, they gave me the opportunity to listen to such artists as Gigli, Heddle Nash, Richard Crooks, Lawrence Tibbett, Norman Allin, and, of course, Caruso. Somehow lady singers didn't interest me – not at that time anyway! Much as I enjoyed listening to those records, my own interest in performing did not start until I was sixteen and my voice broke.

By that time I had left school and was employed as a junior clerk at the Wolverhampton and District Permanent Building Society. I still remember the chill horror that swept through me after my mother had taken me for my interviews and I had been told to report for my first day's work the following Monday. 'You've got a job there for life,' she said, her face beaming, 'and a pension at sixty-five'. I was just fourteen and the prospect seemed both daunting and endless. However, I began work at the appointed hour. My duties consisted of being the general run-around, delivering the local letters by hand, cycling to the directors' residences to get cheques signed, and running the post book.

I hated it, but there was little else I could do and I had to stick at it. My only escape was on the football field and at the local cinema, to which I went twice a week.

My voice at that time was quite high-pitched. One irate customer had actually phoned the office to complain that I had been rude to him, and threatened that he would 'get that girl the sack'. Then one day, soon after my fifteenth birthday, I was in the strong room with a friend from a solicitor's office, filing deeds, when, without warning, my voice dropped from boy soprano to bass. It immediately returned to treble again until a few days later when I was playing football. I was on the wing and called for the ball. The game stopped dead. No one could believe that the bass voice they had heard had actually come from me. Half the fun of the rest of that game was in waiting to hear me call for the ball. My voice had finally broken, not, as so often happens, sliding through the octaves, but descending straight to a basso profundo.

Among my cousins' record collection were several songs by Paul Robeson and I suddenly found I could sing along with him. I became fascinated by Negro spirituals and without telling anyone, I went out and bought the music for them. I soon found that none of them were printed in Robeson's key and I had to transpose them all down a third or fourth. Both my cousin Marjorie and my sister Edith were extremely good pianists, and often accompanied me in these spirituals. I gradually widened my repertoire to take in the popular songs that people like Peter Dawson, Norman Allin and Bob Easton were singing – 'The Floral Dance' was always a great favourite. Of course everybody said that I was magnificent, but then families tend to say that about one of their own and I never once had any thought of becoming a professional.

I was, however, far from happy at the Building Society. My way out came in 1940. For six months after the start of the Second World War, I became increasingly restless, feeling that I ought to be doing my bit for King and Country. Finally I decided I must join up. I was nineteen and didn't tell my mother what I planned for I knew she would do everything in her power to prevent me.

Lunchtime the following day found me on my way to the local Army Recruiting Office. It was closed. On my way back down the stairs, I passed an RAF Warrant Officer in uniform.

'Want to join up?' he asked me. I nodded, still too disappointed to speak at finding my plans to defeat Hitler thwarted.

'Forget that bloody mob up there,' he went on. 'RAF's the thing.' By 2.30, I had signed on the dotted line and was a member of the Royal Air

Force. My service career followed a similar pattern to that being experienced by thousands of other young men at that time: Blackpool for basic training, followed by a posting to an airfield, in my case the De Havilland airfield at Hatfield and then Stradishall in Suffolk, and then a transfer to Fighter Squadron 136. My twenty-first birthday found me on board the ship 'Capetown Castle', sailing out of Liverpool, bound for – we knew not where, though the rumour was that we were going to Rhodesia. That voyage was to change my life, for it was on board the 'Capetown Castle' that the idea of singing for a living first entered my head.

We had sailed from Liverpool out into the Atlantic and then down the west coast of Africa, and were anchored outside Freetown harbour. It was a sweltering hot night, the moon was shining, and everyone was very restless. An officer came round asking if anybody could do anything – tell a few jokes, play the mouth-organ, do impressions – for an impromptu concert he was organising to keep the men entertained. As I had occasionally sung some spirituals and ballads for my mates below decks, I was volunteered.

When my turn finally came, I stepped very nervously onto the raised portion of the deck that was being used as the stage, to find myself facing six or seven hundred men; and I had only ever sung to a handful of people before. I had decided to sing two songs and the fact that there was no piano or accompaniment of any sort made me even more nervous. I had had no training at all and not having perfect pitch, I had to take a chance that the note I began with would be the right one. Everything went perfectly. Somehow I managed to get the right note and the lack of accompaniment seemed only to enhance the mood of the song. I had chosen as my first piece 'Water Boy', and the dark, hot night, completely still, gave it an air of authenticity I have never managed to recapture since.

As I sang my last note there was a moment's silence, and then a thunderous burst of cheering and applause from the assembled company. I felt as though I was standing on air. The applause began to die away as they settled down for my second song, and then a remarkable thing happened. From a sister ship anchored some hundred or more yards away came the sound of further applause and cries of 'More! More!' The still night and the silence on board my own ship while I had been singing, had allowed my voice to be carried across the reflective water so that they could hear me as well as if they, too, had been on the 'Capetown Castle'. I was in a state of complete exultation and followed up 'Water Boy' with two more songs before bowing my way off and going down to my bunk. I was completely drained but filled with a joy I can still recall even now without any effort. I don't think, in all honesty, that I have ever, not even in my greatest triumphs on the operatic stage, experienced that same thrill again. That night was very special and as I lay on my bunk, trying to work out what had happened to me, I think I knew, for the first time, that I wanted to be a singer.

The morning after that wonderful experience we set sail, making our way further south. A few days later we received the news that the Japanese had bombed Pearl Harbour and that America had entered the war. Wherever our original destination may have been, we were, within a few hours, heading for Rangoon. We arrived there in January 1942, just in time to join the British retreat from Burma. We were driven back up the Arakan coast through Akyab and over the Indian border to Chittagong. I was to be in India and Burma for the best part of four years, and suffered the usual hardships and dangers. Like 90% of servicemen in that part of the world I contracted malaria, and wasted away to just over 140 lbs., a ridiculous weight for a man my size. It is the good times that I remember best, and one time in particular. We were in Secunderabad for rest and re-equipment and were entertained by a visiting concert party. A magnificent tenor took part in the Miserere Scene from *Il Trovatore*. We all roared our appreciation, but I never managed to meet him, for like all artists he was whisked away to the Officers' Mess immediately after the concert. I had to wait almost six years before getting the chance to congratulate him, and it was in the Chorus Room at the Royal Opera House, Covent Garden, where we were both busily rehearsing the chorus parts for the new season of 1948/49. His name was Charles Craig!

That concert gave me the idea of applying for concert party work myself, and I duly put in an application and was sent on a two day train journey to give an audition for an elderly colonel. I went straight from the station to the audition and sang one of my favourite songs, 'The Floral Dance'. I think I sang it rather well. The colonel listened politely and then said that he thought I was all right for taking part in barrack-room sing-songs, but not for appearing on a stage. 'Anybody can sing that sort of thing,' he remarked. And so I returned to the station and caught the next train back to Secunderabad. Altogether it took me four days of solid travelling to sing that one song, and be turned down.

I eventually sailed for home in August 1945. As I walked up the ship's gangplank, I experienced a long moment of nostalgia for a part of the world in which I had spent nearly four years and for the friends I was leaving behind, but I was young, the dangers were past, and I was on my way home. Life seemed good.

The war may have been over but I was still in the RAF and had to wait my turn for demobilisation. After a few weeks leave, I was posted to Sutton Coldfield to fill in my time and managed to land myself a sinecure in charge of the airmen's mess. This meant that I could, within reason, obtain anything I wanted to eat, and after the deprivation of India and Burma, it was like being in heaven. It was not only the food that I found to my liking, for it was there that I met the girl who was to become my wife. We came face to face over the coffee urn one morning, and I was smitten! Her name was Vera Duffield, she was a sergeant in the WAAF, and she didn't seem very keen to date me when I finally plucked up the courage to ask. I didn't know what to do next. It was then that I was asked to take part in a camp concert. In the early days of a singer's career one inevitably tries to mould one's voice and style on that of another singer. I've found few singers who have not been influenced by some famous singer of the day, and, even now, at the National Opera Studio, I can tell when certain young singers have been listening to records of famous artists. At the time of this particular concert I had abandoned Paul Robeson and was into a Nelson Eddy stage. I sang 'At the Balalaika', 'Wanting You', and ''Neath the Southern Moon', to such effect that afterwards Sergeant Duffield agreed to come out with me!

Our romance was nearly over before it had begun, for almost immediately I was demobbed. Fortunately, however, Sutton Coldfield is not far from my home town of Wolverhampton and we were able to meet in Birmingham, a suitable half-way point. Even after Vera was also demobbed and had returned to her home in Norwich, we continued to meet with one or the other of us making the long journey to the other's home.

After demobilisation, I went back to my job at the building society. I was twenty-five and knew immediately that I couldn't stand it. The problem was not mine alone; it happened to thousands of us. We had gone away to war as boys and came back as men. We had lived in an unreal world which had changed our lives completely; we had travelled; and yet we were expected to go back to the humdrum jobs we had held before the war and continue as if nothing had happened. Very often, as in my case, we found ourselves being told what to do by men much younger than ourselves, not long out of school. I just couldn't take it. Besides, I still remembered that night in Freetown harbour and I was determined that somehow I was going to be a singer.

While I had been at Sutton Coldfield, a family friend had put me in touch with Joseph Yates, a singing teacher who lived in Walsall, and I had started taking weekly lessons with him. My plan at that time was to work in pantomime at Christmas, for there was always a spot for a straight singer playing the Baron, the Wicked Robber, an Island Chieftain, or whatever, and then try to get a summer season somewhere on the coast. I mentioned this to Joe Yates and he was horrified. 'It's much too precarious on the stage,' he told me. 'Forget it. You have a good voice and you can make a nice living doing part-time concert work for which you could be paid as much as three guineas a concert! Forget the stage.' But I couldn't forget it.

Two months after I returned to the society, in November 1946, I received a call from Peter Marwood, the manager of the Grand Theatre, Wolverhampton, asking me if I would like to sing in a quartet he was arranging for that year's pantomime, *Dick Whittington*. He had heard about me from my Aunt Rose, who ran the Circle Bar in the theatre and was possibly the only member of the family who believed I might have a future on the stage. She was not only a great encouragement to me, she also badgered Marwood into giving me a chance. I promptly threw up my job with the building society and signed on as a member of 'The Lyrical Four'.

We must have looked faintly ridiculous. I am over six feet tall and looked fairly impressive, but my companions consisted of a small, thin man, a very fat one and one of medium size. We were dressed in togas, slashed across one shoulder. I wasn't too concerned about how we looked. It was enough for me that I was actually appearing on a stage. Naturally, I sent to Norwich for Vera to come and witness what I knew would be a remarkable and impressive debut. Our big number was called 'Men of steel, as tough as steel', and we did our best to look the part, flexing our muscles and causing our right pectorals to ride up above the slanted line of togas. Vera, who was watching all this from the back of the Dress Circle, suddenly became aware of muffled laughter. She turned to see Peter Marwood and a group of his friends. 'What did I tell you?' Marwood was choking. 'This is the funniest part of the whole bloody show. I call them the Titty Men.'

I was at last appearing on the stage as a professional singer, and being paid ten pounds a week, double the amount I had been earning at the

18

building society. I had, I felt, arrived. One other important thing happened to me during my engagement at the Grand, Wolverhampton, and that was that I changed my name. I had been born Frank Birtles and had every intention of staying that way. It was Peter Marwood who told me I ought to change. 'People will call you Beetles, Bottles, Battles, everything but Birtles,' he said. At that very moment he happened to look out of his office window and saw a bread van going past. On its side was emblazoned 'Langdon's Bread.' 'That's it,' said Marwood. 'Langdon. That has a nice ring to it. Now what about a first name? How about Michael? Michael Langdon sounds right.' And so Michael Langdon I became.

I stayed with *Dick Whittington* for twelve weeks until the pantomime season came to an end and was then out of work. I managed to pick up the occasional concert, but I was hardly setting the world on fire. Just to complicate matters, Vera and I had decided to get married. I had proposed to her while I was still working at the building society. We were sitting in a pub at the foot of the Lickey Hills. I had intended climbing to the top to plight my troth in a more suitably romantic manner, but, being August, the rain was falling and the wind was howling, so we sat in the pub instead. We shared our table with a man who insisted on telling us how he had won the war single-handedly, and, while he was talking, I romantically slipped the ring to Vera under the table. It was, I suppose, an impetuous thing to do. I didn't have any money, I wanted to give up a secure job and become a singer (though I didn't then know how I was going to do it), and our entire courtship could not have added up to more than a couple of months. But at that time we didn't consider the future. The war had taught us to live for the present and not to worry about what might or might not happen the following week.

I did not, at first, tell my mother about our engagement. Although I was twenty-five, I was still her little boy and she had not then realised that I would one day be leaving home. By the time I did break the news to her, my job in the pantomime did not reassure her as to my future prospects and she felt it was no time to be thinking of embarking upon marriage with a girl I hardly knew. Wedding bells seemed a long way off.

Then came an incident that was to change everything. I had caught a cold and my Aunt Rose, who lived with us, suggested that I should put some glycerine into my nose to ease the soreness. I had never tried that before but did as I was told. The result was agony! I felt as though my

19

head was on fire. My mother and aunt began to giggle and the more I writhed in pain, the more hysterical they became. I struggled up from my foetal position on the settee. 'That does it', I roared. 'I'm leaving home! I'm getting married.' I went straight to the Post Office and sent a telegram to Vera arranging the wedding day.

We were married on 19th June 1947 and went to Worthing for our honeymoon. We planned to live in London where I would pursue my career as a singer. While we were in Worthing we received a postcard from an ex-WAAF friend of Vera who lived in London and had assured us that she could arrange accommodation for us there, to say that she hadn't been able to find anywhere. Vera and I decided we must go ahead as arranged, that something would turn up, and so, our honeymoon over, we caught the train to London. We arrived at Victoria and stood on the platform, our worldly possessions in two wooden cases, with nowhere to go and no job. Vera turned to me. 'What do we do now?' she asked. And I realised, for the first time, that my responsibilities as a married man had commenced.

As a temporary measure, we booked into a small hotel near Euston Square while I looked around for somewhere to live. I had managed to save a little of my pantomime pay but the thing I remember most about that hotel was lying on the bed, staring at the cornice work, trying to work out just how much I had left and how long it would be before I would have to admit defeat and either return home to Wolverhampton or find alternative employment. To ease our financial situation a little, Vera went back to Norwich to stay with her mother, while I wrote letter after letter asking for auditions.

Eventually I managed to find a place to live in South Lambeth Road, run by a man with numerous children. Vera came down to join me and we had a room on the top floor. It was an incredible place. Mealtimes in the basement were like a scene from a Dickens novel. There weren't enough chairs for all the children and they would stand round the table eating their food. I never did manage to discover exactly what our landlord did for a living. Strange people would appear at night, leave packets and parcels, and then disappear, and the next day he would ask me if I wanted a new pair of shoes, a new coat, or whatever. (I bought a beautiful music case from him for £2 which I used until quite recently.)

For a while I did no singing at all. I had to give up my lessons since I could no longer afford them, and although I wrote off to everybody I could think of for an audition, I was offered nothing. In order to keep us, Vera had had to go out to work and had taken a job at Bon Marche in Brixton. Then, I *did* manage to land a job, in the chorus of a new touring musical called *Cyrano de Bergerac*; at least, that was the title it started out with. The show was directed by a man called, I think, Lynn Seeley, who had also written the book, the lyrics and the music, and, with his wife, was going to star in it. One day during rehearsals, a gentleman in a dark business suit suddenly appeared, and after an earnest, whispered discussion with Seeley, left. Seeley then announced to the company that since Alexander Korda was planning to make a film of *Cyrano de Bergerac*, we were unable to put on a stage show of that name. Since the posters had already been printed with a picture of a man with a long nose, what he proposed doing was calling the new show *Son of Cyrano* and keeping it exactly the same except that it would be about a character who looked exactly like his father. Not surprisingly, Korda took exception to this, too, and for some reason which none of us could fathom, the show suddenly became *Gardenia Lady*. There was never any further mention of Cyrano de Bergerac, even though his picture continued to adorn the posters.

Gardenia Lady opened in Leeds. The climax of the production was a scene in which Seeley was supposed to be killed by a Bowie knife thrown from one of the boxes. A professional named Kit Carson whose act consisted of throwing knives and flaming axes at his wife standing against a board, had been engaged especially for the scene. Early on in the dress rehearsal I saw him standing backstage and he was trembling with nerves. 'I don't like this at all, mate,' he said. 'I've been trained to *miss.*' When the moment came, Seeley swept on stage, a cork pad on his back hidden beneath a flowing cloak, and turned his back to the box where Carson was. Carson threw, and instead of the clunk of a knife hitting cork, there was a horrible squelching sound as it sank, up to the hilt, into Seeley's backside. I was standing next to him and couldn't believe it. He turned white, pulled the knife out and said faintly, 'Is there a doctor in the house?' Up until then, there had been hardly any tickets sold for the production but as soon as the news of Seeley's misfortune got out, the house was packed with people wanting to see if he would die during the performance. He was pumped full of drugs and staggered on, his eyes glazed. He managed to get through it and received a massive ovation. Bookings remained good for the rest of the week and it was only when he began to recover that they started to drop. It really was an awful show and as soon as the audiences realised that he wasn't going to drop dead on the stage, they lost interest.

From Leeds we headed north as far as Aberdeen, then turned south and came back to Coventry where I resigned. The show still had two more weeks to run but it had gone beyond a joke. In Aberdeen the wrong sets had been put up; songs were being given to people regardless of whether they could sing or not, or whether the songs had any relevance; and people were putting in their own lines, making every performance a complete shambles. I could see no point in continuing and so returned to Vera and to our room on the third floor in the South Lambeth Road. I was never more pleased to get home.

One good thing did come out of *Gardenia Lady*: I met another singer called Jack Curzon. Jack and I decided that we would get together a variety act to play the music halls. He also introduced me to his aunt who lived in a house in Swinton Street, off the Gray's Inn Road, and had two rooms spare. Vera and I moved there in November 1947. Almost immediately I was contacted by the management that had put on my first pantomime, *Dick Whittington*, and asked if I could appear in the production of *Babes in the Wood* they were opening at the Alexandra Theatre in Birmingham. So, no sooner had Vera and I unpacked in our new rooms in Swinton Street than we were off to the Midlands. Vera was by then pregnant and we had no wish to be parted again so quickly, so she came with me, taking a part-time job at the Odeon Cinema in New Street while I went to the theatre to rehearse.

I was again engaged as a member of a quartet, only this time I was also given the job of understudying the Wicked Robber. It was a lovely part, acting as straight man to a comedian named Eddie Connor, who had just gone solo after being one half of the double act, Connor and Drake. Some understudies spend all their time waiting to go on. Indeed, there are stories of people who have spent two years understudying in a West End run and have never got on once. That didn't happen to me. It was as if I had a guardian angel who always made sure I wasn't forgotten, for I always went on in every role I understudied. Later in my career it got to be such a habit that people would ask me not to understudy them because they knew something would happen to them.

The first time this occurred was in Birmingham. After *Babes in the Wood* had been running six weeks, Colin Lawrence, the Wicked Robber, was tragically killed in a car crash. Derek Salberg, the owner of the theatre, sent for me.

'We want you to take over the role,' he said. I was delighted, thanked him and turned to leave. 'Just a minute,' he went on, 'we haven't discussed terms. Will £25 a week do?' I was then on £11 a week and he knew that I would have done it, even without a raise, but he had been paying Colin Lawrence £25 a week so that's what he paid me. Derek Salberg was that kind of man.

For a time everything seemed wonderful. I was enjoying my first experience of being a soloist and was earning what was then a very good salary. With a baby due in a few months, the extra money came as a godsend. But pantomimes, of course, don't run for ever and when the season finished I was once more 'resting'. Vera and I returned to London and I set about trying to find work. While in Birmingham I had made my first radio broadcast, for the BBC Midland Region, and I had high hopes that this would lead to a lot more broadcasting, but, strangely, I heard nothing. I wrote asking when I might next be considered. Vera brought me the reply one morning when I was still in bed. 'I hope you're not going to be too disappointed,' she said as she handed me the letter. 'Dear Sir,' it began, 'I regret to say that as a result of your broadcast on the 1st January 1948, I cannot recommend your further inclusion in our broadcast programmes.'

I was, naturally, very disappointed for the only work I had to look forward to was a summer concert in Pimm's Park, Edmonton, appearing with Frank Sandford's Palm Court Orchestra. It was not much but it *was* a future engagement, something to make me feel I was still 'in the business'. On the afternoon of the concert, I put on my full evening dress, wrapped myself in an overcoat and scarf so that I wouldn't appear too conspicuous, and set out by bus for Edmonton. It was a lovely day and my fellow travellers, dressed in light summer clothes, stared at this unhappy, muffled figure who was growing more and more uncomfortable in the heat. But I didn't dare disrobe. Just before I reached Edmonton, there was a torrential downpour. I arrived in Pimm's Park to find it empty except for the orchestra and the organiser. I offered to come back on another day but the organiser insisted, so that he could pay me, that I sing at least one song. And so I sang 'Asleep in the Deep' to row after row of empty deckchairs, awash with rainwater, with the orchestra accompanying me. It was the only time in my career that I have ever sung to an audience of nil. There was not even a man out walking his dog to stop and listen. As I finished there was desultory applause from a few nurses leaning out of the windows of a distant hospital; that was all.

Although I was still hoping to land a lucrative engagement in a summer season somewhere, I had to face up to the fact that I was not successful enough as a singer to support myself, let alone my wife and the baby that was almost due. I had to get a job of some sort and eventually I took one as a clerk in an office in Great Queen Street, just off Covent Garden. I was immediately reminded of the building society and I could hear my mother talking about security and a pension at sixty-five. I felt the same chill of horror that I had had when I was fourteen and I knew that no matter how great my responsibilities as a family man, no matter how regular my salary was, I could never so easily abandon my ambition to be a singer. One lunchtime I went for a walk and suddenly found myself in Bow Street looking up at the façade of the Royal Opera House. I remembered something that someone had told me in Birmingham, that the newly-formed Covent Garden Opera Company was looking for choristers. I had never considered singing in opera before, but it occurred to me as I stood in the street outside, that if I could get in, it would be a job in music and it would tide me over until I could land that plum engagement in a summer season. And anything would be preferable to working in an office. I took a deep breath, went in through the stage door and asked for an audition.

Chapter 2 The Understudy Who Always Went On

I was lucky with my timing. They were about to hold new auditions and I was asked to report back in two days time with my audition piece. When the time came, I slipped away from the office and hurried round to the Opera House. The auditions were taking place in the Crush Bar and I joined a long queue of other young hopefuls waiting to do their bit. When my turn came, I sang Sarastro's aria, 'O Isis und Osiris', from *The Magic Flute*. Douglas Robinson, the Chorus Master, who was holding the audition, thanked me and said they would let me know the results later. Two weeks passed and then I received a letter asking me to go back for a further audition. This time there was to be no creeping away from the office and I had to ask for time off to attend.

The auditions again took place in the Crush Bar, but as well as Douglas Robinson and members of the music staff, Karl Rankl, the Musical Director, was also present. I again sang Sarastro's aria from *The Magic Flute*. When I had finished, Douglas Robinson beckoned me over to where he and Rankl were sitting. 'I would very much like him in the chorus,' he said to Rankl. Rankl considered for what seemed an age and then nodded. He turned to me. 'You realise,' he said, 'that you are either a chorister or a principal? There can be no changing over.' I didn't know what he was talking about, but I said I understood. 'Very well,' he said to Robinson. And I was in, a member of the chorus at the Royal Opera House.

I promptly gave in my notice at the office and spent what remained of the summer learning the music of the operas scheduled for the forthcoming season. I also began to take singing lessons again. Being a naturally deep bass I had never had any problem with the bottom of my register but I was still having difficulties with the top notes: a top E Flat being about my limit. I was introduced to Samuel Worthington, who agreed to take me on. Sam had sung supporting roles at Covent Garden before the war and had also sung in Italy under an Italian name. His knowledge of vocal technique was formidable and he soon gave me the confidence, and the know-how, to sing higher than I had ever sung before. He told me to practise Ramphis's cry of 'Folgore, morte', from the Consecration Scene in *Aida*, in order to get used to singing the high F, and I used to do this *ad nauseam* in the basement of our lodgings in Swinton Street. I had no idea just how far my voice carried until one evening, when I was returning home, I rounded the corner into our street and came across a crowd leaving the pub opposite. As soon as they spotted me, one of them said, in a very loud voice, 'Oh, look! There's bloody old folker immortae!' Apparently it had taken them days to find out where this strange noise had been coming from.

Our daughter Christine was born on 29th July 1948, and one month later I reported to Covent Garden ready to begin life as a chorister. Our immediate task was to learn, with all possible speed, the chorus parts of the ten productions that were already in the repertoire and were due to be staged that season, and to make a start on new productions of *Aida* and *La Bohème*. Special attention was paid to the revival of *Boris Godunov* (in which Paolo Silveri sang Boris), for it is a very difficult work for a largely untried chorus, and the idea was to feed the chorus newcomers into the company in this opera. This was the famous Peter Brook production in which I was asked to crawl across the stage and got hit on the head! After the careful, painstaking work of the summer, both on my own and with Sam Worthington, the actual rehearsals and production seemed to happen very quickly, and almost before I had realised it, the curtain was going up on my first ever appearance on the stage of Covent Garden. Although it was October, I became very hot dressed up in heavy furs, and during the Coronation Scene I was standing in front of a chorister who was tolling the bell when something went wrong and the rope began to saw up and down the back of my neck. Later, when Boris entered, he threw coins at the crowd and that night I received a face full of pennies. It was not a very comfortable debut.

Although singing in the chorus was, to begin with, just a job, it didn't take long before I was beginning to enjoy it. There was a very special feeling about Covent Garden in those early days. The chorus was made up largely of untried amateurs, many of them from Wales, and a tremendous amount of hard work went into those first productions. The rebirth of Covent Garden as an opera house (it had, of course, been used as a dance hall during the war) had taken place only a year before I joined, and everyone, from the top to the bottom, was fired with a deep sense of enthusiasm which it was impossible to ignore. I was almost immediately caught up by it and it quickly changed from being just a fill-in job to being something I was desperate to do. Above all, there was a tremendous amount of fun in what we were doing. And the musical side, although we may have been raw, was of an extremely high standard. One has only to think of just a few of my fellow choristers at that time: Charles Craig, Kenneth Macdonald, Ronald Lewis, and then, a little later, Patricia Johnson, Josephine Veasey and Iris Kells. The overall sound made by that chorus in those early days was probably the best I have ever heard anywhere.

Many people made invaluable contributions to the formation of the Covent Garden company but, in my opinion, one man stands head-and-shoulders above the rest: Karl Rankl, the Musical Director. Rankl was an Austrian with fluffy grey hair, a diffident manner, and rimless glasses which he would lift up to peer at you. If you had to cast a typical Austrian professor in a film you would have chosen Rankl. As a conductor he may not have been the most imaginative – he certainly wasn't one to demand attention from the audience – but he had few peers as a musician and his great achievement was to set the company on the road. I do not think (and I know I am not alone in this) that Covent Garden would have got away to such a flying start under any other person. Some people now say that many of those early performances would be unacceptable today but I don't think, for one moment, that this is true. Some of the run-of-the-mill productions, put in to build up the repertoire, may have been less than perfect, but there were productions and performances that would stand comparison with any seen today. The early *Salome* performances with Welitsch, Shacklock and Lechleitner, for instance, and those of *Boris* in which Christoff made his debut, would grace any stage in the world. And how about the first *Bohèmes*, with Schwarzkopf, Welitsch, Schock, Silveri and the young Geraint Evans singing his first Schaunard? *Tristan* with Flagstad, Svanholm, Schoeffler, Shacklock and Norman Walker, or *The Marriage of Figaro* when Geraint Evans first sang Figaro with Schwarzkopf as Susanna? No, the overall standard during Rankl's regime at the Garden was always good, and occasionally very good. As the 'complete' musical director he was obviously far from perfect. A musical director has to be something of an ambassador as well as a conductor; he has to go to the right receptions and please the right people. And it was clear that Rankl, a very private person who kept himself to himself, did not please some of the people who mattered. But no matter what his shortcomings may have been on the social side, it was Rankl who established the musical side of the company, it was Rankl who breathed life into it and created a living organism that wasn't

27

going to wither. His personal enthusiasm for the project and for the company permeated the whole structure of Covent Garden. He imposed upon himself an exhausting schedule, rehearsing not only his orchestra and principal singers, but frequently cramming in extra sessions with the chorus, for it must be remembered that 80% of them were untried professionally, and Rankl was determined that style should be allied to sound. In my opinion it is quite disgraceful that when he finally departed as Musical Director in 1951, he was never invited back to conduct even one guest performance.

My love of opera developed soon after becoming a chorister. I found myself on the same stage as some of the greatest singers of the time and it wasn't long before I knew that I wanted to be out there singing solo myself. The turning point was probably the first Ring cycle I was in, with Hotter, Flagstad, Ernster, and Svanholm. Hearing those glorious voices at close quarters used to send a shiver down my spine and I knew that I would not be happy to remain a chorister for ever. Singing in a chorus can be invaluable, if you use it properly. You see the very best people in action, you get to understand what opera is all about, but it's important that you don't stay too long. Being surrounded by other people all the time produces a block of constant sound which blankets what you are doing yourself; you don't hear yourself and you can do bad things with the voice without realising it, forcing it out of shape. But, for two or three years at the beginning of a career, it can be a marvellous experience, provided the time is spent watching and learning. If you are receptive you can learn not only the things that are effective, but also, on occasions, the things to avoid! The danger time comes after about three years. If you stay in the chorus beyond that, you tend to remain a chorister for the rest of your career.

I had decided fairly quickly that I didn't want to stay as a chorister. To be working at close quarters with such famous singers made me realise not just that I wanted to be out there with them, but that they were also human beings, and, most of them, extremely nice people. It really was a revelation to discover that the voices I had heard about or heard on record, actually *belonged* to someone, to someone I could speak to, have a cup of tea with or watch scratch their nose. I remember walking to Covent Garden one bitterly cold day to rehearse the Ring, with Eric Thornton, a fellow chorister, when a taxi pulled alongside us. The window wound down and Kirsten Flagstad put her head out.

'Aren't you two boys in the chorus?' she asked. And she told us to jump in and gave us a lift.

28

On another occasion, the last act of *Tristan und Isolde* was being rehearsed on the main stage. The large dock doors by which the scenery is moved in and out of the theatre were wide open. Flagstad, who was singing Isolde, had been held up and the rehearsal had started without her. Just as she got out of her taxi outside, she heard the cue for her off-stage singing coming from the stage, and from where she stood she turned and sang, with resonant emotion, 'Tristan! Geliebte!' Everything in the fruit market stopped as, from inside the building came the reply from Set Svanholm: 'Wie, hör' ich das Licht!' The scene carried on without a break as Flagstad walked through the scene dock and onto the stage exactly on cue. It was a magical moment that makes my skin prickle whenever I think about it.

Events such as these made me realise that these marvellous people were real, that they were ordinary people who had been gifted with magnificent voices, and I began to think that maybe it could be me. I became so preoccupied with the idea of being a principal that I didn't always concentrate on my work as a chorister as much as I should have done. During one performance of *Götterdämmerung*, I was a torch bearer in the Immolation Scene, standing two or three yards from Flagstad. She was in superb voice and I was utterly entranced. Halfway through I heard somebody whispering and I thought, 'How can they do that while Madame Flagstad is singing?' Suddenly I realised that the whispering was directed at *me*. I had completely forgotten where I was and was standing with my torch pointing at the ground, the "flames" directed downwards, completely ruining the effect. The whispering was from a furious stage manager telling me to hold it up again.

Again, during a performance of *Aida*, I became so carried away with the idea of singing Ramphis that when, in the last act, he sings 'None can his doom' (we sang it in English then), a phrase which is immediately echoed by the chorus, I actually sang the solo line with David Franklin who was singing the role. Not only that, but I was so convinced in my mind that I was Ramphis, that when the line was repeated, I again sang it. As we came off, Douglas Robinson grabbed me and told me to go straight up to David Franklin's dressing room and apologise. I climbed up to Room 7, a room I was later to occupy, and knocked on the door. Franklin wanted to know who was there and when I told him, asked what 'Michael Langdon from the chorus' wanted. Through the still-closed door I made my apologies for singing his line with him. There was a pause, during which I half expected him to fling open the door and confront me. Instead, I heard him say, 'Well, if I was singing it too, I wouldn't have heard you, would I? Good night.'

It was only after I had made up my mind that I must try to become a principal that Rankl's remark at my audition came back to me. He had said that I could be either a chorister or a principal, and, as everyone kept reminding me, I was a chorister. I knew, however, that no matter what odds were stacked against me, I *had* to become a principal or leave. I still hadn't got the top of my voice in order and there were few roles I could actually have done well at that time, but one which did lie comfortably within my range was that of the King in *Aida*. I had already studied it and sung it through to myself. Once again the incredible luck that has followed my career took over. Marian Nowakowski, who was singing the King, couldn't make a rehearsal and, for some reason I now forget, his official understudy wasn't there either. After some time, Warwick Braithwaite, the conductor, irked by the lack of a voice for the part, suddenly said, 'My God! Can't anybody sing it? Isn't there someone in the chorus who can do it?' I didn't want to seem too pushy or over-confident, but when no one else spoke, I said that if I could have a score, I would try sight-reading it! I was given a score, which I didn't actually need, and, of course, sang the part note-perfect. When the rehearsal was over, Braithwaite called me over, thanked me, and said that he was going to speak to Rankl about getting me a principal's audition.

Braithwaite was as good as his word. He spoke to Rankl, but Rankl still held to his view that there was a division between chorister and principal which could not be bridged; and nothing came of it. This rejection-without-trial made me all the more determined. I was now in my second season as a chorister. Although my first contract had been just for one year, as soon as I had been invited to re-sign for a second, I had agreed without hesitation. All thoughts of working at Covent Garden just as a temporary measure while awaiting the big offer of a pantomime or a summer season to sing 'At the Balalaika' had vanished. I was obsessed by opera.

One of the productions we performed during my second year, the 1949–50 season, was Sir Arthur Bliss's *The Olympians*, with a libretto by J. B. Priestley. In it was a lovely bass part of the Nightwatchman. It was Peter Gellhorn, Rankl's assistant, who suggested to me that I should learn the role. He warned me that I would not be an official understudy, but that if anything should happen, he would expect me to be ready to go on. In those early days part of each season was spent on tour. We were in Manchester, due to perform *The Olympians*, when

30

Langdon's guardian angel fluttered his or her wings again. Rhydderch Davies, who was singing the Nightwatchman, contracted bronchitis. Peter pulled me on one side and told me I was to go on. He also told me that he did not intend telling Rankl, who was conducting. So, I went on as the Nightwatchman. I was sitting on a darkened stage, warming my hands over a brazier, when my first line, 'All is well', came. Rankl, who had no idea it wasn't Rhydderch sitting there, gave me my cue and I began to sing. He immediately peered over the top of his spectacles, trying to make out who it was, while continuing to beat time. At the end of the performance we took our curtain calls and although I looked at Rankl, he said nothing. I knew I had sung well, even though it was a small role, and I felt a great sense of anti-climax. The following day I went to the theatre to prepare for a performance of *Aida* (back in the chorus, of course) and there was a note waiting for me at the stage door. It was from Rankl. 'I feel,' he had written, 'that you have nothing to lose by giving a principal's audition.' At last, Rankl, the one great stumbling block to my career as a soloist, had seen the light! And I gave the worst audition it would be possible to give. It took place on the Covent Garden stage and several well-known basses were also audition-ing that day. I was over-awed by the company I was in, and each preceding singer seemed to me to have such a magnificent voice that by the time I was due to give my piece, I was so nervous and full of self-doubt that I was unable to sing properly. Afterwards, I heard nothing and I knew that my dream of becoming a principal was over. I was so depressed that I decided, there and then, to give up singing. I had no idea what I would do instead but anything had to be better than suffering the agonies I was going through. I went to Douglas Robinson and told him that when my contract expired at the end of the season, I would be leaving.

'You can't do that,' he said.

'Why not?' I replied. 'You heard my audition.'

'Yes – and you weren't very good, were you?' he said.

Suddenly I realised that he had not been too displeased by my failure for he wanted me to remain in the chorus. He didn't make me change my mind and I was still determined to quit; but I did decide to go and talk to Rankl personally. I didn't need to be told that I had given a bad audition – I knew that – but I also knew that it is the performance that matters and I had been all right in performance. Like all choristers, I had been allowed to take time off to sing in concerts outside the Garden, and I had been taken on by an agent in Wales who got me quite a lot of work with famous Welsh Male Voice choirs. I had also made my debut as Mephistopheles in *Faust* for the Welsh National Opera, singing at a schools' matinee in Swansea. At the end, when we took our curtain calls, I, as the villain, had been cheered while the 'goodies' – Faust, Valentin, Marguerite and Siebel – had been hissed, and I knew that good reports of me had gone back to Covent Garden. On the only occasion I had sung solo for Rankl, in *The Olympians* (a part I was kept on in for Birmingham and Edinburgh) I also knew that I had acquitted myself well. Perhaps, I thought, Rankl could help me decide where my future lay.

The meeting took place in Room A, which was then the Musical Director's room. Peter Gellhorn and Norman Feasey, the chief repetiteur, were also there.

'What's all this nonsense about leaving the chorus?' Rankl began.

I explained that I wanted to be a principal and that if I couldn't be one, I had no wish to stay.

'Why are you so desperate to become a principal?' Rankl asked. I tried to explain. Finally, he interrupted me. 'Have you anything to go to?' I shook my head while he looked away and polished his glasses. 'Then what *have* you got?' he asked. 'Ambition,' I replied. I had obviously·struck a chord for he smiled and asked me my age. I told him: 28.

'You're a baby,' he murmured, 'a baby.'

'I may be from your standpoint,' I said indignantly, 'but not from mine.'

'I'll tell you what I'll do,' he went on. 'Mr. Robinson is very keen that you stay in the chorus. . . .' I started to speak but he stopped me. 'Stay in the chorus, sign on for another year, and I will give you all the performances of the King in *Aida* for next season. You will be paid an extra £5 for each performance.'

With ten performances of *Aida* scheduled for the season, I would be given an excellent opportunity to show what I could do, and I had no hesitation in agreeing, particularly since he also mentioned that I might be able to cover for other parts. And so I signed on again as a chorister for 1950–51. The season turned out even better than I could have imagined for not only did I sing the King in *Aida*, but I was also asked to understudy Varlaam in *Boris*, Sparafucile in *Rigoletto* and Zuniga in *Carmen*, and – Langdon's guardian angel – I got on in every one. Ten days before I was due to make my official debut as a soloist, Howell Glynn fell ill and I had to take over as Varlaam. Later in the

32

season, Ernest Davies dislocated a shoulder and I had to sing Zuniga, while Nowakowski simply put the wrong date in his diary for *Rigoletto* and I had to go on as Sparafucile. This last performance was by far the most difficult because it happened before I had finished learning the role. We were on tour in Liverpool and I had gone to the theatre late one Saturday afternoon to see if I had won the football sweep. I wasn't performing that night and wouldn't normally have been there. While I was at the stage door, I met John Gardner from the music staff. He grabbed me by the arm. 'Come on,' he said, 'you're on tonight, doing Sparafucile.'

'But,' I protested, 'I don't know it.'

'You know the first duet, don't you? We'll learn the last act after you've done the first duet.'

I rushed into the theatre and prepared for the performance with just twenty minutes to go before curtain up. It transpired that Nowakowski was still at home in London thinking his performance was the following night. The first act duet, with Tom Williams as Rigoletto, went well apart from a mistake we made in the text. We were still singing in English at that time and Tom, instead of singing 'How do you lure them?' sang 'How do you kill them?' I found I was replying, 'With my sister.' However, we got through it all right and then, while the second act was on, I learnt the last scene with John Gardner. Thanks to John's hard work and the enormous help I received from Emanuel Young, the conductor, I managed to get through it with, as far as I can recall, only one error. I was also helped by the fact that I had learned the scene at such short notice. One hour after the performance I had completely forgotten it, a phenomenon that all opera singers will recognise.

Officially I was still a chorister but I found myself doing less and less chorus work. Although I had been signed originally only to do the King in *Aida* (making my debut with Joan Hammond singing the title role) and to understudy three other parts, I not only got on in them all but was also cast as the Gaoler in *Tosca*, as Ferrando in *Il Trovatore*, as Titurel in *Parsifal* (with Flagstad and Weber), as Narumov in *The Queen of Spades* (under Erich Kleiber), as The Minister in *Fidelio* (with Flagstad as Leonore and Patzak as Florestan), as Sleep in *The Fairy Queen* and as Apollyon in the premiere of Vaughan Williams' *The Pilgrim's Progress*. I did not find Apollyon much of a challenge since my part was all on one note. I was, however, asked to wear a huge rubber head which made it impossible for me to sing, and eventually we compromised with a fellow chorister appearing on stage while I sang through a megaphone from the side. I still treasure one review which says that I made a brief but impressive appearance!

Altogether during that season I made forty-four appearances as a soloist and in between, returned to singing in the chorus. Pay day for choristers at that time was far from discreet. We had to line up outside the company manager's office, exactly as if we were in the services, and wait for our names to be called out, along with the amount due to us, so that everyone knew exactly what everyone else was getting. As a general rule no one got more than about £13. When it was my turn one pay day, because I had been receiving a performance fee for each solo role on top of my basic salary, and because my back-pay had accumulated, the amount due to me was £74. No one could believe it.

I had had my first real taste of what it was like to be a principal and I had enjoyed it. More than that, I had proved myself both to Rankl and to those members of the music staff who shared his view that once a chorister, always a chorister. The result was inevitable: at the end of that season I resigned from the chorus and was re-engaged as a principal for the 1951–52 season. When I thanked David Webster for my new contract, he replied, with typical Websterian whimsy, 'I'm glad you're pleased. And, as for us, well, it's cheaper this way.'

Chapter 3 Rankl: Establishing The Garden

As if to prove Webster's point that I had been costing the company too much by being paid both as a chorister and as a soloist, I found myself, at the beginning of the new season, cast in the same performance of *Tosca* not just in the role of the Gaoler, a part I already knew, but also as Angelotti, the political prisoner. Two for the price of one!

I now realise, more than ever, just how much I owed my chance at principal roles to two men: to the vastly experienced Warwick Braithwaite and to Peter Gellhorn, neither of whom ceased in championing me to Rankl. Without them, I doubt whether I would have made my breakthrough when I did. Looking back over those years when I was both a chorister and a soloist, I am amazed to discover that, between them, Rankl, Braithwaite, Gellhorn and Reginald Goodall (the fourth member of Rankl's team) conducted more than ninety per cent of the performances. Two other young members of the music staff were given their first chance at this time: Emanuel Young with *Rigoletto* and Leonard Hancock with *The Pilgrim's Progress*; and there were the occasional guest conductors such as Erich Kleiber (who came in for performances of *Der Rosenkavalier*, *The Magic Flute*, *Tristan und Isolde*, *Rigoletto* and *The Queen of Spades*), Clemens Krauss (who gave four performances of *Tristan*), and the talented, tragic Constant Lambert from the Ballet Company (who conducted the first performances of *The Fairy Queen* and of *Turandot*). By the time I got to work with Lambert, on the 1951 revival of *The Fairy Queen*, he was already very ill. One day, during rehearsals, he asked for a glass of water but was shaking so much that before he could get it to his mouth, the glass had been emptied. He had already done wonders with the ballet company and was held in very high esteem, and although I had comparatively little to do with him (my role of Sleep being very straightforward and not requiring a great deal of his attention) I always found him marvellously sympathetic. His death was an enormous loss. And then there was Sir Thomas Beecham, who conducted *The Bohemian Girl* and *The Mastersingers*. But the main share of the work fell on Rankl, Braithwaite, Gellhorn and Goodall, and I am in no doubt that without the help of the other three, Rankl would not have been able to perform his miracle.

I seemed to work with Reginald Goodall much less during my early days as a chorister and principal than I did with the others, and it was only later, when I began to work on the Wagner roles with him in his studio high up in the Royal Opera House (christened, inevitably, Valhalla) that I got to know him well. Quite apart from benefiting from his tremendous knowledge of, and feeling for, the music of Wagner, I enjoyed many laughs over operatic life in general. He, too, possesses a keen sense of the ridiculous and the fact that he insisted on speaking in German for 90% of the time somehow made his comments on the inhabitants of the Opera House even funnier. He was always a very shy, private person. I once remember him refusing to take a solo call after a performance. The stage manager grabbed him by the shoulders to drag him on and was left holding an empty jacket while Reggie was off upstairs to get changed. It may even have been for that same performance that he had arrived at the Opera House without his dress suit and been forced to borrow one that had been left hanging in the conductors' dressing room. It was several sizes too large and when Reggie lifted his arms to conduct, all we could see were two inches of baton poking out from the end of his sleeve. Reggie is a typical example of an artist whose talent is recognised only late in his career, for it was not until he began to conduct Wagner for the Sadler's Wells Company (later the English National Opera) that many people realised what a unique talent had lain dormant at Covent Garden for so long.

I remember little about the producers of those first three years except, of course, for Peter Brook, who seemed to notice me, for not only did he pick me out to be a cripple in *Boris*, he also decided that I should lead the band in Act II of *La Bohème*. I remember, too, being taught the seamen's dance in *The Flying Dutchman* be Heinz Tietjen, who had been brought in especially from Germany to produce the opera, and the fantastic set and costumes designed by Salvador Dali for *Salome*. What a furore they caused! A stuffed hippopotamus was lowered from the flies at one point but so outraged people that it was later dispensed with. Poor Constance Shacklock was made to wear a head-dress so huge that if she turned quickly, she overbalanced. Above all, when I look back on that period, I remember the sheer hard work involved in putting on thirty-two productions, twenty-seven of which were to become part of the standard repertory, and the feeling of camaraderie which suffused the company, then, and indeed, for many years to come.

When it comes to personalities from that time, it is still the shy, diffident figure of Rankl who sticks most in my mind, and one moment especially towards the end of his reign as Musical Director. It was on the 25th July 1951, when the company was on tour in Liverpool and Kirsten Flagstad made her final appearance on any operatic stage in a Wagnerian role. The opera had been *Tristan und Isolde*, with Set Svanholm partnering her as Tristan, and after the final curtain David Webster came on stage to announce to an audience still in the clouds following her magnificent performance, that she had, indeed, made her decision to retire from the operatic stage and that they had been privileged to see her final performance. There were groans and shouts of 'No!' He immediately went on to inform them that although Flagstad was withdrawing from Wagner, Constance Shacklock, who had been singing Brangaene, was approaching her best and had that night given her fiftieth performance in the part. This brought renewed cheering. But my eyes were on the little grey-haired man standing in the stage line-up and politely clapping each announcement. I waited for Webster to tell them that this was Rankl's final season as Musical Director, that he would be leaving in a week's time, and to pay some sort of tribute, but he said nothing. Everyone bowed and made their final exits. I wanted to call out, 'What about Rankl?', but I lacked the courage. I was young and had my future to think of; I kept my mouth shut. We returned to London at the end of that week and I wrote to Rankl, thanking him for all the help he had given me and wishing him well in the future. He sent me a reply which I picked up from the stage door and took across the road to 'The Nag's Head' to read. 'My dear Mr. Langdon,' he had written, 'It is awfully kind of you to write to me like that. I am convinced that you, with your voice and musicality, will make a good career as an opera-singer. All my good wishes accompany you.' I finished reading, left my drink on the table and hurried back to the theatre to have a last word with him before he left for home, only to find that he had already departed. I never saw him again. On his final day as Musical Director he was conducting a concert in the provinces while I was on stage at Covent Garden making my debut as Sleep in *The Fairy Queen*. He was never invited back to the house, and, indeed, only returned to it once before his death in 1968 – as a member of the audience on the first night of *Moses and Aaron*, composed by his former teacher, Schoenberg.

No Musical Director was appointed to succeed Rankl and the 1951–52 season began with a succession of guest conductors. The first I worked with was Sir John Barbirolli, who conducted *Aida* in which I again sang the part of the King. Barbirolli was a Sir John Falstaff in miniature, a superb raconteur, with a fund of marvellous stories about his career and the personalities he'd worked with. I remember one occasion, after a concert performance of *Aida* in Newtown, Montgomeryshire, when the entire cast and Kenneth Loveland, the music critic, who was then also the Editor of the *South Wales Argus*, were regaled by one hilarious anecdote after another until three in the morning. In particular I remember his story of another performance of *Aida*, given in an English provincial theatre. The toilet for the lady principals in this theatre was right next to the stage, and there was a notice in it asking that the chain should not be pulled while the curtain was up. An Italian mezzo, who could not read English, had decided to use the toilet during the performance and when, on stage, the impassioned cry, 'Aida, where art thou now?' was heard, back came the sound of a flushing lavatory! Sir John was still in full flood, and still sipping brandies, when with aching sides, I was the first to depart for bed. The continuing noise, however, would not allow me to get to sleep and at about four o'clock, mindful of my long drive back to London later that morning, I was compelled to go downstairs in my pyjamas and point out that it really was time they also retired to bed.

Barbirolli was a superb musician but he did make one terrible mistake, at least as far as I was concerned. I happened to be walking through the Crush Bar at Covent Gardent one day when he was in there rehearsing the orchestra for the last act of *La Bohème*. He saw me, stopped the orchestra and called me across. 'Do you know this part?' he asked, pointing at Colline's music. I admitted that I had looked at it. 'Then just sing this bit, will you?' he went on, indicating the end of the famous Coat Song. He played the accompaniment for the end of the aria, then looked at me. I sang the next word, 'Schaunard', and waited. He continued to look at me, while I looked back at him. 'What are you waiting for?' he demanded. After that word, there is a chord before Colline begins to sing again. 'I'm waiting for the orchestral chord,' I replied. 'My God!' he exclaimed. 'A bloody musician. Gentlemen, we have a musician!' Apparently Inia te Wiata, who had been cast in the role, rarely waited for this particular chord. On the strength of that incident I was cast, on Barbirolli's insistence, in a role for which I was completely unsuitable. The Coat Song, which is, after all, Colline's showpiece, lies just a shade too high for me to handle in the way Puccini intended, and my fellow Bohemians knew I hated it. They would leave the stage, glancing at me with mock pity, while I remained to blast my way through it. I must have been the worst Colline ever to appear at Covent Garden for I was never asked to repeat the role, in spite of the note Barbirolli sent me after the first night. 'Bravo Langdon,' he wrote. 'You were magnificent.'

I came to know Barbirolli really well on the Covent Garden tour to Rhodesia in 1953, when the company was invited to take part in the Rhodes Centenary celebrations in Bulawayo. The full company of more than 200 musicians and stage staff took four productions – *Aida*, *La Bohème*, *Gloriana* (which Britten had written for the Coronation) and *The Marriage of Figaro* – and we opened at the impressively named Theatre Royal with *Aida* on 30th July. Hilde Zadek sang Aida, Shacklock was Amneris, James Johnston the Radames and Norman Walker, Ramphis; I was the King and the performance was conducted by Barbirolli. The reception was fantastic. In spite of its name the theatre was little more than a converted aircraft hangar. The week before a visiting drama company had played there and had had to partition off half the auditorium; because of its size, their voices wouldn't carry to the back. We had the partitioning removed and every available inch of space was occupied by one of the most enthusiastic audiences I have ever played to. It was the same for every performance.

As well as conducting *Aida* (sharing the performances with Emanuel Young) Barbirolli also took charge of *La Bohème*, in which I had not been asked to sing Colline! At the end of the opera, as Mimi dies, there is a pause before the final death chord. Barbirolli used to hold this pause for what seemed an eternity. Some distance from the theatre was a railway line and on the first night of *Bohème*, just as he reached this pause, there came the sound of a prairie whistle as a train hooted its way down the track. Barbirolli's effect was ruined and he never had the courage to hold that pause so long again. As the moment approached in subsequent performances, you could see the hairs on the back of his neck beginning to rise, his ear would incline towards the track, and Mimi was always compelled to die a little more quickly than he would ideally have wished!

Not only were the houses good throughout our six week stay in Bulawayo, we were also treated like royalty when off stage. We were constantly entertained, given picnics at which whole pigs were roasted, and taken on trips round the Wankie Game Reserve. Geraint Evans and

39

many of the cast of *Figaro* managed to get stuck there on the day they were due to sing and only just got back in time for the performance. We also organised company football and cricket teams to play local sides. Barbirolli would occasionally stand as umpire in these cricket matches and some of his l.b.w. decisions were distinctly strange. When questioned about them afterwards, he simply replied that he had 'never understood the bloody l.b.w. laws'. I sprained an ankle quite badly while playing football and had to hobble on in *Aida* with my foot encased in plaster, while James Johnston had his two front teeth knocked out during a cricket match and spent the rest of the day hunting for a dentist who could cap them so that he wouldn't have to sing 'Celeste Aida' that evening with a gap showing. In fact, our outside activities so interfered with our performing opera that David Webster felt compelled to put up a notice informing us that we were in Rhodesia to sing, not to injure ourselves while indulging in 'other pastimes'. The wonderful thing about that tour was that it was a real company tour; it was not a collection of principals brought together from around the world to sing under the name of Covent Garden. It was a chance to get to know one another properly, to form lasting friendships; and a company spirit was fostered which was reflected in the performances. In my experience the best performances are always given when all the principals happen to like one another.

Another guest conductor who came to Covent Garden during the 1951–52 season was Benjamin Britten, who took charge of the first performances of his new opera *Billy Budd*. With the exception of Billy, who was played by the American baritone Theodor Uppman, the entire production was cast from company singers and I took the role of Lieutenant Ratcliffe. I am, at heart, a blood-and-thunder man; I love big ensembles and great arias; and I have to admit that it took me time to get to know and love *Billy Budd*. I had already sung in *Peter Grimes*, as a chorister, and I knew that Britten was a brilliant man of the theatre, but I could find no immediate appeal in the music of *Budd*. In fact, none of Britten's works ever had the same instant appeal that I found in the operas of Verdi, Puccini or Wagner, for example. (Even when we first began rehearsals for *A Midsummer Night's Dream*, and even though Solti was conducting, I found it hard to be enthusiastic. It was only later that I came to recognise what a magnificent piece it is.) And so it was with *Billy Budd*. The more I worked on it and the more I performed it, the more I was able to see in it. The reason for this may partly have been that I had been hearing everything played on a piano

40

during rehearsal, and Ben's music sounds completely different when played by an orchestra. Partly, it may have been that he wrote for the theatrical effect. He knew exactly what would be happening on stage and his music both complemented and enhanced the action. It was only after the two had been slotted together, and the music had become a part of the broader pattern, that the whole picture became clear. It was like a jigsaw in which the individual pieces seem meaningless until they are placed in their correct relationship with the others. This was very much my individual reaction, for there was, during the rehearsals for *Budd*, a great sense of excitement in the company, a feeling of exhilaration that we were in on the birth of a masterpiece.

The inevitable difficulties presented themselves during rehearsals. There were what seemed like hundreds of little boys running around, always under foot. These were the 'powder monkeys', and when they weren't rushing about, they were being marched up and down endlessly. It all took a long time, particularly with the meticulous attention given to it by producer Basil Coleman, whose understanding of the opera helped to make it the great success it proved to be.

Undoubtedly the greatest help on the production came from being able to work with the composer. Although I am down on the cast list of *The Pilgrim's Progress* as having 'created' the role of Apollyon, I had done nothing but sing on one note while sitting in the wings, and, as far as I was concerned, it was on *Billy Budd* that I really worked first with a composer on creating a role. I learnt, for the first time, that the written note is not as sacrosanct as some musical purists would have us believe. Britten would adjust his tempo to accommodate the singer, he would suggest singing perhaps a little softer or a little louder than he had marked in the score, he would mould the part to suit the character and ability of the person playing it. If necessary, I am sure, he would even have transposed a sequence or written in different notes. What concerned him was not that we should recreate exactly what he had put down on the page but that we should give a 'performance'. (This was the same with Stravinsky as well. When I took part in a concert performance of *Oedipus Rex* at the Royal Festival Hall, with Stravinsky conducting, I remarked that he had adjusted many of his dynamic markings during rehearsal. 'Yes,' he replied, 'I've had time to think about it since I composed it.')

I did not find Britten particularly inspiring as a conductor. He knew exactly what he wanted and he could make his intentions very clear, but his performance was not the soul-shattering experience of doing, say,

Don Carlos for the first time with Giulini. He could flare up on occasions and use surprisingly direct language, but generally I would describe him as typically English. His great value to the production was the insight he brought to the score.

The year after *Billy Budd* opened at Covent Garden, we were invited to Paris to give two performances of it as part of a Festival of Twentieth Century Art. In the opera there are several disparaging remarks about the French – one line we sang was 'Don't like the French; don't like their hoppity-skippity ways' – and at least half the audience spoke English well enough to know exactly what was going on. During a quartet between Peter Pears as Captain Vere, and Geraint Evans, Bryan Drake and Hervey Alan as the officers, in which they were being particularly sarcastic about the French, I could hear, from where I was standing in the wings, a hiss beginning to run round the auditorium. It grew louder and louder, and the singers finished the quartet looking quite startled, as if they expected the stage to be rushed at any moment.

Although I sang the part of Lieutenant Ratcliffe in those early performances, it was as John Claggart, the Master-at-Arms, that I was to become best known. I had worked with Britten again on *Gloriana* and also appeared as a soloist with him in a concert at Torridge in Devon, but there was never any suggestion that I might be suitable for Claggart. I was then invited to take part in a concert at Rosehill for Miki Sekers, compèred by Lord Harewood. Edward Downes, who was accompanying and arranging the programme, suggested that I might like to include Claggart's aria. Afterwards, Lord Harewood said he hadn't realised how well the part lay for my voice; and he later went on to speak to Britten about me, as Claggart. So, on Britten's invitation, I sang the role when the opera was broadcast on radio, when it was televised, and when the Decca recording was made. And yet I never performed it on stage, even though Britten asked for me to be cast in the part. Quite why is still a mystery to me.

Gloriana had been written especially to celebrate the Queen's coronation and opened with a gala performance, at which both the Queen and Prince Philip were present, on the 8th June 1953. I sang the Recorder of Norwich and appeared in only one scene, during which I had to deliver a long speech of welcome to the visiting Queen Elizabeth I (played by Joan Cross). As an extra piece of 'business' I had arranged with producer Basil Coleman that I would roll up my scroll in the long flowing beard I was wearing, and then have surreptitiously to remove it without the Queen (Elizabeth I, of course) noticing. It got the desired

42

laugh. Afterwards the cast was presented to Queen Elizabeth and Prince Philip. When Prince Philip got to me, he asked if the business with the scroll had been intentional. I assured him it had. 'Are you sure?' he insisted. 'Positive,' I replied. He shook his head. 'Pity,' he said. 'You've just lost me ten shillings.'

Immediately after the première of *Billy Budd*, I embarked upon another twentieth century masterpiece, Alban Berg's *Wozzeck*. This was the opera's first production in Britain and was conducted by Erich Kleiber, a friend of the composer, who had taken charge of the 1925 world première in Berlin. I was cast as the First Journeyman and when I opened the score to see what sort of part it was, I was horrified. Its range went from the B Natural below bottom C, all the way up to a top A Natural – a range of almost three octaves (the natural bass range is two to two and a half octaves). I went immediately to the repetiteur and said that I couldn't possibly sing it. He told me not to take the score too literally, that I should just growl in the lower register and sing falsetto in the high parts. I did not know what he was talking about. I was still very inexperienced and to me opera meant singing the notes that had been written, *how* they had been written. I went away very puzzled and very unhappy, not knowing how I would be able to cope.

I discovered the answer when I went for my first piano call with Kleiber. He explained that the notes were only an indication of where the composer wished the voice to go, and that in order to perform it I had to practice the speech rhythms and then allow them to follow the shape of the music. 'I won't argue,' he said, 'if you don't get up to a top A, and when you have to go down to the bottom B, just let your voice sing down as low as you can until it stops.' The character I was playing had to deliver a drunken sermon and I began to half-recite, half-sing the words, as Kleiber had directed: 'And yet, if a wanderer, who is leaning on the stream of time . . .' The effect was startling. Without even trying my voice was going all over the register and I began to sound as if I was drunk. This was my first introduction to *Sprechgesang*, and to Kleiber. Although I had already sung under him in *The Queen of Spades*, I had had only a few lines to sing, and one of those, 'I trump it,' I managed to get wrong one night! In fact I had hardly met him. He was clearly pleased with my performance in *Wozzeck* for, apart from Christel Goltz, the German soprano who sang Marie, the production had been double-cast. Kleiber insisted, however, that I sing the First Journeyman in every performance. Many years later, when I was in Stuttgart for performances of *Der Rosenkavalier* conducted by Erich's son

Carlos, he told me that his father had often played a tape of me in *Wozzeck* as an example of how *Sprechgesang* should be performed!

Erich Kleiber was a marvellous man to work with. He was one of that handful of conductors who are able to give something on top of their musical ability, something which turns them from being merely good into great, who can inspire and generate an excitement which gives a performance a special edge. It was a talent possessed by such men as Kempe, Barbirolli and Beecham. Beecham could lose his place in the score and end up flapping his arms aimlessly until he managed to pick up the beat again. With most other conductors this would have killed a performance, but not with Beecham. Somehow the mere fact that he was there did it all. Of the present generation of conductors, Solti also possesses this indefinable quality, as does Giulini, whose great strength is his concentration and his ability to send a laser beam straight from the pit to an artist so that you respond almost without realising it. Carlos Kleiber, too, is capable of producing tremendously exciting performances, although I know, from my own experience, that he can sometimes be erratic in his direction of singers. Where Erich Kleiber scored for me was in his participation with what was happening on stage. He invariably reacted to everything that occurred, his face mirroring the various moods, from rage to sadness to laughter. A wonderful gift for any conductor to have.

Shortish, thick set, and with a round, cherubic face, Kleiber always reminded me of a Westernised Buddha. He was usually a very patient man but one thing roused him to anger: if a singer arrived at rehearsal badly prepared. Vocal shortcomings he would forgive, but not lack of preparation, and if this did occur he would be extremely scathing. Fortunately these occasions were rare for we all knew better than to appear at his rehearsals without knowing our parts, and most of the time he was in an impish mood. This could be seen in a long-running battle he had with Morris Smith, the Orchestral Manager. Morris's office was directly below the conductor's room and every time Kleiber passed his door, he would knock and continue on his way without pausing. On the way back he would do exactly the same thing. Morris never seemed to be able to catch him and grew steadily more annoyed. One day, when he knew Kleiber would be passing, he positioned himself behind the door and, as the inevitable knock came, threw it open and enquired respectfully whether the Maestro wished to speak to him. 'Oh, no,' Kleiber replied. 'I just saw the notice on your door which says "Please Knock" and so I knocked.' He paused. 'I always do,' he added.

Kleiber also knew exactly how to put his artists at their ease before a first night. He would make his way round everyone in the cast and tell them, 'Go on tonight and do not worry. All the mistakes tonight are mine. I have never yet conducted a musically perfect performance and I do not expect tonight to be the first. Remember, I have the score. If anything goes wrong, look at me, and it will all come right.' He would smile reassuringly. 'It always does.'

It was with a certain amount of trepidation, therefore, that I made my way to his room one afternoon after receiving a message that he wished to see me. He had returned to Covent Garden to conduct three further performances of *Wozzeck*, and although he had been kind enough to praise my work I could not be certain that I had not done something to incur his displeasure. I knocked on the door and waited for the high-pitched voice to bid me enter. I went in and waited. He suddenly smiled and waved me to an armchair. 'It's nothing bad I want to talk to you about, Langdon,' he said, seeing the expression on my face. 'Quite the contrary. I wanted to tell you that I've spoken with Them.' He pointed at the ceiling. 'I have told them that I think you have a fine talent and should be encouraged. There are certain roles I feel you should study. Continue with the Verdi bass roles, of course, and also Sarastro and Osmin. And, as you have a comic flair, look at Kecal in *The Bartered Bride*. Lastly you should think about Ochs von Lerchenau in *Der Rosenkavalier*. You will need a long period of study for this so the sooner you start, the better. Do the same as you did for *Wozzeck*: get the speech rhythms first, don't bother with the notes. Speech rhythms, speech rhythms. Do as much as you can and when I return I shall want to know what progress you've made.'

To gain the approbation of a famous and influential person is every young singer's dream, and I was being counselled by a man who was, and still is, considered to be one of the most illustrious conductors of the century. I was overwhelmed. I had only recently been made up to principal and here was Kleiber talking about my performing the major bass roles. At that moment I saw my name in large letters outside the great opera houses of the world. I don't remember the journey home that night for my head was still too full of plans for the future. And yet I failed to take Kleiber's advice. I did continue with the Verdi roles, I studied Sarastro and Osmin, and I even looked at Kecal, but I did not bother with Ochs von Lerchenau, the role that was eventually to introduce me to those foreign opera houses.

At about the same time, Sir John Barbirolli had suddenly said to me, after a performance on tour, 'You know, Langdon, you do a lot of things well but if you're going to get to the top in this business, you've got to *specialise*. As soon as you get the chance, specialise.' If only I had linked this advice with Kleiber's suggestion to look at Ochs – but I didn't. I had sung in the chorus in *Der Rosenkavalier* and had thought the part of Ochs to be rather dull. I had no wish to learn a role which was both extremely long and, in my view, boring. In any case that was not the direction in which I saw my career going. Although I had always enjoyed playing comedy, I did not see myself as a singer of comic roles. I wanted to be out there performing the 'pure' roles, the big impressive bass parts in Verdi, Mozart and Wagner.

I saw Kleiber privately only once more, in the summer of 1953, just before he left Covent Garden. After his last performance of *Wozzeck*, I went to wish him *bon voyage*. Mrs. Kleiber opened the door of his room and seemed reluctant to let me in even though I could hear Kleiber in the background telling her to. I saw the reason the moment I entered. Kleiber was standing in front of the mirror tying his tie but minus his trousers. I pretended not to notice as we shook hands. Before I had a chance to speak, he was saying, 'Don't forget, Langdon, with Ochs it's the speech rhythms. Speech rhythms all the time.' I waited for him to continue, but he held out his hand again and I realised that he had said all he wanted to say. We wished each other all the best and, feeling somewhat let down, I made my way down to the Stage Door.

Chapter 4 Keeping Good Company

I often felt guilty about not making a start on Ochs and used to tell myself that I really ought to have some of it ready to show Kleiber when he next returned to Covent Garden. But, after those 1953 performances of *Wozzeck*, he never came back. In spite of Webster's wish that he should, his terms were too high for a house that was still struggling to justify its existence. And then in January 1956 came the news of his sudden death at the age of 65. I was deeply saddened for I felt that there had been a rapport between us that would have been of incalculable benefit to me as a singer had he lived, and his loss to opera as a whole can never be measured. At the same time, I must admit that I felt a certain shame-faced relief that I would not have to explain why I had not begun studying Ochs. I have sometimes wondered what would have happened had he returned. My impression is that I would have studied and later performed Ochs under his direction, for he was a man who rarely took No as an answer. That, however, would almost certainly have meant singing the role in English (after the last war it was not done in German at Covent Garden until December 1959), and would I have had quite the same success with it that I did in 1960? I rather doubt it, for no foreign opera house is much interested in a British singer who only knows a role in English. It is, perhaps, useless to speculate on what might have happened, and in any case, in 1956 I was far too busy carving out a career for myself as a company member to worry about a role that did not interest me.

We were, at that time, still singing the majority of performances in English. Indeed, it was a house rule that no foreign opera should be given in its original language. There were exceptions. The Ring Cycle was given in German, and when Boris Christoff made his debut as Boris in 1951, two performances were given in Russian. Sometimes, too, last minute replacements had been allowed to sing their roles in the original while the rest of the company performed in English. Set Svanholm, for instance, sang Walther in *The Mastersingers* in German, and when I made my debut as Varlaam in *Boris Godunov* there were no less than three languages to be heard on stage: Ludwig Weber was singing Boris in German, the rest of us were singing in English, while some of the chorus, who had forgotten the words, sang in Welsh! Generally, however, artists visiting Covent Garden were expected to learn their roles in English. Even Kirsten Flagstad (for whom an exception was made with *Tristan*, which was given in German in her honour) had first sung Brünnhilde, with Hans Hotter as Wotan, in English, and such international artists as Schwarzkopf and Paolo Silveri had, in becoming company members, agreed to re-learn all their roles.

During those early seasons, the company was beginning to make strides towards international recognition. British artists like Constance Shacklock and Sylvia Fisher were starting to secure regular engagements abroad and it was gradually being realised that to be British did not mean you could not sing at the highest level. It was clearly ridiculous to expect British artists to have to learn their roles in two languages and for foreign artists to have to do the same just to accommodate us. If Covent Garden was going to be an international house in the true sense of the word, then operas had to be performed in their original language. This move didn't happen overnight and it took some years before it became the rule rather than the exception. Indeed, for some considerable time after much of the basic repertory had gone into the original, we would revert to performances in English if there were no foreign guests in the cast, a situation which tended to produce a great deal of confusion.

One of the earliest works to go into repertory in its original language was *Il Trovatore*, in which the eminent mezzo Ebe Stignani sang four performances of Azucena in 1952. I was cast as Ferrando and the conductor was Franco Capuana from La Scala. The value to the company of being able to perform the opera in Italian was quickly demonstrated for not only did it bring Stignani to the house, it also enabled the work to be revived the following season for a new young soprano who was setting the operatic world alight, Maria Callas.

I first appeared with Callas during the same season in *Aida*, also in Italian. I again sang the King, and during the ballet sequence of the Triumphal Scene, Callas and Giulietta Simionato, the Amneris, were sitting at my feet. They kept up a non-stop conversation in Italian throughout it without moving their lips. (A really practiced opera singer can carry on a perfectly normal conversation without moving his lips, believe me. Audiences have no idea the sort of information that is passed on during a performance. Football results can be circulated, and I remember being informed by Donald McIntyre, as we stood in front

1. Sgt. Frank Birtles – taken in Secunderabad, 1945.
2. Making up as Sarastro for the Budapest State Opera production of *The Magic Flute*, 1964.
3. At the party given for me by Scottish Opera to mark my official retirement from the opera stage, 4 January 1979.

4. A moment of repose during rehearsals for the world premiere of Robin Orr's *Hermiston*, in which I played the title role.

5. As Count Waldner in *Arabella*.

6. As Rocco in *Fidelio*.

7. In the title role of
   Scottish Opera's *Don Pasquale*.

8. As the drunken apprentice
   in Berg's *Wozzeck*,
   Covent Garden, 1952

9. My first appearance as Ochs, Covent Garden, 1960.
The costume is from the original 1947 production.

10. As Ochs four years later,
wearing the costume for
my one and only appearance
at the New York Met.

of the curtain, taking our calls following a performance of *Fidelio*, that the pound had just been devalued. Few people will have realised that Rocco's gasp of horror came, not because I was still 'in character' but because I had quickly computed just how much I had lost by changing my dollars into sterling that very morning!) With Callas and Simionato in earnest conversation, and with my Italian being very sketchy, I was fascinated to try and make out what it was they were talking about. I couldn't follow them at all until I suddenly heard the words 'Marks & Spencer', and I realised that they were discussing the price of underwear in that famous store. I became so engrossed that it was with utter horror that I looked up to find the ballet finishing and my next phrase imminent. My mind had gone a complete blank. I looked at the prompter but he was busy congratulating the ballet, clearly not expecting to have to prompt a singer who has just had a quarter of an hour to think about his next line. I stared at him with blazing eyes à la Christoff in *Boris*, but he refused even to glance in my direction. I stood, my heart punching my costume in and out, and opened my mouth. Somehow I began to sing but I didn't know until the phrase was over that I had managed it correctly.

People tend these days only to remember Callas as an artist who went from crisis to crisis, a 'prima donna' in every sense of the word. And yet the thing I remember most about her in those early days was her delicious sense of humour. She and Simionato were always going off into peals of laughter. There was one incident during the rehearsals for *Trovatore*. I still had a habit, at that time, of counting the beats on my fingers during rehearsal. Some artists tap their feet but I used my fingers, my hands clasped behind my back. I was in the conductor's room rehearsing with Alberto Erede, and counting away as usual, when I suddenly felt my hands being grabbed tight from behind. It was Callas. 'Now,' she hissed in my ear, 'you won't be able to sing, will you?' She held on to me as we all dissolved into laughter throughout my aria, with Erede trying to work out what was going on.

Did Callas have a beautiful voice? Not, I feel, in the true sense of the word. But what a compelling and unmistakable sound it was – and what a brilliant artist. To get the full impact of Callas one had both to hear and see her. After she slimmed down, her tone, which always carried a hint of metal, seemed to me to become somewhat harsh when under pressure and I preferred the sound she made in her earlier days. But to hear her at *any* time during her career was always a thrilling experience.

As well as engaging such singers as Callas, Stignani and Simionato,

49

the Garden also began to import more foreign conductors and producers in its attempt to become a front-rank house. A distinguished producer who arrived in 1952 for his one and only production in the house was Gunther Rennert from the Berlin Opera. He produced *A Masked Ball* with John Pritchard conducting at Covent Garden for the first time. The opera was given in English and I was cast as Count Horn, one of the conspirators. It was beautifully directed and designed, but it suffered from more than its share of disasters: no less than four Amelias sang in the first six performances. A stunning set had been designed for the second act in which Amelia goes to have the spell cast at the foot of the gallows. The only problem was that Frederick Dalberg, myself, and about thirty choristers, had to be in our positions beneath the stage before the act began in order to make our entrance as Rennert wanted over the skyline, where rotting corpses were hanging from gibbets. It was a marvellous effect but there was no way we could get on if we weren't already waiting under the stage. Freddie was furious with this arrangement because it meant we had to sit under the stage while Amelia went through her great aria, while the tenor joined her for a duet and while the baritone joined them for a trio. We finally made our entrance after about thirty minutes of being crammed together in a confined space. One night, Freddie was so bored that he began playing with some pieces of rope, untying the knots and then retying them. It so happened that, unknown to him, these pieces of rope were attached to one of the rotting skeletons on the stage above. The Amelia (I forget *which* Amelia) was in the middle of her big aria when this skeleton suddenly dropped and hung grotesquely. It was a wonderful if unexpected effect to which she reacted while continuing to sing. The trouble was that it was completely ruined a minute later when Freddie decided to re-tie the knot, and the skeleton shot back up into its correct position.

One of our Amelias during this series was the soprano Constantina Araujo, who was to make an entrance that has since passed into operatic folklore. Freddie Dalberg and I were on stage with Jess Walters in the scene in which the conspirators put their names into an urn to decide which one is to kill the king, proceedings which Amelia is supposed to interrupt. On this particular night there was no sign of Araujo when the moment came. John Pritchard slowed down the orchestra as much as possible and Freddie was muttering to Jess Walters, who had his hand in the urn, 'Feel about a bit, Jess. She isn't on yet!' Finally Freddie exclaimed, 'She's here! She's come through the bloody fireplace!' We were standing in a room with a huge open fireplace in which a fire was roaring. It was mock, of course, but it looked so realistic that people would ask us afterwards if we didn't get too warm working so close to it. We swung round and, sure enough, there was Araujo entering through the flames. She had been called in as a last minute replacement and had not even seen the set. When the time came for her entrance, she had been unable to find the door and her English was not good enough to ask any of the backstage staff. So, hearing her cue and seeing a spill of light from what she assumed was a very low doorway, she ducked her head and entered – through the middle of the fire!

Another soprano who took over Amelia in that production was a young singer who had just joined the company: Joan Sutherland. It has always been a mystery to me why it took so long for audiences to recognise Joan's talent, for it was not until she played Lucia in 1959 that she became a superstar. I don't think it is simply hindsight that makes me say this, for I remember saying to my wife Vera, the first time I heard Joan, that if I was an agent I would sign her up because she would be taking the world by storm. But somehow, nothing seemed to happen. She received consistently good notices but no one said, 'Here is a future superstar.' And then, suddenly, on that February night in 1959, that wonderful alchemy that can only happen in the theatre, took place. I don't think her singing was any better that night – she was always a marvellous singer – and it was not as if she had been doing only small roles before and hadn't had the chance to be noticed. She had already demonstrated her tremendous range in *The Midsummer Marriage*, she had appeared as Aida, had sung all three leading roles in *The Tales of Hoffmann*, had played Gilda in *Rigoletto* (I had to carry her on, and she was a big girl!), Eva in *Die Meistersinger*, Agathe in *Der Freischütz*, Pamina in *The Magic Flute*, Micaela in *Carmen* and Desdemona in *Otello*. She played all these star roles before she was 'discovered'. A lot of people say that much of the credit for her enormous success in *Lucia* was due to the fact that Tullio Serafin was in the pit and that Zeffirelli was producing, and I think this is true. I certainly think that Covent Garden had decided to go to town with her, to promote her and make a star of her if possible. I was singing Raimondo in the production and one day I was walking through Leicester Square when I met David Webster. Although he always seemed loath to enter into a conversation inside the theatre, once he was outside, Webster would often permit himself to have a long, friendly, and sometimes intimate, chat. We began to talk about the production.

'Is Joan going to be very good, Langdon?' he suddenly asked. (He always called me Langdon, never Michael, except once when he seemed to do it almost by accident and became very embarrassed, reverting at once to Langdon.) 'Absolutely,' I replied. 'Good,' he said, nodding his head in agreement. 'I think so too; I think so too.'

Convinced though we were within the company that Joan was going to be very good, none of us was quite prepared for what actually happened. Her singing was magnificent, the production caught fire, and when the curtain came down on her Mad Scene, the house erupted. We had rehearsed two picture calls for the end of that scene, during which we stayed motionless. The curtain came down on the second and Joan began to get up. I was kneeling by her side, bending over her. 'Stay there, darling,' I hissed as the curtain went up again. Each time it came down she would move as if to get up and each time I prevented her physically. 'How much longer, Mike?' she kept asking, one eye open to see if the curtain was going back again. It did – seven times, if I recall correctly. When she eventually went out to take her solo call in front of the curtain, the house went wild and it was at least twenty minutes before we could start the final scene, a scene I shared with the tenor Kenneth Neate (a last-minute replacement for the indisposed Brazilian, João Gibin). We sang to a constant buzz of conversation, not, I hope, because we were bad, but because our presence was quite superfluous to the evening. A star had been born.

Why hadn't it happened earlier? It comes down to what Sir John Barbirolli had once said to me, that if you're going to get to the top you have to specialise. It is not enough to be very good in a number of roles, you have to be superb in one. And with Joan that one role was initially Lucia. She had never been acclaimed as the greatest actress on the operatic stage, but in *Lucia* Zeffirelli brought out talents no one realised she possessed. He built the entire production around her and used the set pieces to concentrate the audience on the voice rather than the action. And it worked.

Seeing her repeat the role some years later at the Metropolitan Opera House in New York, I realised just what assurance such adulation can give to an artist. At Covent Garden she had been shattered and stunned by the reaction. In New York she came out to take her solo call and hung on the curtain with apparent exhaustion! The audience responded by going crazy.

Taking a curtain call is an art in itself. I dislike seeing an artist who has just died in the most tragic circumstances bounding out to take a

52

call with a broad grin. The illusion one has spent the previous few hours trying to create should be broken gently and I think it is most important to remain 'in character' for the first two or three calls, only gradually re-assuming one's own identity. The greatest master of the curtain call I ever saw was Boris Christoff. He would take his first curtain call after, say, *Boris* or *Don Carlos*, looking completely exhausted, and then step out of sight, listening to the applause. The moment it died a fraction he would go out again, this time, his hand on his heart. Off he would come and again gauge just the moment to reappear with a deep bow of gratitude to the audience. This would continue, ending, on one occasion, with him in a kneeling position! Audiences feed on their own applause, especially in an opera house, and Boris certainly knew how to evoke the maximum response.

There are several levels of achievement to which an opera singer can aspire of course. There are the superstars, the stars, the eminent singers (those artists who have an international career in a certain number of specialist roles; the level which I attained), the well-known all-round singers, singers who are well-known in their own country, and so on, down to good company singers. In 1952, I had no thoughts of rising much higher than becoming a good company member, someone who was both reliable and respected as an artist, and my main concern was simply to increase my repertoire of roles.

Over the following three years I was able to do this. I appeared as the Hermit in *Der Freischütz*, as the He-Ancient in Tippett's *Midsummer Marriage*, as Calkas in Walton's *Troilus and Cressida*, and as Fafner in the 1954 Ring Cycle produced by Rudolf Hartmann and conducted by Fritz Stiedry. And I continued to appear regularly in my more familiar roles. I was also beginning to increase my work away from Covent Garden, appearing in celebrity concerts, on radio and television in Vic Oliver's *Variety Playhouse* and *This Is Showbusiness*, and singing Mephistopheles in a televised production of *Faust* under Charles Mackerras. We gave two performances of *Faust*, both transmitted live, and during the second, the worst smog London had seen this century decided to descend. Some of it managed to get into the studio and made life very difficult. We spent the entire performance trying not to cough while we were actually singing.

In the summer of 1952, I had been engaged to appear in *The Desert Song* at the Open Air Theatre in Scarborough. Four years earlier this would have been the height of my ambition. Pleasant though it was, it was only an interlude, and I could not wait to get back to opera and to *real* singing. If I *did* have an ambition as the next three years unfolded, it was not connected with musical comedy; it was to sing Wagner at Bayreuth. By 1955, I was, I thought, working towards this. But then Rafael Kubelik was appointed Musical Director.

Chapter 5 Out of Favour

Rafael Kubelik was a tall, well-built Czech, going thin on top, with flowing hair at the side and back which would fly forward whenever he gave a big downbeat. A composer as well as a conductor, his experience of opera was somewhat limited. He had run the Brno Opera for two years at the beginning of the war, had conducted the Glyndebourne production of *Don Giovanni* at the 1948 Edinburgh Festival, and had made a deep impression with his handling of Janáček's *Katya Kabanova* when Sadler's Wells put it on in English to celebrate the composer's centenary, but his reputation was chiefly as a symphonic conductor and he came to us as something of an unknown quantity. My only knowledge of him, in fact, was that he was the son of the famous violinist, Jan Kubelik.

His appointment as Musical Director came after a gap of four years without one and was not universally welcomed, at least not by such people as Sir Thomas Beecham and his supporters, who complained that once again a foreigner had been given the job of leading our national company. Indeed, there were rumours that Kubelik had not been Webster's first choice to fill the vacancy but that both Erich Kleiber and Rudolf Kempe, the men he preferred, had turned him down. Politically, Webster had had to make an appointment, and since there were no British conductors capable, or willing, to take on the responsibility, he had been forced to look abroad, and had settled on Rafael Kubelik.

His appointment was announced at the end of 1954 and he took up his post at the start of the 1955–56 season, having come in two months earlier to take charge of a new production of *The Bartered Bride*. The arrival of any new Musical Director is always viewed with a certain amount of trepidation by the established members of the company. It doesn't matter if the stage door keeper thinks you are good, or your aunt thinks you are wonderful, if the man at the top doesn't share their opinion. The liking, or not liking, of a person's voice is so much a matter of individual whim that no one knows exactly what will happen when a new man arrives, how the appointment will affect them personally.

Soon after Kubelik's arrival at Covent Garden we were all asked to go on stage and sing for him. Lord Harewood, who was the Administrative Assistant at the time (later to become Controller of Opera Planning), told us we should not be worried by this request. We would not be singing for our contracts, he assured us, only to let Kubelik know what voices he had available in the company. There's no doubt, however, that in spite of this reassurance, what happened at those auditions – and they *were* auditions – had an important bearing upon Kubelik's attitude towards us. When the day came we lined up in the wings and, one by one, went out on stage to sing our piece. Although I was quite experienced by now, I was still very nervous when my turn arrived. I had decided to perform an aria from Halévy's *La Juive* – 'O Faithless Men' – because I thought the range, from bottom E to middle C, would show my voice off well. The choice of an audition piece is all important, as I have discovered since becoming Director of the National Opera Studio where I have to sit through audition after audition. The first piece you sing should make the listener sit up; it must pin him back in his seat. Impressions are formed very quickly at an audition and if your initial impact is poor, you are unlikely to be asked to perform a second piece. If I had known then what I know now, I would never have chosen that Halévy piece to sing for Kubelik. It is, in retrospect, extremely dull and I think, probably because of nerves, I sang it in an extremely dull way. Kubelik was clearly not impressed.

Shortly after this public audition I was asked to go and sing for him again in the conductor's room. This time I chose Beethoven's 'Ich liebe dich' because I thought it would demonstrate my control of the mezzo-voce. I shall never know what mental quirk caused me to do this for it was another totally inappropriate choice. One should not sing German lieder for the head of an opera house unless he asks for it. Kubelik must have thought I was mad.

His reign opened officially with an all-star production of Verdi's *Otello*, with Ramon Vinay as Otello, a role he had sung and recorded with Toscanini, Gré Brouwenstijn as Desdemona and Tito Gobbi cast as Iago. One of Kubelik's declared intentions when he joined Covent Garden was to continue building up the company by concentrating on ensemble work. He was not in favour of mounting productions for international stars to fly in and join, and he soon made his intentions quite plain. When Tito Gobbi, who was still recording in Italy, failed to make the first rehearsals, Kubelik promptly sacked him. The news created a furore. Gobbi was a world star, one of the 'names' the public was expecting and wanting to see. To sack him was a calculated risk. It was tantamount to a declaration that Covent Garden now considered itself to be a major house, able to dictate terms to international stars and no longer having to rely on their goodwill to create its reputation. It was a gamble that paid off, for not only did Covent Garden find a new star in Otakar Kraus, the understudy who took over the role of Iago, but Gobbi was also persuaded to return to the house in later years, most notably to portray Scarpia in the wonderful Zeffirelli production of *Tosca* with Maria Callas.

I had been cast as Montano in *Otello*, a small, very frustrating role. He is on stage for about the first ten minutes of the opera, has a sword fight with Cassio, is wounded and helped off, and then returns some four hours later to make the important interjection 'Sciagurato!' Although Montano was by no means the leading bass role I was not too worried about being given it for they were early days and at least my sword fight with John Lanigan was impressive! For the second new production of the season, *Tannhäuser*, produced by Sumner Austin and conducted by Kempe, I was again given a small role, that of Reinmar von Zweter, one of the knights, but after only five performances I moved to the leading bass role of Landgraf; and when *Madam Butterfly* was revived the same month I made my debut as the Bonze, at the request of Kempe who was again conducting.

It seemed at first as though my career was continuing its upward path, but an element of doubt began to creep in when *The Magic Flute* and *The Ring* were revived. I might reasonably have expected to be offered Sarastro or The Speaker in *The Magic Flute*, but instead I was asked to do the Second Armed Man. I had already sung Fafner in *Das Rheingold* for Stiedry, but this time I was not even considered for it. There is always a polarisation into an in-group and an out-group whenever a new Musical Director takes over, and it soon became apparent to me that I was veering towards the out-group. Whether this was due entirely to Kubelik and my auditions for him, or whether there were other influences at work, I am not entirely sure. I was told, however, that when *Rigoletto*, which was to be performed in Italian that season, was being cast, I was the almost unanimous choice for Sparafucile, a part I had been singing regularly since 1951. Lord Harewood, though, was not keen and in the event, Fred Dalberg was given the role even though he confided to me that he didn't want it and would have much preferred me to sing it. I have learned since that time that, although Lord Harewood always praised my stage work and my acting, he was never very thrilled by the actual sound of my voice. Never having liked it much myself, I can understand his point, but it certainly didn't help me at that time. My rapid progress had come to a halt.

This feeling of being passed over was not just my imagination or pique at not being offered roles I wanted, as an examination of the work I did at that time clearly shows. There were other indications also that all was not well. Up until the time of Kubelik's arrival my contract had increased financially every year. It now stayed the same. And then the attitude of people within the opera house altered. People in minor administrative posts, who would usually say good morning and exchange a few words, would just nod and walk past. It was not that they were rude, it was as if they knew something that I didn't. I was not the only person affected by this polarisation. One of the greatest losses to Covent Garden was the eventual departure of Freddie Dalberg, who suddenly found that the roles he had always performed were being given to newcomers. And Adele Leigh was another artist who found she was no longer being cast in plum roles and decided to move on.

Kubelik's second season confirmed my worst fears. Although my volume of work did not decrease, I was continuing to play minor, supporting roles. When *Jenufa* opened in December 1956 I played the Mayor, a very small part, and when *The Mastersingers* was given a new production in January 1957 I took the role of Schwarz, a character who sings only four solo words in the entire opera. Berlioz's *The Trojans*, which confirmed the young Canadian tenor Jon Vickers, making only his second appearance with the company, as a star, was the major production of the season. I was in it as Pantheus, the secondary bass role after Narbal. These were all parts one would expect a good, solid, small part artist to perform, and it was clear that that was how I was considered at best. I was certainly not looked upon as a person with enough talent to progress towards the major bass roles.

I had, in effect, regressed to the situation I had been in in 1951, just after I had been made a principal, and as a result my voice and my performance began to suffer. No one seems to know quite why some people have a voice while others, with apparently the same physical apparatus, cannot sing a note. But one thing that every performer knows is that the first part to be affected if you are under any kind of emotional strain is the voice. A singer must be relaxed and confident in order to maintain a free flow of sound. If he is worried or tense, the delicate muscles of the throat are affected and the sound becomes tight.

58

This can occur even though you are performing music you know well and have sung a hundred times before, and even though it might be easy and right for your voice. And, of course, once you start to anticipate trouble for the voice, you will invariably get it. The whole business compounds itself.

Just as you will not sing well if you are worried or lack confidence, so your acting suffers as well. You must believe, as a singer, that the sound you are making is authentic, good, pleasing, and even thrilling, to your audience, for only if you have this belief can you relax sufficiently to be grand, commanding, comical, or whatever the work demands. If, however, you feel that you are not singing well, even in the middle of a performance which might have been going well up until that point, your stage presence flies out of the wings, your stature diminishes, and you are left on stage as a very small figure. Once I had realised that I was not a member of Kubelik's 'in-group', that someone up there didn't like me, this sensation began to happen to me more and more, and because I felt that I was not satisfying people, that those who mattered were unimpressed by all I did, I began to give mediocre performances which only confirmed their belief. They looked at what I was doing and said, 'We're right. He's *not* very good.'

I went to see my agent in a mood of deep depression. She listened to all I had to say and suggested that the best place for me to continue my career might be in Germany, away from Covent Garden, and she undertook to go and see Webster on my behalf to find out exactly what the position was. When she asked him whether I should consider a German contract for the forthcoming season, he replied that he thought I would be wise to accept one. His reply really upset me for it was tantamount to saying that my career at Covent Garden was over. There were still six months of the season, and my contract, to run and so I could not contemplate going to Germany for some time. It was an agonising wait during which I continued to turn in mediocre performances.

One incident did help boost my confidence during this period. I received a call from my agent that Sir Thomas Beecham wanted to see me. I made my way to his apartment in Portland Place, to find myself in a queue of well-known basses. Eventually I was shown into his study, where he was sitting at the piano, smoking a long cigar. 'I'd like you to sing the first Sarastro aria from *The Magic Flute*,' he said. He paused, obviously expecting me to ask which aria that was. Instead I said, 'Yes, Sir Thomas.' 'Good start,' he replied, opening the score. 'I will play it for you myself, making countless errors of which you will not apprise me.' And he began to play the accompaniment to 'Isis and Osiris', making several mistakes, even though it was only in one flat, no doubt because he couldn't see the keyboard through the swirl of smoke that came from the cigar still clamped between his teeth. When I had finished he said, 'Very good, Langdon, very good. Tell me, have you sung this role yet at Covent Garden?' I replied that I hadn't. 'No,' he went on, 'it suits you too well. Well, thank you very much.' I left and went home rather disappointed. I thought he must be planning a production of *The Magic Flute* somewhere but obviously I hadn't made a hit and would not be in it.

When I got home, my wife said there was a message for me to call Sir Thomas. I phoned immediately and spoke to his secretary, who said that Sir Thomas wished to engage me for the recording he was due to make of Haydn's *The Seasons*. (It still puzzles me why he chose a Sarastro aria for the audition. Quite by coincidence, I was suddenly asked to sing Sarastro with the Covent Garden company, first in Manchester and Southampton, and then, for one performance only, in the main house itself with Joan Sutherland as Pamina.)

When the Beecham recording eventually took place, we spent the first day rehearsing. On the second, Beecham said to me, 'You're singing very much better today than you were yesterday, Langdon. Why's that?' 'Because,' I replied, 'yesterday I didn't know what to bloody well expect.' He looked puzzled for a moment then he began to smile. 'Ah,' he said, 'you mean those Beecham stories?' He paused. 'You know, if they're good enough, I collect them myself.'

Beecham was a delight to work with. When we came to record he observed that Aria No. 12 would suit my voice better if it were transposed down. He turned to his assistant and told him to get all the parts transposed down a tone, ready to record first thing the following morning. 'But that means working all night, Sir Thomas,' the poor man exclaimed. 'Quite right,' replied Beecham, 'quite right.' The next day the parts were ready and we recorded it a tone down. The actual transposition was made in the last two bars of the preceding recitative, and we then continued through the aria itself in the new key. When someone suggested to him that the critics would comment, Beecham replied that he would give five pounds for every one that did. To the best of my knowledge he never had to pay out a penny.

I could no longer escape the fact that my career at Covent Garden had come to a halt, and so, as soon as the season was over, I embarked on a

60

boat from Harwich to the Hook of Holland, and then by the Rhinegold Express to Munich where my agent had arranged for me to sing for Herr Schmidt of what was then the Schmidt-Ballhausen Agency, one of Germany's best. Herr Schmidt was sufficiently impressed to send me to audition at the Opera House in Düsseldorf, after which I was told that there would be no problem in my joining the company provided I signed on for a minimum of three years. I said that I would think it over and let Herr Schmidt know as soon as possible.

The fact that they liked me in Düsseldorf and were prepared to offer me a contract did much to reassure me that I did still have a future as an opera singer, but I was not at all certain that I wanted to move to Germany. My return journey to London was taken up with a lot of serious thought about just what such a move would entail. Vera and I had bought a house in Sutton on which I had taken out a mortgage. Christine, our eldest daughter was now almost nine and Diane, our second child, who had been born in 1950, was almost seven. I could forsee enormous difficulties. My knowledge of German was rudimentary. I would not only have to learn the language fluently but so would Vera and the girls. We would have to find suitable accommodation and schools. We would all have to make new friends. It would mean a tremendous upheaval and a complete alteration to our lives. Worst of all, from my point of view, I realised that I would no longer be able to go and watch Wolves playing football. As soon as *that* consideration entered my arguments, I knew that I was really only looking for excuses not to have to uproot my family and settle in Germany. I put all of this to Vera when I got home and she simply said that she would do whatever was best for me and my career. So the decision had to be mine and mine alone. I decided to consult David Webster before committing myself to a course of action I might later regret.

Webster's method of conducting an interview was unique in my experience. He would take up a position near his office window, his back towards the person in the room, and gaze out across Mart Street at the fruiterer opposite. His hands would be thrust into his jacket pockets, thumbs out in perfect alignment, and he would intone, in his rather high-pitched voice, 'And what can I do for you today?' On this particular occasion I went through my story carefully, explaining how unhappy I was with my lack of progress and ending by mentioning that I now had the opportunity of joining a German house. He knew, of course, that I was desperate for some measure of reassurance but he heard me out in silence. When I finally finished he began to speak, still without looking at me. He said that he was aware my career had suffered a setback and that if I felt my prospects would be improved by going to Germany than I should not hesitate to go. My heart fell. This wasn't what I wanted to hear at all. Suddenly he swung round to face me. 'My dear chap,' he said, 'you *must* know that the most important thing in this business is to be liked by the right people at the right time.' He paused for so long that I felt he was waiting for me to depart. 'Times do have a habit of changing,' he suddenly added enigmatically, before returning to his scrutiny of the fruiterer opposite. I knew then that the interview was finally over. I thanked him, though I was not sure what for, and took my leave, trying to work out exactly what his advice meant. Almost twelve months had elapsed since he had told my agent, in effect, that if I should leave Covent Garden I would not be missed, and now came his pronouncement that 'times have a habit of changing'. Did he know something he was not yet prepared to tell me? It was not much on which to base a decision that would affect not only my career but also the future of my wife and daughters, and yet I felt that it did offer me some hope. I decided not to pursue the German contract but instead to stay on at Covent Garden for one more season and see what happened.

The 1957–58 season began with a revival of *The Tales of Hoffmann*, in which I was given the two minor roles of Crespel and Schlemil. I also continued with the other small roles I had been singing for some years. There was one small glimmer of hope when I found that I had been cast as Dr. Bartolo in *The Marriage of Figaro*, and was then asked to sing Ramphis in a revival of *Aida* conducted by none other than Kubelik himself, but I soon began to doubt the wisdom of my decision to stay on. It was clear that I was still considered as nothing more than a run-of-the-mill house artist hoping for the better roles but spending his time doing the basic work, including understudying, often for parts I had already performed with a measure of success.

One of the new parts I was given to understudy was that of the Grand Inquisitor in the new production of *Don Carlos* being mounted by Visconti and Giulini. It was an exciting prospect for the cast included Christoff, Gobbi, Barbieri, Brouwenstijn, Vickers and Neri, and the chance of sneaking into that company, even if only to watch, made life a little more bearable. All the cast, with the exception of Giulio Neri, the Grand Inquisitor, who still had an engagement to fulfil in Italy, assembled in London in April ready to begin rehearsals for the opening in May. One fine morning I was out in the garden doing my deep breathing exercises when I was hailed over the garden fence by my neighbour, who asked if I had seen the news about some opera singer. He handed me a copy of his newspaper, opened to an inside page. Tucked away at the bottom was a single short paragraph saying that Giulio Neri, the eminent Italian bass, had died in Rome the previous day. Almost before the news had had time to sink in, Vera was calling me from the house: I was wanted on the phone urgently. It was Edward Downes, calling from Covent Garden. Without wasting any time he told me that since I was Neri's official understudy, Giulini wanted to hear me sing through the part from the Opera House stage that morning.

I rushed up to London and got to the theatre at about ten thirty, only to find that Giulini was already in rehearsal and I would have to wait for two and a half hours before he would be free to hear me. While I was waiting I found out what had happened earlier that morning. Ted Downes and John Matheson, another young member of the music staff, had both reached the Opera House at the same time, full of the news. They waited for Giulini to arrive for the morning's rehearsal to ask him what should happen about a replacement, and only when they saw him walking in in his usual manner did they realise he hadn't yet heard of Neri's death. When told, he was terribly upset and it was only after he had had time to compose himself that the subject of Neri's replacement was broached. Finding out that I was the official understudy, he immediately asked to hear me.

Under normal circumstances I would have become so nervous during that long wait that I would probably have sung badly and ruined any chance I might have had of getting the part, but, in a curious way, my two years in the wilderness began to work for me. I knew there were people at Covent Garden who did not expect me to impress a man like Giulini, and I knew I had nothing to lose. This knowledge had the effect of calming my nerves and when I finally walked out on stage I felt relaxed and in good voice. The music for the Grand Inquisitor suits me well and I believe I did it justice. Giulini certainly seemed pleased. He thanked me warmly and told the assembled company how impressed he had been. I was almost certain the part was mine; but something told me not to be too confident.

I was right to be wary for I soon discovered that in spite of Giulini saying he would be very pleased to have me in the cast, the Covent Garden management had redoubled their efforts to find someone, anyone, other than me, to sing the part. But although they phoned round the world, it was difficult to come up with someone of sufficient eminence at such short notice and it began to look as though I would get it after all – even if only by default. But then they discovered that Marco Stefanoni, who was singing Pistol at Glyndebourne, just fifty miles south of London, knew the role and he was immediately signed up. My feelings can probably be imagined! To have come so close and then to be denied was almost too much to bear and I knew that whatever happened I would be leaving for Germany at the end of the season.

I still had a handful of performances to sing, of Sparafucile, of Ramphis, of the Mayor in *Jenufa*, and I was still the official understudy in *Don Carlos*, not now to Neri but to Stefanoni, and so I had to remain at the house, otherwise I think I might well never have gone back. In my mood of utter dejection I had completely forgotten one thing: that I had never failed to take over in a part I had been understudying, though I doubt whether the thought would have proved much comfort even had I remembered it. But I was standing at the back of the Stalls Circle one day, watching a rehearsal of *Don Carlos*, my arms resting on the seats in front of me, when I became aware of someone next to me. It was David Webster. 'I hear you sang a very fine audition for Giulini the other day,' he murmured. 'He seemed to like it,' I replied, resisting the impulse to add, 'and a lot of bloody good it did me!' 'Well, don't despair,' he went on, as if he could read my thoughts, 'something may come of it.' And he drifted away. I didn't have to wait too long to find out what this particular remark meant for the same day I was told that Stefanoni had found he could not manage two performances and I would be singing them in his place.

My first appearance was on the 12th May 1958. I travelled up to town early in the afternoon but I didn't go to the theatre. Instead I went to watch a film, and I eventually arrived at the Opera House some time after the performance had started. I spent about an hour putting on my elaborate make-up and then decided to warm up by singing through my entire part. I was in a dressing room on the same floor as Christoff, Gobbi and Vickers. I felt a little self-conscious about vocalising in such company, and so I began to look around for somewhere a little quieter. I found it eventually in the basement, amongst the dustbins awaiting collection (an area which, superstitiously, I was always to use for warming up after that night and which became known as 'Langdon's Studio'). I sang through the part, felt good, and then went back to my room to have a cup of black coffee and smoke a cigarette. I felt surprisingly calm. I knew that I was singing in a production with one of the finest casts available anywhere in the world; I knew that it was my opportunity to show the doubters that I could live in such company; and yet I did not feel over-awed. If I felt any emotion at all, it was one of anger; anger at the frustration I had been suffering right up to that performance, anger at the way I had been forced into giving mediocre performances because of my self-doubt and uncertainty, anger that even after my audition for Giulini they had still been scouring the world for another bass. I was, above all, angry at being afraid. The resentment of the previous two-and-a-half years came welling up and for the first time since the war I felt that old RAF feeling of 'Here we go, boys. Shit or bust!'

As soon as I heard Christoff being called for the beginning of Act IV, I made my way down to the stage and stood in the wings listening to him singing his great aria, 'Ella giammai m'amo'. He was in superb voice and I knew how difficult it would be to follow him effectively. The scene between the King (Christoff) and the Grand Inquisitor is short but crucial and is probably the finest scene for two basses in all opera. Several references have been made to the Grand Inquisitor earlier in the opera, each accompanied by the most magnificently sinister music. Eventually, in Act IV, he is announced, the music again growls and he finally appears, ninety years old and blind, to confront the King. It is a marvellous entrance which Visconti had staged, as he had the rest of the scene, brilliantly. At first he had the Inquisitor standing immobile and then, after his first phrase, being led to his seat. The rest of the scene was then played with him sitting still, light being played up from the side to limn the face, with its hooked nose, the blind eyes and the cowl, while the King was involved in all the movement. And when, finally, the Inquisitor makes his judgment, Visconti had him standing for the first time, rising slowly, like a huge exclamation mark. It was a wonderfully effective scene in a production that was to set new standards not just at Covent Garden but throughout the operatic world, and to carry it off in harness with such a superlative artist as Christoff was a daunting prospect. He came to the end of his opening soliloquy, I heard my cue and I was on.

A singer knows when he has given a good performance and I knew it that night. The confidence Giulini gave me was tremendous. Towards the end of the scene, after I had stood up to give my judgment, I had a very daunting phrase, a slow ride up to a high F. Giulini knew that it was difficult for me and literally willed me through it. He looked at me throughout, setting his feet as though in concrete, and lifting me through the phrase. My only blemish that evening was a small musical error early in the scene, and when it was all over I felt on top of the world. As I came off, Tito Gobbi, who was on the other side of the stage awaiting his entrance, walked round the back of the set to clap me on the back and say 'Wonderful', before hurrying back to compose himself for his entrance – a marvellous gesture. My other colleagues offered their congratulations and later Giulini came to find me to say how pleased he had been. A measure of the man's confidence in his singers is that he made no reference to my small mistake. He knew that I would go away and check where I had gone wrong, and when, in my second performance, I got it right, he just nodded and smiled up at me from the pit.

My second performance was three days later. Normally a stand-in doesn't get much notice unless he or she is a big international star, but this performance happened to be the Gala Night of the year, celebrating one hundred years of the present Covent Garden building. The house was packed with distinguished people and, more importantly for me, with the press. After my successful first appearance, I was now well into the part and probably sang with even more confidence. I certainly got noticed, with excellent reviews in every major paper. All the tension and doubt of the previous seasons drained away. I had been pitched in at the highest level and had shown everyone, myself included, that I could hold my own. The fact that I had done nothing of any real consequence at Covent Garden for so long must have helped. The danger for any artist singing with a company year in, year out, is that people get too used to you, that they come to expect a certain standard and very often do not realise how high that standard is. Because I had been relegated to minor roles for such a time, no one was expecting me to be much more than a stand-in; it was almost as if I had come in as a guest artist. Maybe, on reflection, those years in the wilderness were to my advantage. All I know for certain is that I could have done without them.

My season finished a couple of months later with a single performance of Sparafucile in *Rigoletto*, and I left London for Scarborough where I had been booked to appear as Joe in *Show Boat* at the Open Air Theatre. I knew by then that I would not have to leave Covent Garden and that my career was again on the up, and I sang my heart out: 'Old Man River' three times a performance. We were working in a local park and producer Ralph Reader thought it would be nice for one of my renditions if I could sing it while being rowed gently across a lake. I was duly wired up with a neck microphone and set off with my boatman. Half-way across the boat got stuck, caught by a piece of cable, and no matter how hard the boatman tried, he was unable to free us. Each time he attempted to go forward, the cable would take up the slack and drag us backwards again. I was singing throughout, and as the boatman became more and more annoyed, his language grew steadily more foul. Every word was picked up by my microphone and the audience that night was treated to 'Old Man River' with profane obligato!

While at Scarborough I received a letter from the well-known agent John Coast, asking me whether or not I was represented, and, if not, whether I would like him to handle my affairs. He had been in the audience on the Gala Night and had heard my Grand Inquisitor. He knew that Stefanoni had been brought in to replace Neri and didn't bother to check his programme, so when he phoned Muriel Kerr, Webster's secretary, it was to ask where he could find Stefanoni. Muriel replied that as far as she knew he was still at Glyndebourne, but what did Coast want him for? John explained that he had been in the Gala audience and had been impressed. 'But', said Muriel, 'that wasn't Stefanoni, that was Michael Langdon, one of *our* basses.' 'In that case, where can I get hold of Michael Langdon?' came the reply.

I have to admit that I had never heard of John Coast but I replied to his letter that I would contact him as soon as I returned to London. We duly met and he became my sole agent from that moment on. If a singer is to stand any chance of getting to the top, it is absolutely vital that he is represented by a good agent who will know who is casting what and where, how much every grade of singer is being paid, how much he can confidently ask for your services, and who can also act as a buffer between you and managements. John Coast is one of the best and I cannot overestimate the help he gave me in reaching the top.

Those two performances of *Don Carlos* were the most important appearances of my career, for out of them came everything that has happened to me since. Not only did I acquire an agent who was to prove invaluable to my career, but shortly before I left for Scarborough, after what, with the exception of the Grand Inquisitor, had been a pretty mediocre season, I received a call from Kubelik's secretary. 'Mr. Kubelik wants to know if you would like to sing Kecal in *The Bartered Bride* when he comes back next season as a guest conductor,' she said (this was the first I knew that he had resigned as Musical Director). 'Are you sure he means Kecal?' I replied. 'That's the *big* bass part.' I heard her turn to Kubelik and repeat my question. 'No, no, no,' I heard Kubelik saying, 'Kecal.' She came back to me. 'He *does* mean Kecal,' she said. 'In that case,' I replied, 'I'd love to.'

Chapter 6 Why Not Ochs?

Kecal, one of the main characters in Smetana's *The Bartered Bride*, is one of the most famous of all bass roles. He's a greedy, money-hungry marriage broker, with the gift of the gab, who sets up and forces through the arranged marriages. He is on stage throughout most of the action and it is his come-uppance which helps produce the opera's climax. It is a part that any singer with a flair for, or desire to play, comedy, longs to be asked to do; and I was being invited to sing it by Kubelik of all people. After the events of the previous couple of years or so such a turn-around may seem inexplicable, and yet had Kubelik stayed on as Musical Director I feel my career would still have got better. There were definite signs during his third and final season that he had begun to revise his opinions of me. I had been given seven performances of Dr. Bartolo in *The Marriage of Figaro* at the start of the season, and had finally been allowed to sing Ramphis in the main house, in a production with Vickers, Brouwenstijn and Shacklock, conducted by Kubelik, after which he had remarked to John Matheson, with an air of incredulity, that I had 'filled the stage'. And then there had been my two performances in *Don Carlos* which had proved at last that I could survive in the highest company. The fact that he personally asked for me to play Kecal shows that he had, by the time of his departure, come to accept that I did possess some talent. I have often wondered just how much my time in the wilderness was due not so much to Kubelik's own antipathy but from the advice of those who were close to him.

In spite of what happened to me, I was sorry to see Kubelik go, for I had always liked him and he managed to achieve a great deal for the company. His productions of *Otello*, *Jenufa* and *The Trojans* demonstrated that Covent Garden had finally entered the front rank of international houses, while the Visconti/Giulini production of *Don Carlos* was one of the supreme operatic achievements of all time. Where Kubelik failed was that, like Rankl before him, he was not a politician. He was, first and foremost, a musician, and he was over-sensitive to the constant criticisms he received, particularly from Beecham and his supporters; criticisms which led to him offering to resign at least once before his actual departure.

No one was appointed to succeed Kubelik and the Garden again had to rely on its own music staff and a succession of guest conductors. Just as the arrival of a new Musical Director can affect your career if he doesn't like you, so his departure can produce the reverse result as people start to re-examine the forces that are left. In my own case, because I had been starved of any worthwhile roles until the very end of Kubelik's tenure, people began to look at me in a new light, and I found myself appearing in roles for which I would not have been considered previously. And so, when the season opened with a Ring Cycle, under Kempe, I was cast as Fafner in *Das Rheingold*, a part I had not sung for four years. My career at Covent Garden was again under way.

I began work on *The Bartered Bride* with John Matheson, who was scheduled to conduct some of the later performances, and soon found that it was a role I could really enjoy. Playing Bartolo in *The Marriage of Figaro* had given me an inkling of what it was like to perform a comic role, but Bartolo is a cameo role, whereas with the character of Kecal I was required to play a sustained comic role for the first time, one which is not only at the centre of the action but which also enjoys a robust sing with plenty of voice – everything a singer asks for.

When Kubelik arrived to take his first rehearsals, I was thoroughly immersed in the part, and he seemed pleased with my work. There was never any suggestion that all may not have been well between us earlier. By the time of the dress rehearsal I was really enjoying myself and I came off stage after it with that feeling of exhilaration that every singer, if he is lucky, experiences: the feeling that, despite the inevitable nerves, when the first night comes, everything is going to be all right. And so it proved with Kecal. After the curtain calls I was making my way back to my dressing room when I met John Matheson at the foot of the stairs.

'Bloody good!' he enthused. 'It's a good part for you. Suits you vocally and the audience liked you. They laughed a lot.' I began to thank him for all his hard work with me and for his constant encouragement, but he butted in. 'What you need to do now,' he went on, 'and I say this with all the vehemence I can muster, is take a good hard look at Baron Ochs and see if you think you could have a stab at it. I personally think it would fit you like a glove and I'd be delighted to work with you on it. If all goes well, I'll talk to David Webster and put him in the picture. They need an Ochs here, you know.' He began to move away, then turned back. 'They need an Ochs everywhere,' he added.

I went back to my room deep in thought. Everything was coming full circle. 'Take a look at Kecal and, lastly, at Ochs von Lerchenau' – that had been Erich Kleiber's advice to me after the *Wozzeck* performances in 1953. 'If you're going to get to the top in this business, you've got to specialise' – that was Sir John Barbirolli. I had just enjoyed a success as Kecal and now I was being advised by John Matheson to study Ochs. I had taken five years to connect those two pieces of advice, but I didn't shout 'Eureka' and suddenly realise I had seen the light. I thought long and hard about everything that had been said, by Kleiber, by Barbirolli, and now by Matheson, and I decided that I ought to study Ochs, not because I was desperately anxious to sing it, but because I knew that if I could bring it off it would help advance my career. One other thing helped me make up my mind and that was listening to Ludwig Weber singing the role on the Kleiber recording. For the first time I began to realise what an artist could actually do with it.

I went back to John and told him I'd like to accept his offer to work with me on the role. He told me to start right away on the first act which, he declared, I would find the most difficult. It may seem logical to begin the study of any role at the beginning but this doesn't always happen. For a variety of reasons an artist may prefer to start work with a scene or act well into the opera. Walter Midgley used to tell me that his method of learning a part was to learn the big arias first, then the duets, then the trios and so on, and finally the patter in between. The 'patter in between', as he called it, could well comprise the bulk of the part, and to adopt such a method of learning Ochs would be to ask for trouble. The first act of *Der Rosenkavalier* is fiendishly difficult and if a singer is to have any sort of success in the part he must bring that to heel first. It is musically very complicated having a range of two and a half octaves, and it requires complete mastery if Ochs is to move easily and confidently around the stage, in tune with and attending to everything the other characters are doing and singing. In other words, if a bass can bring off Act I, the rest of the part is downhill by comparison. There is another aspect of the role which is of the utmost importance in Act I, and that is the overall tessitura. Although in general Ochs is quite a hard part, staying around the top third of the bass range for long periods, Strauss has also given him some extremely low notes. His final exit in Act I is to a low C natural, and although it is permissible for the singer to growl an approximation, it is infinitely better if he can produce the legitimate note. (Most composers give difficult notes, high or low, as options; Strauss makes low C his first choice with the alternative middle C in brackets.) One eminent singer of my acquaintance *did* make the great mistake of not beginning his study of Ochs with this act. Skimming through the score he noticed that Ochs has some music of his own in Act II – the famous waltz theme – and was so taken with it that he began work from that point. Having mastered Act II he moved on to Act III, and it was only after some months, when he returned to look at Act I, that he discovered he couldn't manage the part.

Remembering Kleiber's injunction to study the speech rhythms first, I began working through the score, carefully pencilling in the beat marks and comparing them with Hofmannstahl's libretto. Just as Kleiber had told me they would be, the speech rhythms were incredibly accurate, flowing naturally with the music. The music, in fact, was so beautifully adjusted to the speech that when, some years later, I was presented with a recording of *Der Rosenkavalier* done as a play, with Helmut Qualtinger speaking the part of Ochs, I was unable to listen to it without hearing Strauss's music as the natural background. And on the odd occasion when, for theatrical effect, a word had been added, a repeat had been omitted or a speech rhythm had been slightly altered, I felt quite cheated.

For about three weeks I concentrated on memorising Ochs's lines in the first act, ignoring the musical progressions to which they were set, and then pronounced myself ready to begin studying the music. The complexity of the music hit me immediately. The danger when learning such a long and complicated role is the almost overwhelming desire to 'get on with it', to let one's voice go to its 'natural' place, even when this differs slightly from the notes the composer has written. I might have fallen into this trap had it not been for John. He would simply not let me become lazy, asserting that it is just as easy to learn the right notes as the wrong ones, and becoming very angry whenever I was careless. He was quite right, of course. An error that is allowed to slip through becomes so ingrained that it is almost impossible to eradicate. There are singers all over the world, some of them very well-known indeed, performing roles much less complicated than Ochs, who have their pet mistakes which recur every time they sing, much to the despair of repetiteurs and conductors alike.

I must emphasise that this work was all unofficial, quite outside my regular commitments at Covent Garden. I was already appearing as

Kecal and was then cast as Raimondo in the Zeffirelli production of *Lucia di Lammermoor*, rehearsals for which took up a lot of time. I was working on a revival of *Salome*, appearing as Ramphis in *Aida*, as the Second Armoured Man and later Sarastro in *The Magic Flute*, and as the Grand Inquisitor in five further performances of *Don Carlos*, again under Giulini. I also made my one and only appearance as the Mandarin in *Turandot* when Rhydderch Davies fell ill and I had to learn the part and take over at twenty-four hours' notice. But my obsession throughout the season was with Ochs, in spite of the fact that no one at the Garden had suggested I should study it much less that I might one day perform it. It was John who continually assured me that the house was desperate to have its own Ochs able to sing the role in German, and that this would be my big chance to convince them it should be me. And so we continued to work together, in snatched sessions at Covent Garden and at John's house in Ealing. I began to doubt whether I would ever acquire even a passable Wiener dialect but John, who had a remarkable ear not just for languages (he spoke fluent French, German and Italian) but also for dialect, kept me at it. We listened to Weber's pronunciation on the recording and worked at it, with John checking and advising constantly, and I slowly began to believe that anything might be possible.

How Vera managed to put up with me during those months, I will never know, for every waking moment was taken up with Ochs. Sometimes, when I slept badly, I would get up in the middle of the night to check a passage in the score. I had devised a system of counting the beats of the bar on my fingers, using the first three fingers for bars in three time and the first four for bars in four time. I tried always to know on which beat I began singing and on which I finished, and if, at the end of a passage, I had somehow finished on the wrong beat I knew I had made a mistake and I just had to know where.

By the time the season came to an end in July 1959, I had memorised Act I and had made a start on Act II. We had rented a cottage for four weeks that summer on the cliffs at Peacehaven and even on holiday I kept working. I would spend every fine day slumped in a deck-chair rehearsing my speech rhythms. Although our cottage was fairly secluded we did get the occasional passer-by, and I hate to think what they must have thought of this large man, sitting alone, muttering to himself in German! But I was making progress and when we returned home I was almost word-perfect.

That August I had one engagement to fulfil outside the Garden, singing Mephistopheles in the Welsh National Opera production of *Faust*. It was in Wales that, for the one and only time in my career, I missed an entrance. Robert Thomas, who was singing Faust, and I were in our dressing room chatting when we suddenly heard some music coming over the tannoy and realised simultaneously that we should have been on stage singing. We ran like hell and arrived just in time for him to say to me, 'Be gone!' and for me to reply 'I shall wait at the door', before I had to make my exit. We were both terribly upset and, as soon as the curtain came down, went to see Ivor John, the conductor, to apologise. 'Don't worry, boys', he said. 'I never realised how bloody beautiful that music was until I heard it without the voices.'

I returned from Wales and even before the 1959–60 season at the Garden began, John Matheson and I were hard at work again on the music of Ochs.

With the hard graft of learning the lines behind me, the musical side progressed much quicker and I began to feel at last that I was getting somewhere. But if I was anxious to get on with it, John kept slowing me down, making sure each passage was correct before he would allow me to move on. Gradually the part began to take shape and I started to see what Strauss was after. There were still one or two places which caused me difficulty, however, and the only way I could master them was to practise them constantly. One such passage was the 'Mord! Mord!' section from Act II.

This enormous cry of 'Murder! Murder!', when Ochs is wounded by Octavian, can be one of the funniest moments in the opera. It is also one of the most difficult vocally. It is written high in the voice and is marked 'brüllend' which means, literally, 'roaring'. It is easy to roar if you can choose your own pitch on which to make the noise, but if you have to do it on a high E natural, it becomes much more of a problem. The voice must sound uncontrolled and yet be *very* controlled. Until I could manage it satisfactorily, I just had to keep practising it, day and night.

Returning home one day after a particularly satisfying rehearsal with John, I went to the bathroom to wash my face and decided, to prove to myself that I had finally got it right, to let out a roar of 'Mord! Mord!' Before I had had time to reach for the towel, our front door bell was ringing furiously. I hurried downstairs, my face still wet, and opened the door to find our next-door neighbour, red in the face with anger. 'That constitutes a public nuisance!' he screamed. 'If you don't shut up, I'll call the police!'

In my single-minded desire to master the part I had quite forgotten that musical phrases, however beautifully and well-sung (and three-quarters of Ochs's music cannot be called 'beautiful' by any stretch of the imagination) can be a terrible bore when repeated *ad nauseam*. I managed to console the man and llater, when Vera, who had probably suffered as much as anyone, went round to make a further apology, she discovered that the neighbour's wife was on the verge of a nervous breakdown and invariably moved out into the garden, no matter what the weather, whenever I came home and started my practice. The upshot of this was that we moved our piano out of our comparatively spacious lounge into a tiny box room on the far side of the house where I would stun myself with the resonance in the confined space. Singing generates a lot of heat – if I sing in the car it invariably steams up – and I used to emerge from my rehearsals with red-rimmed eyes and a blinding headache.

The noise I made during these rehearsals must have been quite terrific for Vera used to say that when she got off the bus at the end of our road, she could tell immediately which place I had reached in the opera. Some years later, after I had been rehearsing Rocco's dialogue in *Fidelio* with Hilde Beal, Covent Garden's German language coach, our conversation over coffee turned to *Rosenkavalier*, and to Ochs's cry of 'Mord! Mord!' Hilde told me that she always found my playing of the scene very funny and that at least one other person must rate it as his favourite scene in the opera for he was constantly playing it over and over again on a record. 'Really?' I remarked. 'He must be a nut. It's hardly beautiful.' 'I know,' replied Hilde, 'but he lives somewhere near me in Sutton and I assure you I heard it almost every day for months some time back, although he seems to have stopped now.' At the mention of Sutton I pricked up my ears. 'Whereabouts in Sutton do you live?' I asked. 'Sutton Common Road,' she replied. 'Then that wasn't a record you heard; it was me,' I told her, and the whole story came out. Until that day neither of us knew where the other lived but it transpired that our houses were some 150 yards apart in Sutton Common Road. If she had been able to 'enjoy' my roaring, what must my poor neighbours have gone through?

The day finally arrived when John said he was going to talk to Webster, to tell him what we had done and to ask him if he wanted us to continue on an official basis. It may seem strange to talk of continuing to work on a role I had just finished learning, but with a part like Ochs it is important not just to know the music but to have it so much a part of you that to hear any section from any part of the opera will provoke a response. You must find yourself singing your own part and everyone else's without having to think about it. The continuation, therefore, was to be the final polishing process, during which I could relax a little and begin to check my memory. John would play a few bars and expect me to take it up correctly without a moment's hesitation.

To our great relief, Webster seemed to be delighted with our work (his grapevine, of course, had told him what was going on). He told John to continue and to give him further reports on my progress. It was this meticulous preparation, lasting almost a year, that was to be the prime reason for my eventual success as Ochs. Some years later a bass colleague, who had been engaged to sing the role with another company, astonished me by mentioning casually that he planned to begin work on it the following month. A quick calculation convinced me he couldn't possibly get it ready for the first night and I suggested that he ought to start immediately and be prepared to work night and day if he was to stand any chance of being even adequately prepared. He replied that he was a very fast learner and that he knew exactly what he was doing. When the production opened, he was woefully underprepared and gave an edgy and inaccurate performance which affected the rest of the cast.

The 1959 season opened with another Ring Cycle, under Konwitschny, in which I again played Fafner, and although I had my quota of old and new roles to sing, the most significant production for me was one in which I was not involved. This was the first production at Covent Garden since the war of *Der Rosenkavalier* in German, conducted by a man new to the House, Georg Solti, and with an international cast of Elisabeth Schwarzkopf as the Marschallin, Sena Jurinac as Octavian, Hanny Steffek as Sophie and Kurt Boehme as Ochs. Although rehearsals had started in November and I was in and around the house, I had heard little of them, simply because I was too preoccupied with my official work and with my own study. On the first day of December, however, John told me that we would be attending the dress rehearsal on the following day so that I could check my memory against a performance and also get some idea of the problems the part posed histrionically.

Most of us can, I imagine, look back over our lives and recognise an event that was to prove a turning point. Few of us, however, are in a position to recognise such an event as it happens. And it happened to me on the 2nd of December 1959. It may seem strange, after all the work I had done on the opera, but I was still not keen to sing Ochs as anything other than a means of advancing my career. I was still not enthusiastic about the role as such, and it had never entered my thinking that I might actually *enjoy* singing it.

The orchestral prelude to *Rosenkavalier* is a short, highly descriptive picture of love-making, during which the music rises to an explosive climax and then subsides into a languorous murmur before the curtain rises. At that point I had always started to lose interest. The idea of the youth Octavian being played by a woman had never appealed to me. On this occasion, however, I was captivated from the moment Sena Jurinac sang her first haunting line. There was such a wealth of boyish appeal in her voice and such a confidence and intensity in her delivery that I felt, against every instinct, that I really was watching and listening to a young man. The idiom of the piece had captured me. Perhaps it was my immaturity vanishing, perhaps it was because I was hearing the opera in its original language for the first time and the inconsistencies seemed softened, perhaps it was because I was desperately keen to like the piece, perhaps . . . . I do not know. I was certain of only one thing: that the opera held me fast in its grip.

If Jurinac was the ideal Octavian, then Schwarzkopf must have been Strauss's dream come true as the Marschallin. She was dignity personified; her face with its fine bones gave her an aristocratic look combined with a sensuous beauty. It was easy to understand her attraction for Octavian. I watched with intense pleasure these two prima donnas playing out their opening scene together. Only one thing clouded my reaction. I remember thinking what a pity it was that Strauss had written such rewarding music for them and left Ochs only difficult music without a hope of getting the audience in the same way. 'Why,' I inwardly groaned, 'didn't he write a bass role to match these two?'

The moment came for Ochs's first entrance and I sat up, ready to begin work. I was there, after all, principally to check on my memorising of the role. After an initial commotion outside the bedchamber had built into a roar, the door burst open and in staggered Kurt Boehme, two lackeys hanging on his arms, two more following nervously. He immediately spotted Octavian in the disguise of Mariandel the serving wench, and was enamoured. Reminded by the lackeys of the Marschallin's presence, he attempted to carry on two conversations at once, one flirtingly with Octavian, the other more dignified with the Marschallin. His every movement was redolent of the countryside from which he had just come, his facial expressions were hysterical, and, most revealing of all, he did not seem in the least worried by the complexities of the music. Everything seemed to happen spontaneously. I suddenly realised that Ochs was not just a long, difficult part, but could be a star role. As the act progressed Boehme managed to become even more funny. His scene with the Notary, in which he was interrupted constantly by the Italian tenor and became steadily more angry, was so funny that I had tears running down my cheeks. As he made his exit, I turned to John Matheson to find him watching me.

'Well?' he asked. 'What do you think of it now?'

I could only lift my eyes to the ceiling.

'I thought you'd like it,' he commented. 'And that's only Act I. Wait until you see the rest.'

By the end of the dress rehearsal I wanted to play Ochs more than I had wanted to play any other role in my life. It was no longer just a means of gaining recognition. I had seen the reactions of those members of the musical staff who had been in the auditorium, I had seen what could be done with the part, and I knew that if I could play him half as well as Boehme, I would be a very happy man. And yet, although I had studied the role and Webster knew that I had learnt it, nothing had so far been mentioned about a possibility I might actually get on stage to perform it. Now that I wanted to play it so much, I was afraid: afraid that my luck, which seemed to have changed, might change again. And the fact that Boehme was so good only increased my fears. He was so certain to be an outstanding success on the first night that I could hardly expect the management to entrust future performances to *me*.

I was even more entranced by the opera on the first night. The singers were magnificent, while Solti in the pit brought out every nuance of the score and clearly enjoyed what was happening on stage. Our own artists singing the smaller roles were inspired by the atmosphere and gave performances far above anything they had previously achieved in the opera. Ronald Lewis, who sang Faninal, a part he had sung at every performance of *Der Rosenkavalier* since Graham Clifford had relinquished it more than ten years earlier, later confirmed my impression. The opera had taken on a new dimension that night, he told me.

As I made my way to the Crush Bar during the second interval, I met Vic Oliver. Vic was a well-known entertainer who had given me my first chance as a soloist on one of his radio programmes. Like many popular musicians, Geraldo and George Mitchell among them, he was a keen opera-goer and was anxious to help break down musical barriers, doing much to popularise opera by always including some in his radio and television broadcasts.

'What do you think?' he asked me, listening intently while I enthused about the performance. 'Do you think you'll ever get the chance to sing Ochs?' he asked when I finally paused for breath. I hesitated, afraid to commit myself. 'Of course you will,' he went on. 'No doubt about it.'

Vic's confidence was a great boost, though it was quite illogical for me to give it any credence. Although he was very influential in his own sphere, and also very knowledgeable, having once coached opera in his native Austria, he had absolutely no say when it came to casting at Covent Garden. But such is the way of opera. The smallest, most ridiculous thing can lift, or lower, the spirits of a singer trying for the top – or even of one already there. What I wanted though was not the encouragement of friends but an assurance from the management that I would one day be permitted to sing Baron Ochs von Lerchenau.

Chapter 7 Why Not Indeed?

Towards the end of January 1960, almost two months after the first
night of that memorable Solti *Rosenkavalier*, John Matheson and I were
having a drink in 'The Nag's Head' when John casually mentioned that
Webster had at last made up his mind: I was to be cast as Ochs in the
revival that October. After I had changed our drinks for something
stronger, he went on to tell me that Webster had also decided to send me
abroad to finish studying the role. Naturally, I wanted to know where
and with whom, but John didn't know. He did, however, say that there
was really only one place in which to study Ochs and that was Vienna.

We decided to consult with Edward Downes, who had had experience of studying on the Continent, and ask him for his advice. Ted had
joined the company in 1952, shortly after I became a principal, and our
first meeting gave little indication of the friendship that was to develop
between us. It took place in Liverpool where the company was on tour.
Rehearsal rooms were in such short supply that a room containing an
old upright piano had been rented in a small terraced house, and it was
there that I had to go to sing through the role of Sparafucile for him. I
found it frustrating, to say the least. Every time I opened my mouth
Ted found something wrong and in a one hour call we barely managed
to get through the Rigoletto/Sparafucile duet. By the time we finished I
was in a state of suppressed fury, and I vowed that if the same thing
happened during our second rehearsal together, I would physically
assault him and walk out regardless of the consequences. The second
rehearsal arrived and to my amazement, after a few stops and starts,
Ted suddenly seemed to find what he was after and we went straight
through the first scene without a break. 'That was very good,' he said as
I finished. I was too surprised to speak, and it was some time before I
informed him that it had been my intention, if the events of the first day
had been repeated, to assault him. He grinned. 'I knew what you had in
mind,' he said. 'I'm very sensitive to atmosphere! But,' he went on, 'you
suddenly began to produce the sound I knew you had and so there was
no need to put you through the mill again.' I often sense that same
'atmosphere' nowadays when I am putting one of *my* young singers

through the mill on the rehearsal stage at the National Opera Studio. After that, Ted and I became good friends. I respected him for his tremendous musicality, his expertise and his mastery of languages, and I think he respected me because he knew I could be trusted to learn my music and that I could get on stage and exist; it was a mutual respect for each other's work, and he was later to be of great help to me during my difficult years under Kubelik.

Ted was in agreement with John over the question of Ochs. He felt that Webster might well be considering sending me to Hamburg or to Berlin, but he too felt that the only place in which to study the role was Vienna. They both made me promise that when the time came I would put my foot down and insist on being sent to Vienna.

I was summoned to Webster's office in mid-March. I had already heard on the grapevine that I was to be sent abroad the following month and I had now convinced myself that he meant to send me to either Hamburg or Berlin. I was determined to hold out for Vienna, and as I stood outside his door I rehearsed the arguments for Vienna and against either Hamburg or Berlin that had been running through my mind ever since my conversations with Ted and John. I knocked on the door and entered. Sir David was in his familiar position, gazing out of the window at the fruiterer opposite. He told me that he had decided I should finish my study of Ochs overseas and that I would be leaving in a month's time. Before he could continue, I plunged in.

'Sir David,' I said, 'I am convinced I should study this role in Vienna. It's a role that requires a Viennese accent and I wouldn't get much chance of listening to a Viennese accent in Berlin or Hamburg. I ask you, therefore, to send me to Vienna. I'm sure it would be best. There must be someone there who will work with me.'

He turned from the window and stared at me. I was disconcerted but knew I had to stand my ground.

'My dear Langdon,' he said, 'we *are* sending you to Vienna.'

I was so surprised I didn't know what to say. Webster went on to tell me that he had arranged for me to work with Alfred Jerger for four weeks beginning on the 16th of April. Jerger was himself a famous Ochs who had sung the role under Strauss, and I was both delighted and thrilled. I was to be responsible only for my living expenses. Covent Garden, Webster continued, would continue to pay my salary during my absence and would pay for my travel. I thanked him and started for the door, but a terrible thought struck me and I hesitated. I turned back to find Webster watching me.

80

'Would it be possible, Sir David,' I asked, 'for this study period to be brought forward a week so that I can be back in London before Saturday the 7th of May?'

Webster looked at me quizzically.

'Possibly, Langdon,' he replied. 'But why should it?'

'Wolves play Blackburn Rovers in the Cup Final at Wembley on that day, and I have a ticket. I'm a Wolves supporter,' I added rather lamely. He looked at me for a few seconds more.

'All right, Langdon, I'll see if it can be arranged. When did you say it would be convenient for you to go?' he added sarcastically.

'The 9th of April,' I told him.

Two days later I learned that the adjusted dates had been agreed and I was to leave for Vienna on the 9th of April, returning in time for the Cup Final. By the time I left Heathrow to begin my study with Alfred Jerger, my period of study had been cut from four to three weeks to enable me to sing in a concert at Rosehill at the end of April, and I was left to reflect that if only I had been a little more patient I need never have revealed my weakness for Association Football, and Wolves in particular, to Webster.

I arrived in Vienna in the middle of a rain storm and made my way by bus to the *pension* where I had been booked in by the Royal Opera House. After lunch I phoned Jerger and we arranged to meet at four o'clock that afternoon to begin work on the rehearsal stage of the Staatsoper. I took a last quick look at Act I and made my way to the Opera House, where I was directed to the big rehearsal room high in the building. It was empty and I sat down to wait. After about ten minutes, the door opened and Jerger came in, his hand outstretched in greeting. My first impression was of a stocky man with a mop of thick, iron-grey hair, a handsome face and a charming smile. He was then over seventy, but he gave no indication of being an old man. There was a spring in his step and an enormous vitality in every movement. As he came up and shook my hand, I realised he was much taller than I had at first thought.

He wasted no time in getting down to business. He said how pleased he was to be working with me and asked when my first performance was due. I told him, the following October. 'Good', he said, 'you have plenty of time to think about what I will teach you, but I must apologise for my bad English. I will not be able to tell if you are saying the right words.' I asked him what he meant, and he replied that he had never worked with anyone in English before. I pointed out that I was supposed to be singing the role in German, or rather Viennese. There was a long, long silence, and then Jerger said, 'I did not understand. I thought you were to study the acting of the role with me but that you were going to sing it in English.' I insisted that I was definitely going to sing in German. He sat down heavily at the piano. 'How can this be?' he muttered. 'Is it possible?' He sat there for so long I expected he was about to call the whole thing off, but at last he raised his head, looked at me with stricken resignation and said, 'So, we begin.'

Those three words heralded the start of three weeks' intense effort and concentration. Just as Matheson had battered me with the music, so Jerger battered me with the acting. It was a good thing I had spent so much time on the music and the speech rhythms because I quickly realised, once Jerger began to show me how to play the part, just how much the music must be second nature if Ochs is to be acted effectively. It was by no means second nature to me then, but it stood the test of our work together – just.

Jerger's method was to take a short section of the music and ask me to sing through it. He would then stand up, leave the piano and ask me to sit and watch him, while he went through the same section with the appropriate movements and gestures, indicating all the time where he would expect the other characters to be. I would then try to follow his example and that was when the real fun began. He would leap up and down from the piano like a yo-yo, explaining why I was doing this or that, why I felt this way or that, why my face must register this expression and not that. It was exhausting but exhilarating.

Jerger was quite an accomplished pianist and so the two of us could work together at our convenience without having to await the availability of a repetiteur. And Jerger's convenience meant morning, afternoon and part of the evening. By the end of the fifth day we had completed Acts I and II. Then came the third act, with its complicated business in the supper scene, and we seemed to bog down. Perhaps we had both been working too hard. Anyway, Jerger suggested that we drop the afternoon and evening rehearsals, and begin again the following day. That evening he invited me to join him and his wife for supper at his apartment in the Hofburg. It was one of the most delightful evenings I have ever spent. We ate, drank and talked, and I felt the tension of the previous few days easing out of me as the evening progressed. Over the second bottle of wine Jerger admitted that he had been in deep despair when he had discovered that he was supposed to teach me to play Ochs in German: he had not thought it possible for an Englishman to sing Ochs in the original language and sound convincing. 'Now', he said, 'I am happier.' At this point, Frau Jerger interrupted.

'He is *very* happy,' she said. 'The first day he came home and said he had been given a terribly difficult task to do. The second day I could tell he was a little happier, and yesterday he said to me "Wir haben einen Ochs gefunden."'

To hear that Jerger believed they had 'found an Ochs' completed my contentment and I felt I had passed my first test. I fondly imagined that within the week we would have done all we could with the role. I was to be proved very wrong. The following morning we were back to three sessions a day and work began on Act III. My confidence was high and things went so well that by the end of the day we had reached the end of Ochs's part. Jerger congratulated me and I was delighted. 'Now,' he said, 'we have gone through it very roughly, it is time to start working on it in detail.' Very roughly indeed! We had spent ten minutes trying to capture one fleeting expression, and now he was talking about 'working in detail'. I was almost ready to cry, but away we went again.

Jerger's vitality was tremendous. He never seemed to tire, in spite of his age, and he had not been joking when he spoke of working in detail. What had gone before was indeed sketchy by his standards. He now asked me to suggest things for myself because, as he was at pains to point out, he did not wish me to be a mere copy of himself in the role.

He continually stressed that Ochs, however seedy, must, above all else, be a nobleman. He talked of his work with Richard Strauss, and of how Strauss would insist that Ochs was not just 'a dirty old man'. When one considers some of the things that Ochs has to say and do during the course of the opera it is difficult to see how one can avoid giving an impression of coarseness, but Jerger managed to explain it. The person playing Ochs must give the impression of an enormous zest for life, for women, and for the physical pleasure the company of women can bring. Everything must be done openly, with a smile. If Ochs wants to feel a woman's bottom, he simply reaches out and feels it with great enthusiasm. None of his actions must be done in an underhand, shifty manner. In this way, Jerger told me, it is possible to make Ochs coarsely likeable.

In spite of this explanation, which made a great deal of sense to me, and in spite of my earnest efforts to follow his instructions, he would often pull me up in the middle of a rehearsal for doing something he considered 'Ochs would not do'. Since assuming the role I have, I suppose, been praised more for my success in achieving this delicate balance between honest vulgarity and plain dirtiness than for any other aspect of my performance, and this is due almost entirely to Jerger. The concentrated, sustained work we did together in Vienna set me off on the right road.

By the middle of the second week I was getting through longer and longer sections of the opera without being stopped. That was a good sign for Jerger missed nothing and our sessions were never fixed by time, only by the completion of the section he had decided to cover in that particular rehearsal. However, due to the intense concentration demanded by his method of teaching, a reaction set in and I began to suffer from headaches and pains in the back of my neck. Jerger fixed an appointment for me with an osteopath.

The osteopath was a keen opera fan and spent the first ten minutes discussing various operas and opera singers. I kept rubbing my neck to remind him of the purpose of my visit, and eventually he made me lie down on his examination table. He began to feel the muscles of my neck. 'Ja,' he said finally, 'I think we can help you here.' He asked me to sit in a chair which looked as though it had been bought second-hand from a death-cell in the United States, and proceeded to strap me in. He then placed a sling round my neck and under my chin. 'Comfortable?' he asked, and disappeared from sight behind me without waiting for me to say I wasn't. I heard a slight cranking sound and felt my head being lifted by the sling. My neck began to extend up and up, until I felt that it must give way at any moment. I was in panic. The strap under my chin meant I couldn't make a sound; I couldn't move a muscle; and the fact that the osteopath was behind me meant he couldn't see the terror in my eyes. Mercifully, the cranking stopped and he came round to my front.

'I think that will be enough for the moment,' he said. 'We will wait and let it take effect.'

I sat sweating, feeling that my head had been separated from my shoulders. My alarm was by no means allayed when the osteopath glanced at his watch, said that I had been there long enough, and announced that he was then about to perform the 'tricky bit'. 'Keep absolutely still,' he said unnecessarily, 'while we try to get it back.' He disappeared from view and the cranking sound started again. Slowly my head settled down.

'How do you feel?' he asked. In fact I felt worse than when I had arrived at his consulting rooms, but I was not going to tell him that. I assured him I felt marvellous, that my headache had vanished, and asked how much I owed him. I would have paid twice the fee he

84

requested out of sheer gratitude for escaping in one piece, and off I went, my head still thumping. The next day, however, all traces of tension in my neck had vanished and my head was clear so maybe he *did* know what he was doing.

Jerger now informed me that for the remainder of our time together we would be having only one extended session each day. He told me it would be very tiring because he wanted me to sing and act through from the beginning to the end every time we rehearsed. 'Without a break,' he added.

Only a singer who has performed a role the length of Ochs will realise just how tiring this is. During a performance a singer at least has a chance to rest between exits and entrances, and between acts, and with a long role like Ochs, one of the longest in the repertoire, you need those breaks. Jerger's intention, in getting me to go through the entire piece without stopping, was to discover just how much I had to spare in terms of physical and vocal stamina, so that I would know where I had to save myself and where I would be 'in the clear'.

Our first complete run-through demonstrated what both of us already suspected, that it was Act I that gave me most trouble. I recovered quickly, however, and the next two acts, although longer, proved to be easier. Our next session was devoted solely to Act I, trying to pinpoint the exact passages which were causing me difficulties. I sang through the act three times, stopping to make adjustments as Jerger directed, and by the end of the session most of my problems had been ironed out.

The fact that Jerger had decided to cut my study period to one main session every day pleased me two-fold. Firstly, it was obvious that he was pleased with my progress and felt that the final polishing progress could begin, and secondly, Vera was flying out to join me for the last week and it meant I would be able to spend some time with her looking round Vienna, of which I had seen almost nothing. And so I completed my studies with Jerger and prepared to return to London. It had been an exhausting but wonderful experience and I knew that no one had ever undertaken the part of Ochs better prepared than myself. It was now up to me.

Before I left Jerger asked me to hand him my score. In the fly-leaf he wrote: 'With friendly memories of our wonderful work together and with best wishes for great successes as Ochs von Lerchenau.' That score, twice rebound since that day in April 1960, is my most treasured possession.

I might have been forgiven for thinking, when I got back to London, that with the exception of the usual refresher music calls, my detailed work on Ochs was finished until the opera actually went into rehearsal the following October. When, however, I went to see Webster to tell him how I had got on in Vienna he again surprised me by telling me that he was sending me to Glyndebourne for the summer, where they were putting on *Rosenkavalier*, to understudy Oscar Czerwenka as Ochs, and to give me a chance to work with the other characters while doing some more thinking about the role. Once again he told me my salary would be paid in my absence but that the Covent Garden management would expect me to hand over to them any fees I would receive for understudying at Glyndebourne as part repayment of the money they had already spent on my preparation.

I drove down to Glyndebourne early one morning and eventually arrived having lost my way (something I kept very quiet since I felt everyone, especially a professional singer, should know how to find it). I was met by Jani Strasser and we began work immediately on the rehearsal stage with the other understudies. Jani was present throughout most of the rehearsal and constantly gave me advice, especially on certain nuances in the text he felt I had missed. After my period of study with Jerger this could have been confusing but I found his ideas on the role tallied with Jerger's to a remarkable degree.

The main value of my time at Glyndebourne was that it gave me my first opportunity to work on a stage with the other principals, especially with Octavian. In Vienna, Jerger had played all the other roles, switching from Octavian, to Sophie, to Faninal in quick and amusing succession, but nothing he could do could make up for the absence of the rest of the cast. Elizabeth Robertson was the Octavian understudy and we were able to go through the Ochs/Octavian scenes many times together. I soon realised how much the principal characters in *Rosenkavalier* are interdependent. More than in any other opera I know, the success of a performance is determined by the teamwork of the cast. Only if everyone is ready to give and take will the performance catch fire. If on the other hand there is someone in the cast who feels that they are the 'star', or the piece is under-rehearsed, then something vanishes and it becomes just another opera. The best performances of *Rosenkavalier*, as far as I am concerned, have always been those that have had adequate rehearsal and a team of principals who were friends as well as colleagues.

After the intense concentration of my studies with Matheson and

Jerger, working at Glyndebourne was relaxed and light-hearted. We were all doing it for the fun of the thing and were well aware that we were unlikely to be called upon suddenly to go on stage and perform our roles. As a result I found myself getting into the part more and more, absorbing it without conscious effort. My preparatory work was beginning to pay off. The music was now such second nature that I could actually begin to enjoy playing the role, exactly as Jerger had told me I must.

A few days later, Regina Sarfaty, who was singing Octavian in the performances, arrived earlier than expected and was kind enough to spend the extra time rehearsing with me. Although neither of us knew it at the time, we were to sing these roles together on many occasions in the future. With the arrival of Oscar Czerwenka my active part in the rehearsals finished and I stayed on to watch the first team in action, and, as Webster had put it, 'to think about the opera'. It was interesting to watch Czerwenka in the role and to compare his performance with Boehme's. Although I still preferred Boehme's way of playing it, there were moments when Czerwenka seemed to bring out a point more clearly. Already I was becoming more demanding in my expectations when watching someone play the part, and the way I wanted to perform it was taking definite shape in my mind.

After the first night, I left Glyndebourne and returned to London to take up my contract with Covent Garden actively again. Walking down Long Acre one day, I bumped into Sir David Webster. We stopped and chatted about things in general and as we were about to go our separate ways, he suddenly asked, as if it was an afterthought, 'Oh, by the way, Langdon, about that understudying fee from the Glyndebourne people. You did promise to pass it on to me, remember?' I had completely forgotten about it. Although John Coast was well-known for being able to secure good fees for his singers, he had only been able to get me a very modest amount from Glyndebourne. They were probably well aware that they had been doing me a favour in agreeing to let me cover the role and, bearing in mind that it was part of my preparation for singing it at Covent Garden, had decided to make the most of it. My fee was, consequently, very small; so small, I told Webster, that I didn't think it was worth mentioning.

'Let me be the judge of that,' he admonished. 'How much?'

I told him.

'Well,' he said, 'it may not be a very large sum, but multiplied by the number of performances, it takes on a more respectable look.'

I then explained that the figure I had given him was to cover *all* the performances. He stood for a few seconds in deep thought.

'In that case, my dear Langdon,' he finally said, 'go and buy yourself a box of chocolates or something.'

The summer break in 1960 was not the most relaxed time in my life. My forthcoming debut as Ochs was never far from my mind and I was acutely aware of how much my future career depended on my success in the role. The cast for the production was to be Régine Crespin as the Marschallin, Hertha Töpper as Octavian, Joan Carlyle as Sophie and Ronald Lewis as Faninal, with Ted Downes conducting, something that pleased me enormously. It was a fine, experienced company, with, in Crespin and Töpper, two internationally recognised exponents of their roles. I was the only raw recruit.

Rehearsals started at the beginning of October. It was the old Joan Cross production, using the old costumes. Shortly after my return from Vienna, Webster had asked me if there was anybody in particular I would like to re-stage the production and I had replied, without hesitation, Alfred Jerger. Much to my surprise, Webster had agreed to the proposal. It was quite obvious to me that Webster was determined to give me every opportunity. He had sent me to Vienna, he had sent me to Glyndebourne and now he had agreed to Jerger producing. Maybe he felt I had had a raw deal during the Kubelik era and, having seen what I could do with Kecal, had decided to give me a real chance to prove myself. If I failed, at least he would not have to feel guilty about denying me the opportunity. Whatever his reasons may have been, Webster gave me enormous encouragement and help.

I began rehearsing on stage with Jerger on my own. A week later we were joined by Joan Carlyle and Ronald Lewis, and with ten days to go before the first night, Régine Crespin and Hertha Töpper completed the team. Everyone gave me the utmost help and I have never seen Ted Downes so patient in the face of so much repetition. It is never easy for an established artist to have to repeat scenes over and over again for the benefit of a newcomer but there was never the slightest objection when Jerger called for a scene to be played 'just once more'.

At supper a week before we were due to open, Jerger told me he was convinced I would have a great success. His confidence was enough to start me thinking of all the things that could go wrong: I could break a leg, I could collapse from exhaustion, I could catch a cold. . . . With seven days to go I did, in fact, catch a cold. I rang the Opera House and was given permission to miss some of the rehearsals and stay at home to nurse myself and try every cold remedy I could think of. If anything my cold got worse. My chest was tight and my singing was difficult and constricted. I managed to get through the dress rehearsal with some difficulty, my voice being reduced in volume, tone and resonance, but at least the cold seemed to be clearing. On the morning of Monday 24th October, the day of the opening, I rose early and went for a long walk on Banstead Downs, humming softly to myself and praying a little every so often. To my immense relief my voice seemed much clearer.

That evening I drove to the theatre and found a pile of good luck telegrams awaiting me, including one from Sir David Webster. I became, for a moment, a little overawed by the importance of the occasion, but that soon passed. Ochs is not on immediately and I had time to stew a little before going down to make my first off-stage noises. Every Ochs I have ever spoken to uses these noises to try out his voice and you can often tell at this point, even before making your first entrance, whether you are going to be in good voice or not. I made my noises, my voice felt in fair condition and on I went.

If I had not felt nervous before going on, I soon felt nervous afterwards. 'Selbstverständlich,' I began, and my voice felt lost and thin. My mouth was dry and I had difficulty in enunciating. Both Crespin and Töpper knew I was nervous and in some trouble, and they did everything they could to help me. At one point, when my lips literally stuck together, Töpper pushed the cup of chocolate that had been used earlier in the scene into my hand and whispered, 'Trink!' As soon as the music permitted, I took a quick sip, my lips unstuck themselves and I felt better. It was the turning point. My crisis was over and, although I was aware my voice was not in top form, I gained in confidence from that moment on. At the end I had a very satisfying curtain call but I cannot describe the relief I felt that it was all over. Most opera singers will tell you that the best part of a first night is the meal afterwards and so it was with me. Vera and I went back to John Coast's for supper with Alfred Jerger and a few friends. My performance was discussed and it was agreed that it had been successful. All that remained to be seen was what the press made of it. The next morning Vera bought copies of all the papers and they were awaiting me on the breakfast table. I opened the first one with mounting apprehension. My fears were unfounded for almost without exception my playing of the role had been warmly praised. Only one thing upset me somewhat. Several critics mentioned that my voice hardly matched up to my acting, that the part required more resonance. They all knew my voice well, having heard me many times over the years. Could they not tell I was singing below form? Only one, Leslie Ayre of the *Evening News*, seemed to realise that there was something wrong, for he wrote that I possessed 'one of the richest bass voices we know at Covent Garden. That it had rather less ring to it last night must be accounted for by his concentration on this extraordinarily difficult character portrayal. Later performances will, I am sure, show him to be a very fine Baron Ochs both in voice and manner.'

So far as the Covent Garden management was concerned, there seemed to be no doubts about my success for when the production went on tour in the Spring of 1961, I was again given the role, and repeated it when we returned to London. Several critics noticed that my tone had improved since my debut. One even commented that I 'had found fuller, more resounding tones in which to sing the music'. Of course I had: I was no longer suffering from the effects of a cold.

Chapter 8 Enter Solti

The main reason for my initial success as Ochs was, I am sure, its element of surprise. I gave an efficient, but by no means finished performance. In fact, I do not think I really began to get into the role until after I had given something like thirty performances. What did surprise people was that an Englishman, singing not just in German but in a Viennese dialect, gave a creditable rendering of the part. Walter Jefferies, a Viennese domiciled in London and a keen fan of *Der Rosenkavalier*, with whom I was to become firm friends, later told me that when he had received notification of the production and glanced at the cast list, he thought that the Ochs had not been cast. He saw my name but assumed I would be singing either the Notary in Act I or the Police Kommissar in Act III. He rang the Opera House to enquire if they had any idea who the Ochs would be and was told it was me. This had given him and his family a good laugh, and they had decided to book for the production just for the hell of it! They were all, he said, tremendously surprised that I managed to bring it off so convincingly.

The one person who had *not* been impressed was Georg Solti. Solti's appointment as Covent Garden's new Musical Director had just been announced and Webster had taken him to see a performance as his personal guest. Afterwards, Webster had asked Solti his opinion. 'Terrible,' Solti spluttered, 'terrible.' It transpired later that he had thought my performance so bad that he had seriously considered whether he ought to take up his appointment. Luckily for Covent Garden he decided to stay. In many ways Solti was right. He was used to conducting the finished article, people like Boehme, and in me he saw only a raw beginner, which was not enough. The element of surprise meant nothing to him for he expected perfection. I did not sing the role under him until six years later. When I asked him why it had taken so long for us to work together on the opera, he replied, 'Because, Mike, *now* you are ready for me.'

Solti took over as Musical Director at the beginning of the 1961–62 season. Webster, aware that the appointment of another foreigner might not go down well with his critics, was determined to ease him in gently, and so Solti was engaged, at the beginning of 1961, to conduct the Covent Garden premiere of Britten's latest opera, *A Midsummer Night's Dream*, a sort of try out to see how we took to him and how he took to us.

Although we knew he would not be taking up his appointment officially for another six months, there was again that unease in the company as everyone began to wonder just how his arrival would affect them personally. We knew he had been at Frankfurt for the previous nine years and we expected him to be rather Germanic in manner and temperament, and so it proved. He was extremely formal and people stood in some awe of him. His appearance did not help dispel this feeling. A man of medium height, very straight and very strongly built, he looked slightly sinister and had about him an aura of energy, a sense of power, which affected everyone with whom he came into contact. When rehearsing, he would seize you by the arm and beat out the time; on one earlier occasion at Glyndebourne he gripped an artist so hard he drew blood. Another of his habits, if he felt that you were too tense to give of your best, was to stand in front of you, bend down and seize you by the forearms while hissing 'Relax!' Very few singers failed to go into an involuntary muscular spasm when receiving this advice.

I got to know him during rehearsals for *A Midsummer Night's Dream* in which I had been cast as Quince. One of his first actions was to try and introduce the continental system of rehearsing, starting with a session in the morning, resting in the afternoon and recommencing in the evening, finishing at about ten or eleven. Such a schedule was all right for Solti who only had to walk to the Opera House from his suite in the Savoy, but there wasn't a principal singer who didn't have a journey of at least forty-five minutes to get home, some considerably longer. For the first few afternoons the Green Room was full of disgruntled singers, trying to find ways of passing the time until the evening rehearsal began; the news cinemas were taken over by bored artists. It was a situation that could not go on and a deputation was sent to request a return to the old schedule. Finally Solti agreed to accept the British way of doing things.

Solti's English when he arrived was awful, and yet he immediately began to criticise our pronunciation in *A Midsummer Night's Dream*. 'Vot ees zis Chineese English?' he would keep saying. 'Vot are you saying?' At one point he said to John Lanigan, who was playing Flute, '*V*oman. Can you not say *V*oman?' John answered that he could indeed and so from then on he would sing, 'Let not me be a *v*oman.' It was only after some time that someone plucked up the courage to tell Solti the correct pronunciation. 'Vy did not somebody tell me? Ve make it *W*oman then.'

I had been watching and listening to this and similar admonitions with some amusement and when it came to my turn to sing, I began my first line, 'Is all our company here?' in a broad Devon dialect. Solti immediately stopped the rehearsal.

'Mr. Langdon,' he said, 'vot ees zis? Zis is awful. I do not understand von single vord you say. Zees opera ees een English – goot English.'

'But Maestro,' I replied, 'I am singing in dialect. These people are rustics; they are all country lads. And I'm from Devonshire.'

There was a long silence.

'Devonshire?' said Solti. 'Zees is a special dialect?'

I nodded.

'I see. So I vould not understand it?'

'No,' I said, 'you wouldn't have a chance.'

'OK,' Solti replied, 'zen you do zees in dialect.'

And so I began again and he never stopped me. When it came to the actual performance, I naturally softened it somewhat so that I could be understood. Somebody obviously told Solti what I had done and that he was having his leg pulled, for a few months later, when I was singing Hunding in Solti's first Ring cycle, I suddenly got my German completely mixed up and came out with gobbledegook. Solti stopped the orchestra. 'Mike,' he said, for I was Mike by then, 'zis also is perhaps in Devonshire dialect?' He waved his finger at me. 'I have been vaiting more than six months for this!'

A Midsummer Night's Dream was produced by Sir John Gielgud, and he and Solti made an effective team. Solti would defer to Gielgud's immense knowledge of the play and the way the characters should behave, but he was determined that the music should register as the prime ingredient and kept reminding us of the way opera singers playing those roles should behave. The major weakness of many producers who come to opera from the straight theatre is that they feel opera is nothing more than a play with music in which the lines happen to be sung rather than spoken. Nothing could be further from the truth. Opera is musical drama and the singer, however good an actor, is confined in the framework set by the composer. An actor can deliver his lines in his own time, he can gauge an audience's reaction, and if he feels he needs to slow a line down, extend a piece of business that might be getting a good laugh, or speed up the action, he can accomplish it easily.

93

A singer, on the other hand, is governed by the music. He has a specific number of bars, occasionally a specific number of notes, during which an action must be completed or an emotion expressed. Solti and Gielgud worked so well together because each knew his own job backwards and at the same time understood the other's problems.

My reaction to the music of *A Midsummer Night's Dream* was similar to that I had had when first working on *Billy Budd*: I failed to see how the individual parts would add up to a whole. But knowing what had happened before I was more prepared to expect something exciting to occur, and I was not disappointed. During rehearsals of the opening scene when the curtain goes up on the forest glade, the music had seemed ordinary when played on a piano. Immediately we heard the same notes being played by the orchestra the effect was magical. You could see the moonlight, see the fairies and strange creatures from other worlds. The first night was an enormous success and Solti brought to it his own brand of excitement and tension. Perhaps under an English conductor we might have had a more 'English' performance, but the evening would have lost that individual Solti magic.

I had particular cause to remember that first night. At the moment Bottom appeared in his ass's head, the mechanicals had to recoil in fear. I had been directed to jump up a couple of steps and as I did so, I heard a sharp report like the crack of a whip. The tendon in my left ankle had, I later learned, sprung from its groove in the ankle bone, taking with it a chip of the bone itself. I was in agony but the opera had to continue. In the last act, when the mechanicals perform their play, a dance had been specially choreographed for us. During the interval I bound my ankle tightly but I was really unable to move properly and could obviously not take part in the dancing. Joseph Ward, who was playing Starveling, had spent hours rehearsing, to great effect, with a gnarled stick, which I promptly commandeered, and instead of taking part I stood in the middle of the circle and used Joe's stick to conduct the dancing. Joe, who was used to having this prop in one hand, suddenly found he had two hands free and didn't know what to do with them!

My ankle healed sufficiently for me to take part in the next new production a couple of months later, of *Falstaff*, conducted by Giulini and produced by Zeffirelli. I felt that I owed Giulini so much for the way he had supported me over *Don Carlos* that I was looking forward with immense pleasure to working with him again, and I would have gone on stage even if both my tendons had gone. Pleasurable though it was to be conducted by Giulini, he was not the same Giulini as in

94

Don Carlos. Marvellous conductor that he is, I found him not quite as effective in comedy as in drama. I often missed the smile that you get from a really good conductor of comic opera, and the impression you get on stage that he is participating fully in everything that is happening.

He and Zeffirelli again worked as a team. They were constantly discussing the placement of the singers, and the timings of their entrances and exits, to fit in with both the visual and the aural aspects of the production. It was a very physical production, very frenetic and very effective, and we all had to work very hard. If I have one criticism of Zeffirelli it is that he could have made our job a little easier by designing lighter costumes. The clothes he made us wear, and he did all the costume designs, were extremely heavy, the heaviest I think I ever had to put on. By the end of every performance we had all lost pounds in weight.

The cast for *Falstaff* was superb, with Mirella Freni, Regina Resnik, Luigi Alva, Robert Bowman, John Lanigan and John Shaw, and Geraint Evans as Falstaff. Although Geraint had already sung Falstaff at Glyndebourne and in France, it was this production that proved him to be a Falstaff of international stature, and indeed the production was hailed as the finest of our generation. I was singing the role of Pistol. It is typical of many roles in the bass repertoire. It is not a star role, but it is one in which a singer can make a big impact. Many basses look down their noses at such parts, wanting only to sing the big roles, but there is only a select band of people who can travel the world doing just a handful of star roles. During my career I performed a tremendous number of Ochses and Osmins, but I would have found it extremely dull to have spent my time concentrating on those to the exclusion of all others, and I loved to get back to the variety of singing, say, Count Waldner in *Arabella*, Don Basilio in *The Barber*, the Commendatore in *Don Giovanni*, or Pistol.

The first scene of the Zeffirelli production was particularly gymnastic, and was the best first scene of *Falstaff* I have ever played in or seen anywhere in the world. Almost invariably it would bring the house down and was a barometer of how well the rest of the opera would be received. At one stage Bob Bowman, who was playing Bardolph, had to escape from Falstaff by diving between his legs, climbing on to a stool, jumping on to a table, then on to the back of a bench and from there leaping up to a balcony. One night the stage hands had set the balcony a little further away from the back of the bench than usual. During the

95

scene, I was on the balcony and I leant over and remarked to Bob that he would never make it. 'I bloody well will,' he muttered. He went through his escape routine and came to the final leap. He made a grab for the balcony rail and just managed to reach it. I could see his fingers going white as he hung on, before I reached down, grabbed him by the scruff of the collar and pulled him up. Such determination is my abiding memory of that production. We were all determined to do the impossible because Zeffirelli wanted it. The audience reaction on that first night on the 10th May 1961 was so overpowering that only then did we realise just how effective the production was. It is amazing just how much discomfort a singer will put up with to hear an audience applaud like that. It's when you've gone through it all and they *don't* applaud that it becomes disheartening.

One week after the run of *Falstaff* ended, I left London for Hamburg, to begin my international career. The engagement came as a direct result of my appearance as Ochs and was the first concrete evidence that foreign houses were interested in me. There are only a handful of singers who specialise in the role and the debut of any Ochs is always of interest to managements. Several other theatres had expressed interest in my performance but wanted to see how I progressed in the role. For an Englishman to sing Ochs in German in London was one thing; to sing it in front of a German-speaking audience was quite another.

During *Falstaff* I had been commuting regularly to Glyndebourne where I had been engaged in my own right to sing the Commendatore and to understudy Osmin in *Entführung*, taking over the last half dozen performances. The last Osmin aria is one of the most difficult for a bass to bring off successfully if he is going to sing all the notes Mozart has written, for it contains bottom Ds. During my first run-through with Jani Strasser, I sang it note-perfect, including a very satisfactory bottom D, and I waited to be praised. 'Yes, my dear,' said Jani, 'that was very good. Now we do it again, but this time I want you to jump on and off a chair while you are singing it. That's how you are going to feel on stage when you come to do it.' And he was right. By the time I got to the bottom D the second time around I had hardly any breath left. I have since come up against producers who have asked me to do all sorts of weird and wonderful things during that aria, and I have always had to say, please let me get that note out of the way and then I'll do whatever you want.

Appearing in that Glyndebourne season were several singers from

96

German houses. Having heard my Osmin in rehearsal they assured me that I had little to worry about singing Ochs in Hamburg. What amused them particularly was that I spent so much time practising my Viennese accent that my dialogue in *Entführung* was liberally larded with Austrian vowels, and they unanimously decided to christen me Osmin von Lerchenau.

I arrived in Hamburg two days before the performance, and there was little time for rehearsal. My first call was with a remarkable pianist named Kunsch, who took me through the part to assure himself and the management that I did, in fact, know it, and then, with the conductor Albert Bittner present, he really went to town. Neatly spliced into Strauss's music were snippets from *Show Boat*, *Desert Song* and *Porgy and Bess*. I still managed to get through it all right, though it was hard to suppress my laughter. Rudolf Kempe later told me that this was Kunsch's speciality and invariably used to startle singers working with him for the first time.

The cast for that production included Clara Ebers and Helga Pilarczyk, who were both very experienced, and once again I felt very much the new boy. I had only performed the role eleven times in my career, and I had never been abroad before as a soloist in my own right. I found the food strange, the language a problem and I felt uncomfortable in the theatre simply because I did not know the building. Corridors never seemed to lead to the place I wanted and I was inhibited at making enquiries in German. I also had very definite ideas by now about the character of Ochs. Jerger had told me repeatedly that he must not be too rough or boorish, and that had Ochs displeased the Marschallin too much she would have thrown him out in Act I and that would have been the end of the story. In Hamburg I found I was not required to do my own make-up. I could have insisted but I was so much the newcomer I did not dare suggest that I could have done a better job than the experts. When my time came to sit in the make-up chair, I told the gentleman as best I could that I wished to look like a nobleman and not like a rough farmer. When he had finished and I opened my eyes I was horrified. I looked like a dandy, with a smooth complexion and a beauty spot on my right cheek. It was too late for me to do anything about it, and when I made my first entrance I could imagine the audience saying, 'So *that's* the way they do it in London.'

I gave a very mediocre performance. I was disappointed even as I sang and anticipated my lack of success. Before the end of the second act

I felt I should have been on the plane home, and by the end of the opera I was not sure I wanted to sing the part ever again. I returned to London very depressed and went down to Glyndebourne to continue the *Entführung* rehearsals. About a week later I discovered that German music critics are as unpredictable as their English counterparts. Heinz Hoppe, who was singing Belmonte with me, produced a Hamburg newspaper with a review of my performance. It was a rave. I had apparently shown Hamburg an entirely new study of Ochs, had thrown a fresh 'shadow' on the part, and so on. A couple of weeks later I returned to Hamburg for a further performance and this time got the make-up I wanted. The food agreed with me better, I knew my way around the theatre a little more, and I again sang below par. I began to have serious doubts as to whether I would ever be a real success in the role.

Solti's musical directorship of Covent Garden began officially in August 1961 (after the summer break), with performances of *Iphigénie en Tauride* (in a new production by Göran Gentele) and *A Midsummer Night's Dream* at the Edinburgh Festival. The company then returned to London for a revival of *Fidelio* under Jascha Horenstein, in which I sang my first Rocco, and to prepare for the opening of a new production of *Die Walküre*. It was intended that this should have been the first of a completely new production of the entire *Ring*. Making his debut as producer was Hans Hotter, one of the finest Wotans there has ever been. The production was not a success. Although Solti was conducting the performances some of the early rehearsals were taken by Reginald Goodall, who had such a serious disagreement with Hotter about tempi that Hotter asked for him to be removed. The designs were downright bad, and Hotter, as a producer, was definitely feeling his way. Although he had many marvellous ideas and obviously knew the work inside out, he found it very difficult to stand outside the production and see exactly what was going on. This was because he was also singing in the performances, a course I would never recommend, for it is virtually impossible for a singer to direct scenes in which he is himself taking part. He was, however, a tremendously exciting person to work with and gave all of us many marvellous tips on how to play Wagner. He explained to me how to make Hunding's realisation that Siegmund is the person he has to kill twice as effective. At that moment I was sitting down and Hotter wanted me to stand up. He watched me do it, then stopped me. 'That's not right,' he said. 'You must always make size for yourself. Diminish yourself so that when you stand up there is more distance to cover.' He then demonstrated what he meant. He sat with his hands on his knees, fingers pointing in, crouching slightly. As he started to get up, he pushed off slowly, rising to his full height. It made him look a foot taller than he was.

Another producer who made his first stab at opera later that season was Peter Ustinov with a triple bill of *L'Heure Espagnole*, *Erwartung* and *Gianni Schicchi*, all conducted by Solti. Once again, it was a case of a theatre man feeling his way and not being entirely successful. In *Gianni Schicchi*, in which I played Simone, we were also hampered by having an atrocious set. It was a terraced effect, quite unlike the inside of any real room you could ever see, and was like working on a rack of shelves. We were literally in tiers – and tears. A further complication was a clash of views between Ustinov and Geraint Evans on how the part of Schicchi should be played. This clash, indeed, extended to practically every aspect of the opera at some time or another. In his book *Dear Me* Ustinov says some rather caustic things about Geraint and his method of playing parts, but my own feeling is that Geraint, much more experienced in opera than his producer, happened to know what worked best for *him* and was determined, if at all possible, to have his way. I am sure that the Peter Ustinov of a few years later, with several successful operas under his belt, would have been much more responsive to Geraint's ideas.

There were other failures in Solti's opening season as well. After the success of *Der Rosenkavalier* the previous year, it had been decided to mount Strauss's little-performed opera *The Silent Woman*. In spite of having Kempe conducting, the production, which opened in November 1961, never really caught fire. I was originally asked to look at Morosus, a part which was considered to be a natural follow-up to Ochs, but it was really too high for me and I ended up playing Farfallo. The opera never came back.

Der Freischütz, which was given its first revival in almost ten years, was another work which didn't really catch on. We sang it in English, which I felt was a mistake. The language was so colloquial that it became embarrassing, and everything that could go wrong with a very technical production did. I played Caspar and at one point had to give my rifle to Max, who pointed it into the flies and shot an eagle which fell to the stage. This, in itself, used to raise a laugh. Arturo Sergi, the American tenor who was singing Max, would then ask me what kind of bullet he had used. One night, he pulled the trigger, the gun went 'phut', but Sergi continued with his line, 'What kind of bullet was that?'

The audience roared with laughter. Kempe, who was conducting, put his head in his hands. A few seconds later the stuffed eagle dropped on to the stage. The audience screamed and the opera was dead from that moment on. There were more involuntary laughs in that production than in anything I've ever done.

There was little indication during Solti's first season of the standards he would later achieve, but at the same time there was an excitement about the house generated by Solti's presence. We all felt we were on the verge of a new era.

If Solti arrived as a Teutonic dictator, it did not take long for him to adapt to English ways and become more English than the English. He never lost his unique accent, but he did develop a pronounced sense of humour and delighted in playing practical jokes. Ken Macdonald, a fine tenor who was never cast in the roles he deserved, was instrumental in introducing Solti to this peculiarly British form of humour. By the time I came to sing my first Ochs with him in 1966, Solti was well into the swing of things. He came to me one day and said, 'Now we must play a joke on Kenneth. What is the worst thing for the Italian tenor to have to do in *Rosenkavalier?*' 'Apart from singing that bloody aria', I said, 'I don't know'. 'To have to stay until half past eleven to take a curtain call,' replied Solti, his eyes gleaming. He told me he was going to speak to Visconti, the producer, and ask him to pretend that when the Marschallin makes her third act entrance she should come on with her complete entourage, including the hairdresser, the flautist, and the singer. 'I will tell Kenneth that it is Visconti's idea, that it is a silly idea, but that we must put up with it,' he said. Shortly afterwards, I saw Ken, blue in the face. 'Do you know what that bloody Hungarian wants me to do?' he spluttered. 'He wants me to stay in make-up until the end of the opera. He wants me to come on with the Marschallin in the third act.' I commiserated with him but pointed out that it was the same for everyone. Ken was not placated. As time went by, Ken became more and more suspicious. The third act entourage was never rehearsed and Solti kept saying it would be done later. The day before we were finally due to do it, Solti told me he planned to put Ken out of his misery. He asked me to bring him in, and said he would meet us at the stage door and tell him it was all a joke, that he wasn't really wanted. So I told Ken I would pick him up the following morning. I lived in Sutton while he lived at Esher, so it was quite a bit out of my way.

The next morning, I pulled up outside Ken's house and he climbed into my car. 'What's going on, Mike?' he asked. 'Why have you come all

100

this way to pick me up? You've never done it before.' I replied that it was a nice day and I felt like a drive. As we began to move off, we saw Ken's wife, Cynthia, waving from the house. We waved back and drove off. When we arrived at Covent Garden, Solti was standing at the stage door like a little boy caught scrumping apples.

'Kenneth,' he said, 'it was a joke.'

'What was a joke?' Ken asked.

'You don't have to come on in Act III. I tried to ring you at home but you were leaving. Cynthia couldn't stop you. Perhaps it wasn't such a good joke,' he added, seizing him by the shoulders and shaking him, 'but it *was* a joke.'

Ken got his own back later when Solti took him to Israel to take part in a concert. The British Fleet was paying a courtesy visit at the time and Solti told Ken how much he adored ships, and how much he would love to go aboard one. The next day Solti's telephone rang and a very British voice asked to speak to 'Mr. Soltee.' 'Sholti,' he replied, correcting the pronunciation, 'Sholti. This is Solti speaking.' 'Commander Willoughby-Smythe here. I've been told you have rather an interest in ships and wonder if perhaps you would like to look over my flagship if you have time?'

'Ah, ha, it's a joke. It's Kenneth, isn't it?'

'I *beg* your pardon?' replied the authoritative voice disapprovingly. Solti later said that it was those four words and the manner in which they had been spoken that had convinced him he had made a mistake. 'I'm dreadfully sorry, Commander,' he said. 'I have this joking singer with me. I would love to come and look round.'

'Are you free tomorrow morning?'

'I make myself free. Where do we meet?'

'If you stand on the bottom step of your hotel after breakfast,' came the reply, 'I will send a cutter down the main street to pick you up.' With which the phone went dead, and Solti knew he had been had.

In return, Solti, well into the swing of things, got a Rabbi to phone Ken and thank him for learning the work in Hebrew; he knew it must have been a tremendous chore but it was a great honour that a British artist should go to such lengths, and so on. Ken was panic-stricken and immediately phoned Solti, who said of course, being in Israel it was understood that they would be performing in Hebrew. He told Ken not to worry, that he had until the following evening to learn it. Only the next morning did Solti tell him the truth, to put Ken out of his misery.

There was about Solti a streak of magnificent selfishness. Nothing else mattered to him except his performances and everything else took second place to them. Anybody looking at the number of rehearsals for any opera in preparation would be able to tell immediately if it was being conducted by Solti or by a someone else. Solti would have two or three times more rehearsal. There was even an occasion when Solti withdrew two singers from a performance of *La Bohème* so that they would be fresh for one of his rehearsals. In anybody else this selfishness would have been a vice but in Solti it was almost a virtue. He was a perfectionist who would leave nothing to chance. He was also very money orientated. Soon after I had started my international career, I was asked to go to Geneva to sing Osmin. Joan Ingpen, the casting director, went to see Solti to ask him to release me from some performances of *Moses and Aaron* in which I was playing the High Priest. Although Joan tried all her powers of persuasion and assured him that someone else could do the part without jeopardising the performance, Solti was adamant! I had to sing at Covent Garden. I told Joan I would go and speak to him.

'I don't know what you're going to say,' she said. 'I've tried everything.'

'I know what you've come to see me about, Mike,' Solti said when I walked into his room, 'but it's impossible; I cannot let you go. This part is so important and you do it so well. We must have you for this.'

'May I just say a few words, Maestro?' I replied.

'OK, but it will make no difference.' He then offered me a drink to show that he was not just being awkward but was taking the action in my own interests. 'What do you wish to say?' he asked eventually.

'It's a matter of money,' I said. There was a long, long pause.

'So,' he said slowly, 'you lose a lot of money if I stop you doing this?' I nodded. 'OK,' he replied, 'who can do it then?'

I had no answer ready for this one and said the first name that came into my head.

'Eric Garrett,' I replied with utter conviction.

'Fine', Solti said, 'Garrett will do it.' And off I went to Geneva. When I got back Solti was furious with me. The part had been too low for Eric and Solti was convinced that I had known it all along.

The selfishness that Solti made almost a religion in his pursuit of perfection was countered by an immense generosity in his private life where money was concerned. More than one person has, to my knowledge, been helped over a rough patch by private donations from him. This was always arranged with the utmost discretion, and with no desire for praise or publicity.

Under Solti Covent Garden was to enjoy its best years since the company was reformed after the war. He consolidated the work of his predecessors and established the Royal Opera House not just as an international house but as one of the finest in the world. He was a man of such great energy, such strength, such dynamism, and such will-power, that he affected everyone around him. He was also a marvellous conductor. If he had any failing in the pit it was that he would occasionally become so wrapped up in the orchestra that he would swamp the singers, but whenever you sang for Solti, you had to *sing*; there were never any half measures. He was not a man to accept second best. At Covent Garden he judged singers purely on their merits and if he thought people were good enough he would give them opportunities. He was never a person to cast a British singer in a role just because he or she was British. If he wanted a foreign star he would get one, but if he felt a home-grown singer was as good *they* would get the part. Before Solti came, British singers had only just started to get around internationally. People like Richard Lewis and Geraint Evans were beginning to widen the trail that had been started by such singers as Eva Turner, Constance Shacklock and Sylvia Fisher. After his arrival, the fact that a man of his ability and reputation was prepared to accept British singers in important roles had a tremendous effect on the operatic world in general and sparked off world-wide interest in 'his' singers. Solti was known as a hard professional who would not accept a singer if he did not think he or she was up to it, and his confidence in his ensemble at Covent Garden worked very much to the singers' advantage, not least my own.

Chapter 9 Ochs Grows Up

My disappointing international debut as Ochs in Hamburg had to some extent been mitigated by engagements to sing the role in Berlin and Paris, and in January 1962, after appearing in a revival of *A Midsummer Night's Dream*, I left Covent Garden for Germany. My fellow artists were Astrid Varnay, Helga Pilarczyk and Edith Mathis. I had obviously undergone a mental change since Hamburg for I went on without a care in the world and really enjoyed myself. To enjoy oneself singing a role is of course the secret. The Berlin public gave me a great reception and the management promptly arranged for me to make further appearances there.

I returned from Berlin to Covent Garden to sing several of my familiar roles, including Rocco in *Fidelio* under Otto Klemperer. I found working with him a joy, for he possessed a wicked sense of humour and hardly a rehearsal went by without a telling quip from him. He once admonished me for not following his beat, to which I replied that I hadn't realized that he *was* beating time. He chuckled, and replied, 'If you look closely, you will see that my right forefinger is moving!' A few years later, while my ankle was still in plaster following an operation, we came face to face at the Stage Door. We were both wearing identical overcoats and hats, and were both walking with the aid of a stick. Being of about the same height we gazed at each other almost like a mirror image. 'Sie machen Spass, vielleicht?' he remarked. ('You are making fun, perhaps?') I learnt more about *Fidelio* under Klemperer than under any other conductor, and we hit it off beautifully. One of my most treasured possessions is a score of *Barber of Bagdad* that he gave me in 1969. In the fly leaf he wrote a most flattering inscription and told me that he hoped one day to conduct the opera with me as Abu Hassan. Following *Fidelio* I went to Paris for *Der Rosenkavalier* again. Singing the Marschallin was Elisabeth Schwarzkopf, one of the greatest Marschallins of all time. I was thrilled and proud to be appearing opposite her only eighteen months after my debut as Ochs. Although I had been in the chorus when she was a member of the Covent Garden company after the war, I had never

104

sung as a soloist on stage with her. I had worshipped her from the ranks of the chorus and had vivid memories of being enchanted by her performances as Sophie.

She was not present at the Paris Opera for the first three days of rehearsal. On the fourth day I was on stage alone, singing the finale to Act II, when I suddenly became aware that she was sitting out front. When I had completed my piece, she stood up, applauded and signalled for me to join her in the stalls. We introduced ourselves and she told me how much she enjoyed my playing of the part. She wanted to know if I would have any objection to her giving me advice from time to time. Any objections! I had never felt so proud. One hears a lot about the selfishness and tantrums of leading opera singers, but I have found that they are almost always ready to offer help and advice, and the help of an artist like Schwarzkopf was invaluable at this stage of my career – I knew there was much to be done. With a part like Ochs, in truth, one keeps learning as long as one is singing the role, and if I keep returning to *Rosenkavalier* over the next few chapters, it is because I can only see now, in retrospect, how the character developed into a fully-rounded portrayal (in every way, not least physically!), and therefore I refer often to this progress in order to pay tribute to some of the people who gave me help and advice with this most complicated of all roles.

It was while I was in Paris that I was to discover just how hectic the life of an opera singer can be. Having been a member of a first class company, I had always had plenty of time to study my parts and prepare for performances (one of Covent Garden's main virtues). My professional life had been comparatively well-ordered, and apart from the occasional crisis I had had no experience of being thrown in at the deep end.

The morning after a very successful first night I was woken in my hotel room by the phone screeching. At the other end of the line was Bernard Lefort, at that time my agent in France. I thought at first he was speaking in French, but soon realised it was English spoken prestissimo. Bernard had a crisis on his hands: Kurt Boehme, who was singing Osmin in Lausanne, had fallen ill. Could I take over? I was looking forward to relaxing and enjoying the short break between *Rosenkavalier* performances, so I was not keen. Bernard was very insistent however, and explained that if I flew to Geneva that day, a fast car would take me to Lausanne in time to go on stage for the dress rehearsal. The following day I would sing the first night, and then the next morning return via the same route to Paris in time for my next performance of *Rosenkavalier*. After *Rosenkavalier*, I would repeat the journey and sing a second performance in Lausanne, returning a day later for another *Rosenkavalier*. That, he assured me, would be it. He paused for my reaction. When I did not answer immediately he said how pleased he was that I was going to do it, and put down the phone.

That afternoon I stepped off the plane in Geneva to find him waiting for me. I hadn't realised that he had not been in his Paris Office. With him was the administrator of the Lausanne Opera House, who owned a Jaguar saloon. We shook hands and piled in to begin one of the most terrifying journeys of my life. On the way, the administrator turned to tell me how I had been sent from God to save the performance. I told him to concentrate on the road otherwise I might be returning to my Maker before I had had a chance to sing for him. We reached the Opera House safely and I went straight on stage for the dress rehearsal. I sang through the part dressed in my street clothes, while my costume was being altered for me. The conductor was Istvan Kertesz, who luckily had a sense of humour, for my dialogue just didn't fit in with the version they were using. That night we sat in a restaurant drinking beer and re-writing it to suit us all. The next day, Gerhard Unger, who was singing Pedrillo, met me at the theatre to go through our scenes together, only to find that the building was locked-up. Whereupon we stood on the pavement outside and went through our lines, much to the amusement and approval of the passers-by.

In spite of the emergencies, the first night went well and as a result I was invited to sing the role in Geneva the following year. After the performance, we went back to the apartment of Jascha Horenstein, under whose baton I had already sung in London. I was really beginning to feel like an international singer, especially when I boarded the plane the next day to take me back to Paris and my next *Rosenkavalier*. My interpretation of Ochs grew immensely during those Paris performances, partly because of the help I was being given by Schwarzkopf and my fellow artists but more because I was becoming increasingly confident in the role and could bring more of myself to it, for the more of himself an artist can bring to a characterisation, the more convincing it will be.

After Paris, the contracts from foreign houses began to come in steadily, mostly for Ochs but also for Osmin and for one or two other roles. All the time I was aware that my interpretation was improving, that I was developing the part. I didn't have to be looking at the music to be working on it. Ideas would come to me in the train, in the bath, anywhere, and as soon as I got the chance I would try them out to see if they worked. I took the best of what producers suggested, always building, refining and trying to improve my portrayal.

There were little things like the scene with the Italian tenor in Act I. In the initial stages I had always played this scene very straight. I would be almost deferential and let the tenor get on with his aria quite undisturbed. Being more accomplished, I began to let him sing his piece through once (it is, after all, his party piece) but then when he repeated it, I would get in on the act trying to hush him up and eventually putting one finger in my ear as I continued my business with the lawyer. It was only a small thing in itself but it helped add to the part, helped give the dimension that Solti felt had been missing when he first saw me.

I was tempted to go freelance after Paris. The opportunity was there, but I weighed up all the pros and cons and decided I preferred to stay on contract at Covent Garden. I am basically a home person. I need my home, football, cricket, the smell of fish and chips, and roast beef. I could never have stood the extended periods abroad that a completely freelance career would have entailed. Going abroad was always just a job, and I found invariably that I was unable to take an interest in anything else. I used to go off my food, off everything, counting the days until I got on the first available plane out. A good example is provided by my third visit to Geneva. Vera came with me for the first time. I had always stayed in the same hotel and as we came out on our first morning, she said, 'Look, Mont Blanc.' 'Where?' I answered. 'There in front of you.' It had taken my third trip and my wife to point out the view. Few people realise the amount of time an opera singer spends in hotel rooms just looking at cracks in the walls. The worst time I ever spent was the Christmas of 1967, when I was in Brussels for performances of *Rosenkavalier*. It was pouring with rain on Christmas Day as I phoned home. From my lonely hotel room I could hear the sound of festivities at the other end of the wire and I could have crawled down it, I so longed to be at home. After we'd finished talking, I went out into the rain to find a restaurant in which to eat my Christmas dinner. This is the side of life the public don't usually see. If you're a superstar, then you always stay in the best hotels and have an entourage to look after you, but for the more ordinary international artist on his trips abroad, it doesn't matter how nice the hotel is, it is still a hotel, how nice the theatre is, it is still a workshop. Your main beat is from the hotel to the theatre and back again. And then you begin to worry whether the central heating is causing a cold to start, and so you begin to worry about your next performance.

When I got back from Paris a note was awaiting me from Lord Drogheda. In it he said he hoped that the 'Gallic charm' would not lure me from my contract. It was not a difficult decision for me to decide to stay. Covent Garden were, however, extremely good to me. There were very few occasions when they refused to release me for an overseas engagement.

In the autumn of 1962 I again left London, this time bound for San Francisco where I had been engaged not only for Ochs but also to do the Commendatore in *Don Giovanni*, Pistol in *Falstaff*, the Doctor in *Wozzeck* and the Grand Inquisitor in *Don Carlos*. I was delighted to be singing roles other than Ochs, and as I signed the contract I had given no thought to the fact that five roles in five different operas in a comparatively short season would mean five separate lots of rehearsals. I did not get much time to look round San Francisco for rehearsals began immediately and did not finish until the last opera had been mounted. My days were governed by my rehearsal schedule, as I soon discovered. We had just finished rehearsing *Wozzeck* (which the stage staff said should have 'God Save The Queen' played at the beginning, since the three main roles were being sung by British artists – Geraint Evans, Richard Lewis and myself) and I was on my way back to my dressing room to change when I received a message to go to another part of the building to sing through the Philip-Grand Inquisitor scene from *Don Carlos* with Giorgio Tozzi. As they were already waiting for me, I went immediately and sang the part still dressed in funeral black and top hat, a sight that almost prevented Giorgio from singing.

Eventually the rehearsals began for *Rosenkavalier*. The Marschallin was once again Elisabeth Schwarzkopf, with Kerstin Meyer as Octavian, Wilma Lipp as Sophie and Thomas Tipton making his debut as Faninal. For once I was no longer the new boy! We all got on well with each other and rehearsals with producer Paul Hager were a lot of fun.

During a run through in full costume one morning I was approached by a gentleman from the publicity department and asked if I would mind giving an interview on a local television station immediately after we'd finished. I said that I had no objections at all, provided I could have time to wash and change. That wouldn't be necessary, he told me, since the station wanted me in costume. As that meant travelling across

108

San Francisco in the middle of the day, dressed as Baron Ochs, I was somewhat reluctant, finally agreeing only when he told me Kerstin Meyer had already accepted.

When the rehearsal was over Kerstin and I made our way to the stage door to await the hire car that had been laid on to take us to and from the studio. It duly arrived and we made a dash across the sidewalk and climbed in as quickly as possible. It is difficult to describe just how exposed you feel, going about ordinary business dressed in courtly costume and powdered wig. Every time we stopped at a set of lights it seemed that another car pulled up alongside us and the looks of astonishment on the faces of the occupants can only have been matched by the looks of embarrassment on our own. One taxi driver even leant across and enquired if we were selling something.

The studio was down a little side turning and since our car dropped us on the corner, we had to dash the final few yards on foot through crowds of shoppers, many of whom hooted with laughter when they saw us. After that the interview itself was something of an anti-climax. For the return journey we at least removed our wigs.

Rosenkavalier opened on the 27th of September and was rapturously received. The next day we all enjoyed rave reviews and I was much praised for my 'underplaying' of the part. I was certainly not conscious of 'underplaying' it; and, indeed, I am not sure that underplaying is a virtue to be extolled. On the second performance, when I felt I *had* underplayed it (though not deliberately) I was accused of *over*playing. You simply cannot win!

One particular incident stands out in those San Francisco performances of *Rosenkavalier*, as the supreme example of how to cope with an emergency on stage. It occurred during my Act I scene with the Notary, in which Ochs is discussing his forthcoming marriage contract. Although the scene is crowded with people attending the Marschallin's levee, I was normally able to hold most of the audience's attention. But not on this night. I could sense a tension in the air, that something was happening elsewhere on stage which was detracting from my scene. I had no idea what it was. I could hear nothing amiss, I could see nothing amiss, I could only feel it, and so I carried on as if nothing had happened. It was only afterwards that I discovered what had been going on.

During my argument with the Notary, Elisabeth Schwarzkopf was having her hair done and generally supervising the business of the day, approving the menu, examining a hat and being shown a few pets by the animal seller. On this occasion she had picked up a small dog and began to tickle it under the chin. The dog, surprised and excited by this unexpected gesture, promptly shat (and that's not a misprint!) in her lap. The Marschallin's retinue watched in shocked disbelief. There was no opportunity for her to go off and either clean up or change, for the Marschallin remains on stage throughout the whole of Act I. Only an artist of Schwarzkopf's experience and coolness could have solved the problem so well. Setting down the delinquent dog, she quietly called for safety pins from the milliner who was attending her, gathered her retinue around her, and efficiently pinned the offending deposit into an improvised pocket. The fact that the audience was unaware of what happened and that I only learned of it at the end of the act proves how successfully she managed to carry it off. The only person who was not too happy with the result was Kerstin Meyer who, later in the act, had to rush over and bury her head in Elisabeth's lap.

On the last night of the San Francisco season I too was faced with an emergency. Ever since my tendon had gone during the premiere of Britten's *A Midsummer Night's Dream*, I had been suffering from it. I had lived in the hope that it would eventually right itself, but this was not to be, and it was during the final performance of *Rosenkavalier* that I decided I must have it put right with an operation. I had just made my first entrance and advanced towards the Marschallin. I bowed low, my right leg thrust forward, my full weight on my left foot, when I suddenly heard and felt the tendon pop out of position again. The pain was excruciating but there was nothing I could do: I had to carry on with the scene. The moment I was able to sit down I tried to push the tendon back under the ankle bone, but I couldn't move it. Three times I tried, and three times I failed.

During the first interval I managed to get it into place and then bound my ankle tightly with an elastic bandage to keep it there for the rest of the opera. Just before my first exit in Act II, after I had swept Sophie into the waltz, it went again. Being already in the middle of the dance I had to keep going. The audience found my one-legged dance very funny, but it's a trick I would not like to have to repeat. Extra binding got me through the rest of the opera, and as I limped out of the stage door afterwards, one man cheered me enormously by saying how hilarious he thought my waltzing had been. 'You must have practised for hours to get that effect,' he said. 'No,' I replied in all honesty, 'it came to me on the spur of the moment.'

A few days later the San Francisco season came to an end with a magnificent impromptu party in Kerstin Meyer's room. Most of the artists had been staying in the Alexander Hamilton Hotel and we cleared our refrigerators of all our unused food and drink for a last supper which went on until the small hours of the morning. The next day the company flew to Los Angeles for a short season, and then down to San Diego for a single performance of *Don Giovanni*. There was a great feeling of team spirit about those performances due, I am sure, to the fact that we had been living and working so closely for such a long period. Being thrown into one another's company off-stage helps draw people even closer together. It was something I had noticed when Covent Garden toured Rhodesia in 1953, and something I was to feel again when we visited Berlin and Munich in 1970.

I arrived back in London shortly after the start of the 1962–63 season, to sing Hunding in a revival of Hotter's production of *Die Walküre*, and found Covent Garden in turmoil. The season had opened with Hotter's new production of *Siegfried*, for which he had got in a new designer, Günther Schneider-Siemssen. Although his designs were infinitely preferable to those that had been done for *Die Walküre*, they had not been generally liked. This had been followed by Sam Wanamaker's production of *The Force of Destiny*, also conducted by Solti. There had again been problems with the designs, no one liked the sparse, almost Brechtian production, and on the opening night there had been loud and consistent booing. It took a superlative revival of *Falstaff* to help balance the artistic books.

After the *Falstaff* performances, in which I repeated my role of Pistol, I again left London, bound this time for Vienna. To sing Ochs before a Viennese audience is, for an Englishman at least, an ordeal. You can sing the part well, you can act it well, but to succeed you must have the accent absolutely right. If you can be faulted on the accent, then it hardly matters how good you are, you will be criticized. For me to sing Ochs in Vienna was, I suppose, the equivalent of a German bass singing Claggart in English in Germany, and then being invited to sing it at Covent Garden. Inevitably there would be a few raised eyebrows, if not indignant letters to 'The Times' and to the musical papers. I felt I was entering a lion's den.

It had been nearly three years since my stay in Vienna studying with Jerger but I found my return to the city, and to the Pension Schneider, a nostalgic experience. After lunch I retired to my room and waited for the phone call to tell me what time to be at the Staatsoper for my first rehearsal. When I had heard nothing by six o'clock, I decided to go round to the Opera House to make sure I had got the date right. To my relief I saw my name on the cast list for the following evening.

Since there was obviously not going to be a call that night, I went to see Alfred Jerger with whom I had arranged to have dinner. He smiled at my surprise that I had not been called for rehearsal, and told me there would be one the following morning at 10.30. 'You are very privileged,' he said. 'Usually there is no rehearsal at all.' He did his best to make me feel at home and to get me to relax for he was well aware of how tense I was about the forthcoming performance, and I must have been rather dull company. He finally made me laugh when he told me that a famous tenor friend of his would never indulge in sex before a performance because he was convinced it had an adverse effect on his voice. The man's wife used to spend all her time complaining that their married life was impossible. 'Before an opera he *will* not,' she said, 'after an opera he *cannot* – and he sings at least three times a week!'

An opera singer's attitude towards sex and the voice is a strange thing. Many male singers, tenors especially, believe that sex before a performance causes the voice to drop, while some sopranos believe it has the reverse effect for them. Most British singers do not seem to have an opinion either way, unless they have given a bad performance, associated it with sex and then decided to give it up for a few months in order to see if they sing any better, which seems to me to be a terrible price to pay.

On the morning after my dinner with Jerger, I was on the rehearsal stage at 10.30 prompt awaiting my colleagues. Only the pianist was there, but by eleven o'clock Hilde Zadek, a former colleague at Covent Garden, who was singing the Marschallin, arrived. We talked over old times for half an hour or so, and then decided that since no one else was going to turn up, we would leave. Hilde, who had only come in to see me, told me not to worry, that no one ever bothered to rehearse in Vienna. But I was worried. I ate a fitful lunch and then went back to my hotel to rest.

It was while I was lying on my bed that a terrible thought crossed my mind: I did not know what musical cuts they were making. Every house has its own ideas on which cuts should be made in *Rosenkavalier*, and it makes for an awkward performance if one sings, say, the Covent Garden cuts in Vienna, or the Berlin cuts at Covent Garden. I decided to relax and leave it to the music staff. After all, they had to tell me some time. But then I began to wonder what would happen if Vienna had decided to put *back* some of the more familiar cuts I hadn't bothered to

112

11. As the Grand Inquisitor in the famous Visconti/Giulini production of *Don Carlos*, Covent Garden, 1958.

12. As Osmin in *Entführung*, Aix-en-Provence, 1962. Stealing the key from me is Luigi Alva as Belmonte.

13. As Hagen in *Götterdämmerung*.

14. Act II of the famous production of *Der Rosenkavalier*, with, left to right, Josephine Veasey as Octavian, myself, Margaret Kingsley as the duenna and Joan Carlyle as Sophie, Covent Garden, 1966.

16. As Don Basilio in *The Barber of Seville*, with Fernando Corena as Dr Bartolo, Covent Garden, 1969.

15. The same production almost ten years later, with Derek Hammond-Stroud
    as Faninal, Gwynneth Price as the duenna and Edith Mathis as Sophie.
    This was to be my last appearance as Ochs at Covent Garden.

17. As Baron Zeta in the 1981 Chicago Lyric production of
    The Merry Widow – a post-retirement appearance.
    With Alan Wilder as Kromow and Victoria Vergara as Valencienne.

18. Baron Ochs

19. As Pistol in the
Zeffirelli/Giulini
production of *Falstaff*,
Covent Garden, 1961.

20. As Osmin, *Entführung*, Aix-en-Provence, 1962.
Luigi Alva as Belmonte.

revise? I phoned the Opera House, to be told that Heinrich Hollreiser, the conductor, would be letting me know the cuts later. I glanced at my watch. It was 4.30; two hours to curtain up, which didn't leave much time. I tried to get Hollreiser's phone number, but the voice at the other end assured me he wouldn't be there. In the great British tradition at times of crisis I ordered a pot of tea, after which I set out for the Opera House to look for Hollreiser. He was still nowhere to be found, and so after leaving a message for him that I had to know the cuts as soon as possible, I went to my dressing room. My dressers were astonished to see me; they had never known anybody arrive at the theatre with an hour and a half to spare before. I put on my first act costume and sat fuming, waiting for the make-up men to arrive.

At six o'clock, half an hour before the opera was due to start, Hollreiser came into my room and apologised for not getting in touch with me earlier. 'Everything will be all right though,' he smiled. 'We do the same cuts as we did when I conducted you in Berlin'. And with that he disappeared. Everything was now clear, except that I couldn't remember the cuts we had made in Berlin. Five minutes later I was put out of my misery when a repetiteur arrived and, with every appearance of having hours to spare, gave me the appropriate cuts.

In addition to Hilde Zadek as the Marschallin, I had the great pleasure of singing opposite Sena Jurinac as Octavian. Jurinac is one of the most sympathetic colleagues one can ever meet, and our scenes together worked beautifully. I felt that I started nervously and took time to warm to the part, for I was aware, if not of outright hostility from the audience, of certainly a 'come on and show us' attitude. But, considering we had not had any rehearsal, and the only principal with whom I had sung in *Rosenkavalier* before was Wilma Lipp, who sang Sophie, the last two acts went off very well, and I got a fine ovation at the end. Jerger, with whom I had supper afterwards, was well satisfied, as were his friends who joined us, and the next morning the 'Wiener Kurier' in addition to praising my singing opined that 'The Sir from London has studied his Ochs not only musically but also in the most subtle of dialect nuances, so that he could *risk* a performance in Vienna where, so to speak, Ochses are at home.' The italics are mine. It was clear that to succeed as Ochs in Vienna one would have to be much better than any Viennese Ochs currently available. I had survived.

From Vienna I moved on to Paris for further performances of *Rosenkavalier* with the same cast as in the previous year. This was the third series of performances in which I had sung with Schwarzkopf.

She had kept to her offer of giving me advice and would sometimes suggest how I could make a point more clearly or the exact moment at which I should try for an effect: 'Not on the fourth beat of *this* bar, Michael,' she would say: 'On the first beat of *this* one'. If I brought something off to her liking she would make sure she told me; and if I failed to get something quite right, she would be equally certain to let me know.

The Paris performances were followed immediately by a series of *Rosenkavaliers* at Covent Garden, with Régine Crespin and Kerstin Meyer in the other main roles and Heinz Wallberg in the pit. These performances marked an important development in my portrayal of Ochs. It was not that I suddenly discovered a new dimension to the role, for I do not think my basic conception had altered very much; it was that at last I was released from the mathematical prison I had built for myself in order to make sure I got the music right.

I had always found the first act the most difficult musically. The fact that I had been able to play my scenes convincingly was due almost entirely to the way in which John Matheson had made me learn the role as one long, interrupted aria. In practical terms this meant that as I finished one phrase I would count through to the beginning of the next, while appearing all the time to be interested in what was being said to me. I found this to be the only cast-iron method I could devise of staying exactly with the music, and if a colleague skipped a couple of beats – not an unknown phenomenon in *Rosenkavalier* – I could still make my entry on time. If I had to look to the conductor for the beat I would cease to be Ochs and become a singer playing a part and in obvious trouble. My mental processes went something like this: '. . . . nach der Hochadeligen Gepflogenheit – *two, three, four; Two, two, three, four; Three* Die Begierde darüber . . . ' While I was counting the Marschallin would be singing her line, and I would appear to be listening with rapt attention.

Although this method worked well it had never satisfied me entirely and I felt that until I could free myself from this mathematical precision, I would never be entirely at ease in the role. I had often considered giving up this counting for a performance to see how I got on, but my courage had always failed me. I was afraid of getting into trouble musically and I took great pride in getting the music exactly right.

During the rehearsals for the Covent Garden revival I found I was hearing things from the orchestra pit that I had never been able to pick

114

out before. I suddenly realised that I could sing and listen to the orchestra at the same time. Perhaps it was the fact that I had been accepted as Ochs abroad, perhaps it was the fact that I was more relaxed being back with my own company, but I decided there and then to stop counting and let the orchestral sound float me into every phrase. For the first time I was able to listen to what the Marschallin was saying to me and not just appear to listen. I literally felt my entire performance round out and take on an added depth. I was delighted to read in the press, the morning after the first night, that my improvement had not been lost on the critics. The 'Times' stated that my performance had 'matured out of all recognition'. It had taken me thirty performances to achieve.

The only new production in which I was involved that season was of *Le Nozze di Figaro*, which opened in May 1963, in a production by Oscar Fritz under Solti.

It had a marvellous cast. Ilva Ligabue sang the Countess, Tito Gobbi the Count, Geraint Evans Figaro, Mirella Freni Susanna and Teresa Berganza Cherubino. I was the Bartolo. Solti took my patter song at an incredible speed. Whether he steadied it later or I got more used to it, I'm not sure, but it was certainly effective. Some years later I recorded the role with Klemperer and that particular aria was taken at half the speed. In its own way that too had a pomposity about it which was very effective, demonstrating how two conductors can take the same piece of music at entirely different speeds and yet both achieve an end result which is perfectly valid.

In spite of its cast, *Figaro* did not receive good notices. Solti, in particular, was singled out for criticism, saying, I think unfairly, that his reading of the score was superficial. Little he had done during his two seasons as Musical Director had managed to meet with the critics' approval, there had been sporadic booing of him from the gallery and the words 'Solti must go' had been daubed on his car. There's no doubt that he was disheartened by the constant criticism, for it became widely known that when his contract ran out at the end of the 1963–64 season he would not be renewing it.

That season opened with a new Hotter production of *Götterdäm-merung*, starring Birgit Nilsson. The electricity Solti was able to generate from the pit, plus the presence of Nilsson, did much to placate the critics. It was followed in December 1963 by the first British performance of Shostakovitch's *Katerina Ismailova*, sung in English by a home-grown cast. Marie Collier was Katerina, Charles Craig was

Sergei, Edgar Evans was Zinovy, Otakar Kraus was Boris, and I was the Old Convict, a short but delightful role. The conductor was Edward Downes, and the production by Vlado Habunek was extremely successful. One month later Zeffirelli's production of *Tosca* with Maria Callas and Tito Gobbi, opened to universal acclaim. His production of *Rigoletto* the following month conducted by Solti, was by contrast, an unlucky one – marred by illness and misfortune, and must have given Solti nightmares! Then, however, came *I Puritani* with Joan Sutherland, and another triumph for the House. Quite against normal expectations the press attitude toward Solti changed. Although the only opera he had conducted out of the last four mentioned was the least successful, the fact that he was Musical Director and ultimately responsible for all that happened in the House, worked in his favour. When Webster brought his persuasive powers to bear the charm worked. Solti decided to stay.

Chapter 10 Always More to Learn

Interspersed with *Katerina Ismailova* during December 1963 were further performances of *Rosenkavalier*, in which Leonie Rysanek sang the Marschallin, Josephine Veasey made her debut as Octavian and Barbara Holt was Sophie.

We were still using the production that Joan Cross had staged originally in 1947. As with all productions, the original conception had become very blurred as a succession of singers came and went in their respective roles. Since the original producer is often unavailable, the task of reviving an opera is given to a staff producer whose job is to try and maintain a continuity of purpose. It is a thankless pursuit and music critics often come down heavily on the poor person saddled with this chore. Some well known opera singers refuse to listen to new suggestions about a role even when a distinguished producer is engaged, so what chance does an unknown staff producer have? The man chosen to re-stage the December revival of the opera was John Copley.

There is no doubt that our production at Covent Garden was extremely tired. The scenery and the costumes were becoming very frayed at the edges, and while the principal artists kept broadly to what had been worked out in the original production, the scenes involving large numbers of chorus and minor characters were frankly a mess. Like most singers who specialise in a role I have often felt I would like to have a stab at producing the opera myself. I have worked with, and absorbed the ideas of, many eminent producers and have my own opinions about the role of Ochs. Naturally I tend to think of the opera in terms of those scenes that involve the principals and Ochs in particular. The scenes that the professional singer, without any experience of producing, nearly always forgets, are those that involve large groups of people on stage; those apparently random comings and goings that need to be timed to the bar. These are the scenes in which a producer really proves his worth, and it was precisely those scenes which in our production of *Rosenkavalier* were the most muddled.

John Copley made up his mind to do something about these scenes before attempting anything else. We had innumerable rehearsals to fix the exact timing of each person's entrances and exits. It was exhausting work simply because nothing is more exhausting than constant repetition, and everybody grumbled and groaned and questioned the necessity of expending so much energy on 'minor' scenes. But Copley forged on regardless. He succeeded completely and those scenes which had always proved a nightmare became highlights of the production. During the rehearsals he proved himself to be a producer of enormous ability, full of ideas and with a single-minded purpose to get everything exactly the way he wanted it. He was helped enormously by the quality of the company at Covent Garden. One of the reasons why production standards became so high at the Royal Opera was that every part in every opera, no matter how small, was cast from strength. This is particularly important in an opera like *Rosenkavalier*.

In Act II there is a non-speaking, non-singing role for a doctor. At first it might be thought that anybody of reasonable intelligence would be able to undertake this, but it is a role that can add much to the humour of the performance. At Covent Garden we had the ideal person in Ignatius MacFadyen, one of the company's original choristers. He and I struck up a perfect understanding and were able to make the scene very humorous, in sharp contrast to an artist I had once worked with abroad. This man was so keen to make the scene hilarious that he had invented all sorts of business, which he barely had time to complete. Between the dress rehearsal and the first night he thought up a few more tricks and was determined to include them as well. After he had finished his examination of me, or so I thought, I sat back in my chair, assuming my look of pain and outrage. To my surprise the 'doctor' then appeared in front of me again and began to examine my right eye. He tugged at the lower lid, and out popped my contact lens. I cursed him soundly and he disappeared round the back of the chair. To my relief, I saw that my lens had landed on my knee but as I bent forward to retrieve it, I felt a sharp tap on my neck. The 'doctor' was improvising some business with his reflex hammer, which, being unexpected, I did not find at all funny. My lens shot off my knee and into a bowl of water standing just in front of me. That was the last I saw of it for, despite a concerted hunt during the interval, it was never found. I castigated him to such good effect that during the next performance he hardly moved and the scene was a flop.

Copley also found time to work in detail on the principals' scenes, giving each of us something to think about. His ideas seemed limitless and, being a superb mimic, he was able to step into each of the characters in turn and show by demonstration what he was getting at. Everyone must know of the occasion when he stood in for Callas during a rehearsal of *Tosca* and a lady visitor, chancing to hear his male soprano seeping through from the auditorium, made the immortal comment 'Ah, the unmistakable voice of Maria Callas.'

Making her debut as Octavian in those performances was Josephine Veasey, who had studied the role with Maria Olszewska, a famous Octavian of former years. From the time she began to sing the part in rehearsal it was obvious that her voice was tailor-made for the role. Thrilling though her singing was, we all knew she had a magnificent voice and had expected her to be good. The real revelation came when we moved from the music room onto the stage. She looked and moved elegantly, giving a fine impression of the young man Octavian is supposed to be. As Mariandel she revealed a dry sense of humour which fitted our scenes together exactly. Nothing was overdone, not even in our supper scene, although that was not for want of trying on my part. I had momentarily fallen into the trap of playing the part for my own amusement and not for that of the audience, and I was rightly rebuked by 'The Sunday Times.'

Immediately after completing the performances of *Rosenkavalier* and of *Katerina Ismailova*, I flew out to Hungary to play Sarastro in *The Magic Flute* and Ochs for the Budapest State Opera. After checking in to my hotel I went straight to the Opera House for a *Magic Flute* rehearsal. I was shown to my dressing room, an old, shabby room with a chair set in front of a mirror. I was told with pride that for forty years this had been the room of the great Hungarian bass Mikhail Szekely. I had had the great pleasure of meeting Szekely a couple of years earlier when I had taken over the role of Osmin from him at Glyndebourne, and immediately the room took on a more glamorous aspect for he had possessed one of the finest basso profundo voices I had ever heard, and his Osmin was a tremendous figure of fun, a delight to both eye and ear. His death the previous year, like that of any great singer, had left a gap that would not be quickly filled.

I was then taken through a series of passages to the rehearsal room to meet my fellow artists. I was the only foreigner in the cast and the introductions were made in German. We began to run through the *Flute* dialogue, starting with Sarastro's message to his priests at the beginning of Act II. At the end of a fairly long speech, two of the priests had to ask me questions. To my amazement, these questions were addressed to me in Hungarian. It turned out that I was the only person doing his role in German, but nobody seemed to be surprised so I just got on with it.

The real problem came with the turn of the Speaker. While the priests' questions were short and obvious, the Speaker has quite a bit to say and obviously enjoyed saying it. Not knowing a word of the language, I had no way of knowing when he had finished. Each time I thought he had come to the end and began to open my mouth, he would launch into a fresh sentence. I found the solution by asking the prompter to look directly at me during the Speaker's lines, with his hand over his mouth. As soon as it was my turn he would take his hand away and point to me. This device worked extremely well and the rehearsal continued. It came as no surprise to me to discover that the music was also being sung in Hungarian, and since no one seemed to care whether I sang in German or not, I carried on in my own sweet way. At the end of the rehearsal everyone seemed delighted.

The first night went well, although I was a little disconcerted, at the end of the first act, to hear a slow handclap. I was assured that this was not, as in Britain, a sign of disapproval, but was the greatest compliment an artist could be given.

The following day we began rehearsing for *Rosenkavalier*. There had been three rehearsals for *The Magic Flute* but only one was scheduled for *Rosenkavalier*. This seemed to me to be the wrong way round, but everything went smoothly, and I knew I was playing with a cast of experienced artists. It is quite remarkable how quickly opera singers adapt to each other. Whatever nationality they may be, whatever background they come from, it does not take long for them to become friends and fit in with the production on which they are working. There are exceptions, of course, but they are mercifully rare. There was only one point at which I encountered a slight problem. During the first meeting of Ochs and Sophie in Act II it is the custom of most Ochses to attempt to draw Sophie down on their knee. The lady playing Sophie in Budapest asked me not to do this. Although I felt that some of Ochs's boisterousness would be lost, she was so insistent that I agreed.

The performance went well. At the end of the first act we received the slow measured handclap of approval and must have taken five or six curtain calls. This so buoyed me up for the second act, which is, after all, Ochs's big act, that I completely forgot my promise to Sopie and tried to sit her on my knee. I encountered an unusual resistance and so gave her a much harder tug in order to bring her down. At that moment I remembered my promise not to attempt this manoeuvre and at the same time realised she was so heavily corseted that I could not have got her to sit anyway. I tried to signal to her with my eyes that I was sorry, but she stepped nimbly aside and refused to have anything more to do with me. From then on, every time I began to move towards her or attempt to establish some kind of physical contact, she was off out of range like a champion boxer. Even when I broke into my waltz I found that she had melted away and left me dancing with empty arms while she observed me from a safe distance. Only at the end of the act when I was able, through an interpreter, to explain how I had come to forget our arrangement, did she relax and smile.

I returned to London for one month and then was off again, this time to Geneva. Although I had already sung Osmin there the previous year, I had not performed Ochs. The series there were to see another important step forward in my characterisation. The cast was Elisabeth Schwarzkopf, Kerstin Meyer, Teresa Stich-Randall as Sophie and Jacques Doucet as Faninal, while the conductor was a brilliant young Swiss, Christian Vochting, who was to die tragically from cancer just as he was coming to the height of his powers. The producer was Herbert Graf. Now that I was establishing myself on the international circuit as an Ochs, I was beginning to appear time and time again with the same artists, for *Rosenkavalier*, like *The Ring*, is a specialist work in which a certain number of singers become famous in their roles and are in constant demand around the world. And so it's inevitable that old friends and colleagues continue to meet in different cities and different countries.

The only member of the Geneva cast I had not worked with in *Rosenkavalier* before was Teresa Stich-Randall. The last time we had sung together had been at a promenade concert at the Royal Albert Hall under Sir Malcolm Sargent, when she had shown herself to be a superlative soprano. Sophie was obviously going to suit her admirably.

Right from the start Herbert Graf took a great interest in me and it became a regular practice, during rehearsal breaks, to sit in the canteen together and swap impressions and suggestions. He immediately noticed one of the comparatively weak points in my interpretation, the end of Act II. I could sing the music comfortably enough but I had never quite made up my mind on the best way to play it. Consequently I tended to drift from one experiment to another, never knowing for certain what I intended to do until the very last moment. Graf told me

121

forcibly that I had to make up my mind and stick to it. At the next rehearsal of this section, he snapped his fingers and stopped us. 'I know what's wrong', he said. 'I've just realised. You are standing up too much.' The final, wonderful sweep of the music as the famous waltz begins must be used to bring Ochs to his feet and into his dance. By spending much of the previous scene already on my feet, I had had to find an opportunity to sit down again in time to stand up at the appropriate moment. It was a movement that struck false and Graf had realised it. From then on, I sang the last scene mainly from a sitting position, only rising to my feet finally as the orchestra swept into the waltz. It made all the difference. I was able to dominate the scene more effectively, because, although sitting, I was relaxed and in command of the situation.

Another difficult scene to bring off is the duel between Ochs and Octavian. Strauss has given them only three bars in which to have their fight, three bars which take about three seconds for the orchestra to play, so how can they have an effective duel? Graf had the answer. He suggested that it is so long since Ochs last drew his sword that it had rusted in its scabbard. (Naturally his servants would be too slovenly to keep this item of his dress cleaned and oiled.) And so, as Ochs attempts to draw his sword and finds it momentarily stuck fast, he would tug at it, it would spring clear and the impetus would take his right arm on to the point of Octavian's sword as he stood in readiness for the fight that never was. This solution had three advantages. It could be done quickly within the compass of the three bars Strauss had allowed; it was very funny; and it was logical, for Octavian could now protest his innocence with utter conviction since the wounding had clearly been an accident. It also had another bonus in that the resultant wound would be so slight as to be almost non-existent, and Ochs's subsequent bellowings and business with the doctor could be made even more amusing. Finally, it did away with the need for Ochs to wear an elaborate and constricting sling in the third act, for what nobleman would take a girl to an assignation if his right arm was seriously incapacitated? A thumb sling was quite sufficient.

Yet another Graf innovation was the insertion of a sudden and unexpected country dance in Act III as Ochs, carried away by enthusiasm sings 'Kreuzustig muss sie sein.' Most people seem to like this, some do not, but it became a part of my performance. There were other ways in which Graf helped me, not just on the more obvious aspects of Ochs but on smaller details of which no audience is ever

122

aware, and his direction, coupled with Schwarzkopf's readily available advice, made the performances memorable.

Working in Geneva at the same time was Ken Macdonald, there to make a record with Helen Watts and Monica Sinclair. Ken and I naturally got together in our off-duty moments and had a fine time. One afternoon we were chatting in his hotel room when he switched on the radio to see if there was anything worth listening to. He chanced to tune in to the middle of an opera, sung in Italian. A bass was singing something both of us knew. 'What the devil is it?' Ken asked. Although I knew I had sung the part and ought to know, I couldn't place it. Our indecision must have lasted a good half minute or more. Then we both said simultaneously, '*Rosenkavalier*'. It was indeed *Rosenkavalier*, in a recording of a performance from Rome with Nicola Rossi-Lemeni as Ochs. I found it incredible that I was there in Geneva to sing that very role, and had not recognised it immediately. Somehow the Italian language had caused the music to take on a different character, to sound like a different opera altogether. I'm convinced that the same thing sometimes happens, though maybe not to such a marked degree, when the opera is sung in English.

I was so pleased with the way the performances had gone in Geneva that I was in a very good mood when I arrived back at Heathrow. 'Anything to declare?' asked the Customs Officer. 'Only my legs and stomach,' I replied. He looked at me stonily and asked me to open my case. On top of my ordinary clothes were a padded stomach and a pair of padded calves to fit under my stockings. I could hardly suppress my laughter.

'Very droll, sir,' retorted the official, allowing himself just the suspicion of a smile. When returning from a trip some eighteen months later, I found myself facing the same man. 'Still travelling with your legs and stomach?' he asked, much to my astonishment. If ever I had had a fleeting desire to smuggle anything in, it disappeared at that moment.

In Zurich a performance of *Rosenkavalier* brought me into contact for the first time with Lisa Della Casa as the Marschallin. Louise Pearl, an American singer, was the Octavian, and Anneliese Rothenberger was Sophie. I had sung with Anneliese in Aix en Provence in 1962 when she had been the Constanze in *Entführung*, and she was the perfect colleague. She proved to be the best Sophie with whom I had up until then appeared. She sang the music beautifully, she looked ideal and she acted so well, that I was completely enchanted. It was such a shame to behave roughly with her in Act II that I really had to force myself to be unkind.

Della Casa was the Marschallin to the life. Every great Marschallin has something different to bring to the part, but the one indispensable quality they must all have is that aristocratic demeanour that sets the Marschallin apart from everyone else. Della Casa had it in abundance, just as Schwarzkopf and Crespin had. Della Casa, however, did have one mannerism I found a little disconcerting. Quite often when she was supposed to be looking at me, I noticed that her eyes seemed to be focused beyond me. It was not noticeable from the house of course. I only discovered later that she was looking past me to where her husband was standing in the prompt corner monitoring everything she did, telling her it was good, it was all right.

As usual, the time allocated for rehearsal in Zürich was laughably short and the entire preparation amounted to little more than a walk-through with the cast. On the afternoon of the first performance I decided to go for a stroll in one of the parks to get myself relaxed. As I walked along I saw a massive figure looming above the skyline, dwarfing the smaller figure beside him. It was Otto Klemperer (also out for a stroll) with his daughter. As we drew near to each other, I greeted him, much to his surprise, for he stopped, peered at me for a few seconds and then turned to his daughter.

'Lotte, who is this man?' he asked.

'Mr. Langdon. From Covent Garden,' she replied.

'Langdon? Langdon?' the Maestro asked uncertainly.

'Yes, father. You remember: Rocco.'

'Ah, yes. Mr. Rocco. Now I remember. What are you doing here in Zürich?'

I told him I was singing Ochs at the opera house that night.

'Who is conducting?' Klemperer asked.

I told him.

'Oh, yes, a good man. A good man.' He paused, and then made as if to move off, before turning back to me. 'A good man,' he repeated. 'The best of luck!'

This time he did move away, and Lotte also waved goodbye. I turned to continue on my way but was stopped short.

'Hey, Langdon,' Klemperer called out.

'Yes?' I replied.

'The *best* of luck,' he cried. 'You will probably need it.' And with a wave of his stick, he was gone.

The performance did not go too well. I felt in good form, I was working with a splendid cast and yet, somehow, I did not find myself able to catch fire, and I gave a below par performance that had little to do with the way I sang. The action seemed to stick, as if a little oil was required, and the timing was that vital fraction of a second out. I gave a performance of fits and starts, and while the reception at the end was good, I did not feel satisfied.

Following these performances I flew back to Birmingham to rejoin the Covent Garden company in Coventry. I had with me a considerable amount of money in Swiss francs, made up of notes of a large denomination, and I immediately went to the airport bank and asked that they be changed into pounds sterling. The clerk counted out the notes and then asked me if I would mind waiting for a few moments. I sat down and was soon joined by another man who sat opposite me. After some ten or fifteen minutes during which nothing happened, I was beginning to grow impatient but decided nothing could be gained by making a scene. I did, however, decide to go to the toilet. As I stood up, the other man in the room asked me where I was going. I told him and asked sarcastically if he had any objections. Whereupon he said he would accompany me. I began to get quite angry until he eventually explained that there was a query over my Swiss francs and he had been detailed to keep an eye on me to make sure I didn't try to get away. Fortunately everything was sorted out soon afterwards. My banknotes were not forgeries, I collected my pounds sterling and drove away to rejoin my colleagues.

During the summer of 1964, my agent had been approached by Rudolf Bing with a view to my going to New York that October to sing performances of Ochs at the Metropolitan. The period, however, clashed with some performances of *Fidelio* for which I was down to sing Rocco. Sir David Webster sent for me and told me that he thought it important for my career to undertake the New York engagement and that he was proposing to bring Josef Greindl from Berlin to take over from me. This was a wonderful gesture that clearly cost Covent Garden a large amount of money.

My agent in New York had considerable difficulty pinning the Metropolitan down to actual dates. It was stressed that I must be in New York for a period of about three weeks, starting from 12th October, in order for me to be there to take over from Otto Edelmann, who was also singing Hans Sachs, should he be unable to complete all his Ochs performances. What worried me more, however, was that I

had not been given a firm commitment as to the number of performances I should be giving in my own right. I still did not know when I
finally left for New York.

My worst suspicions were confirmed when I arrived and Larry
Wasserman, from the Thea Dispeker office, picked me up from the
airport and told me my *performance* would be on 2nd November. That
happened to be my last day in New York for I was booked to return on
the 3rd. It was quite clear that Bing had engaged me, not because he
particularly wanted me to sing Ochs, but to provide an insurance policy
in case anything went wrong with Edelmann, otherwise he would at
least have shown me the courtesy of offering me several performances. I
was furious, but what could I do? I was under contract to the Met for
three weeks and I had to grin and bear it.

The prospect of three weeks in New York with plenty of free time on
one's hands may seem idyllic, but not if you are an opera singer making
your debut at the New York Met. Every day leading up to the
performance is a strain, and at the end of it, I knew I had just the one
performance. It is rare for a singer to give his best performance in a
strange house on the first night of an opera; he needs a series to relax
into the role. Add to this the fact that I knew I was being used by Bing,
and that my solitary performance, good or bad, was unlikely to do me
any good, and I was unable to treat my three weeks as a holiday.
Sightseeing has never been one of my favourite occupations but I did
my best to fill in the time, walking the streets, peering into shop
windows, trying the various cafes and restaurants, and seeing just about
every film in the city.

And, of course, I attended the *Rosenkavalier* performances, which
only helped increase my frustration. Schwarzkopf was the Marschallin,
Della Casa was Octavian, Rothenberger was Sophie; there is not an
Ochs who would not give a quart of his blood to sing with that cast. I sat
in a box at the Met and saw each succeeding performance with ever
increasing anger. It was not that I imagined I would be better than
Edelmann, only that I knew I was different and I wanted more than one
performance to try and impress the public with my conception of the
role.

After a week of this, my appetite disappeared. I did not feel ill, I just
had no desire to eat. Eventually I decided to consult a doctor. He
thought at first that I was sickening for jaundice but after making tests
he pronounced that I was debilitated. He gave me some vitamin
injections and the address of Keen's Chop House where, he said, I

126

could get a typically English meal the moment I felt better.

Georg Solti had arrived in New York to conduct some concerts at Carnegie Hall and hearing that I was under the weather, rang me. He gave me strict instructions not to sing if I did not feel up to it. While the Met may be annoyed by a last minute cancellation, he said, they would be even more annoyed if I gave a bad performance and I would never get another booking. Since I suspected that this was a decision that had already been taken, I thanked him for his advice and promised to follow it. In fact, I was strongly tempted to plead illness and fly back home, but I knew I was capable of singing and felt that I had to honour my side of the contract.

Gradually I began to feel better and went along to Keen's Chop House for a most enjoyable meal, and thought that perhaps my only trouble was the lack of familiar food. I went for a costume fitting, and the day before my performance we walked through the opera on the rehearsal stage. Thomas Schippers conducted and surprised me once or twice with some unusual tempi, but all in all it went well. I could not have wished for better co-operation from my colleagues who insisted that I should play the role the way I was used to, and they would fit in. More than ever I longed for a few more performances with such a team. I was unable to do all I would have wished because the production would not allow it, but the producer, Dino Yannopoulos, helped me as much as he could during our brief session together, and on the 2nd November the performance went on.

It went better than I had any right to expect under the circumstances and Act II, in particular, was a great success. As I returned to my dressing room after taking my curtain calls I met Rudolf Bing, who congratulated me most warmly and asked me to carry his best regards to Sir David. The next morning, while awaiting my plane, I read through my reviews. The 'Herald Tribune' did not rate me as much of an Ochs; the 'Times' thought I was good, my performance being 'admirable in every respect,' and I 'should be heard from again.' The 'Journal' headed its review, 'Langdon in Fine Form' and at the end of an excellent notice, commented 'It will be interesting to see him in other roles.'

Upon my return to Covent Garden I went immediately to report to Webster. He was furious at what had happened and wrote a very stiff note to Bing. Whether that note compromised my future in New York or not, I don't know, but I was never asked back. Webster was kindness itself to me. He could see how disappointed I was with the entire business. As I was about to leave I remembered Bing's last comment to

127

me. 'By the way, Sir David,' I added, 'Mr. Bing sends you his best regards.'

'Does he indeed, Langdon?' Webster murmured. 'Does he indeed?'

Chapter 11 Everything in The Garden is Lovely

A few days after my return from New York I went into hospital to have the much delayed operation on my ankle. The injury I had sustained back in 1961 in *A Midsummer Night's Dream* had so damaged the ankle that it was found necessary to cut the tendon, bore a new channel through the ankle bone, thread the tendon back through this channel, and then rejoin it. It took much longer to recover than I expected and as a result I spent the rest of the year in plaster.

I was able to return to singing however, long before the plaster was removed. The first piece in which I was scheduled to appear was a revival of *Katerina Ismailova*, under Charles Mackerras, in which I again played the Old Convict. I was able to wrap lengths of rag around the plaster, and using a crutch to support me, was able to go on stage and play the part without too much trouble.

As I left the stage door after one performance, still with my foot in plaster and supported by my crutch, I heard a voice in the crowd outside remark that he thought I was overdoing it a bit.

The public's reaction to opera singers generally is interesting. Those who gather outside the stage door to collect autographs usually know what most singers look like without their costumes and make-up, but the majority of the audience have no idea who you are. I have often sat on a train home in the same compartment with people who have been to see a performance I have just taken part in, and listened while they were discussing me. It's a most unnerving experience. Part of me relishes this anonymity, part of me wishes occasionally that I was recognised. The situation is completely different in Germany. Going out for a meal after a performance of *Rosenkavalier*, for instance, as soon as I walked into a restaurant near the opera house, the pianist would strike up a few bars of the Waltz music, everybody would stand up and applaud and people would come to my table to say how much they had enjoyed the performance. But in London once you are away from the opera house you are just another face in the crowd. One Saturday afternoon I was on my way to Stamford Bridge to watch a football match. At the bus stop in Sutton I noticed a man looking at me rather strangely. We both got on the bus and at Wimbledon I changed onto the District Line, only to find this same man strap-hanging next to me. He was still staring at me. Finally he spoke. 'Excuse me,' he said, 'don't you live in Sutton Common Road?' I said that I did, and he told me that he also lived there. 'My wife and I have been having an argument about you,' he went on, 'about what you do for a living. You come in at odd times, sometimes you're in all day, sometimes you disappear for days on end, sometimes you go out early, sometimes you go out late. Now *I* think you're a policeman. My *wife* thinks you're a burglar.' 'Actually,' I replied, 'I'm an opera singer. I sing at the Royal Opera House, Covent Garden.' He stared at me. 'Ask a silly bloody question and you get a silly bloody answer,' he said, turning away.

I was very relieved, when my plaster was finally removed, to discover that the operation had been a complete success and that I could for the first time in four years, walk without favouring my left ankle. My first engagement afterwards was in Berlin singing Ochs with Crespin as the Marschallin. There were no rehearsals and I was sitting in make-up when my old friend, conductor Heinrich Hollreiser, poked his head round the door and told me we would be making the usual cuts. A few moments later an intense young repetiteur arrived with a score and proceeded to go quickly through the cuts. I assured him that I knew them all and that I was quite happy. He laid particular emphasis on my remembering to cut Ochs's Act I narration. I continued to assure him that it was a cut I was used to and that it would not be a problem. He apologised for harping on the subject and explained that they had recently been experimenting with the narration by having Ochs sing it in full and had found, not surprisingly, that it was too long. This performance was to be the first for several months in which they had reverted to the customary cuts. I agreed with him that no Ochs should ever be asked to sing the narration in full and he departed well satisfied.

I returned to my room, completed my dressing, and was on the point of going to wish my colleagues 'toi, toi' when he reappeared with his score and again reminded me that the narration would be sung with the cuts, not in full. He seemed obsessed by this cut and so I once more told him, as firmly as I could without being rude, that I would on no account sing any more music than the Deutsche Oper required of me. And so the performance began.

Everything went well and I was enjoying myself immensely. The narration arrived and off I went: 'Wollt ich könnt sein wie Jupiter, selig im tausend Gestalten, wär Verwendung für jeder.' I then made the cut and prepared to continue. To my horror the orchestra seemed to have gone into a completely different opera. It was like a bad dream, for they were playing music that was quite unfamiliar to me. For a moment I did not know what to do and then it dawned on me; they were playing the narration in full, without cuts. The repetiteur had told *me*, but whoever was responsible for telling the orchestra had not told *them*. I decided to fill in time by chasing Octavian round and round the stage while listening desperately for something familiar from the pit. Crespin stood in mute amazement with her back to the audience, and as I passed her on each circuit, repeatedly hissed, 'Mon Dieu, what is 'appen?' I was much too busy to explain and I needed all my breath for running. At last I heard something I recognised. 'Muss halt ein Heu,' I sang, 'In der nähe dabei sein.' I was back on course again. The audience, well versed in their Strauss, broke into spontaneous applause. They treated that hiatus as a huge joke and an extra treat. Several people told me later that they will never forget the sight of Ochs chasing Octavian round and round a bemused Marschallin while the orchestra bashed away at top speed, trying to get rid of several pages of unwanted music. It was the highlight of their evening.

Back in London, Covent Garden had decided to mount a new production of *Arabella*, to be produced by Rudolf Hartmann and conducted by Solti. The role of Count Waldner is traditionally a role taken by basses who sing Baron Ochs, and the fact that Solti had no hesitation in casting me, showed that he had, as far as Strauss was concerned, overcome his reservations about me. He even went so far as to say he thought I was very good in the part, a compliment indeed.

Arabella was given a beautiful production and had two marvellous artists in Dietrich Fischer-Dieskau as Mandryka and Lisa Della Casa as Arabella. Fischer-Dieskau is a superb musician and a superb stage artist, and our first scene together was one of the most satisfying I have ever done. It was also the only occasion I have ever been on stage with a singer who has sneezed in the middle of a phrase. It is one of those strange phenomena, but it doesn't matter how much of a cold you have, how heavily you are sneezing, you usually only sneeze when you are *off*-stage. On this occasion, however, during our duet, Fischer-Dieskau sneezed and blew all the money off the table between us. One minute it was there, the next it had gone. We got down on our hands and knees and picked it all up, putting it back in the wallet, without missing a beat of the music. An appreciative audience gave us a round of applause. I've

131

sung with quite a number of Mandrykas, and Fischer-Dieskau was, without doubt, the best.

As an indication of Covent Garden's generosity in allowing me time off to pursue my international career, I was allowed to depart for Marseilles after the first four performances of *Arabella*, to sing Rocco in *Fidelio*, with Gwyneth Jones and Fritz Uhl in the other leading roles. The performances were remarkable for two incidents. The first was during the final duet in the dungeon scene between Gwyneth and Fritz. The stage crew began to lower the curtain, realised they shouldn't have but couldn't stop it. It descended slowly as Gwyneth and Fritz moved forward, holding hands, and they finished the scene, peeking through what looked like the opening of a bell-tent, just as the last note came and the curtains whooshed together.

The second incident came after the entire cast had been out for a meal. Gwyneth was struck down by a stomach bug and spent the whole night being sick. She came on for the matinee the following day, looking as white as a sheet, and sang a magnificent performance in one of the most remarkable examples of stamina I have ever witnessed. You would think that being ill all night would have weakened her, but no. Stamina in opera is a strange thing. To a certain extent it can be cultivated but I believe it is something with which you are born. To be an opera singer requires a combination of stamina to sustain the bigger roles and audibility, which does not just mean a 'big' voice. A well-placed voice, like that of Luigi Alva, for instance, is able to penetrate almost any fabric of orchestral sound. This has nothing to do with the so-called 'size' of the voice. The tragedy of opera is that many beautiful but 'soft grained' voices cannot be heard, and many beautiful voices cannot last out. Some artists are limited to the smaller roles simply because they do not possess the stamina for the larger roles. This is, I'm afraid, one of those sad facts of operatic life.

Covent Garden now took a very adventurous step, in June 1965, with the British premiere of Schoenberg's *Moses and Aaron* which brought Peter Hall to the house for the first time. Hall was given seven weeks of rehearsal and *Moses and Aaron* took over the house, dominating everything. It was an incredibly complicated work and after a while even Solti's enthusiasm began to wane. He sat in the canteen one day at the London Opera Centre, where we were rehearsing, his head in his hands, muttering, 'Should we have done it? It is all my fault. If it goes wrong, it is all my fault.' But we persevered and it came together in a brilliant production which was a sell-out, due not, I believe, to the fact that thousands of opera goers were desperate to hear Schoenberg but because of the marvellous publicity it received.

I was playing the High Priest and at one stage I had to sacrifice four virgins, played by Elizabeth Bainbridge, Yvonne Minton, Morag Noble and Cynthia Johnston. During rehearsals Peter Hall had told them that they were to be naked for the scene: 'No clothes, no body-nets, nothing,' he said. 'You come on in cloaks, they take the cloaks away, and you'll be absolutely naked.' The girls looked at one another and promptly refused. So Hall had the brilliant idea of bringing in four strippers from the West End. He didn't tell anybody, just sneaked them in through the stage door for the dress rehearsal. They came as they were, wrapped in their black cloaks, with nothing on underneath. I was standing centre stage, with my knife poised, ready to cut the first throat, when the cloaks went down and these four girls stood before me, stark naked. The chorus missed a beat and I went through the ritual, somewhat stunned. Afterwards one of the chorus remarked that my hand hadn't even trembled!

There was also an orgy scene in which Hall said, literally, that anything could happen, and it did. After the rehearsal, the prompter came out of his box white and shaking. He had never seen anything like it. Word soon got round that the production was more interesting than most. Forbes Robinson and I were having a drink in 'The Nag's Head' when we were approached by a reporter for our comments on the orgy scene. Forbes, in mock horror, threw up his hands and said, 'I've never seen anything like it.' That night one of the evening papers carried the headline 'Covent Garden bass has never seen anything like it.' The result was a rush on the box office. When Vera left me at the stage door on the opening night and made her way round to the front of the house, people were shoving bundles of notes at her, desperate for tickets.

But it wasn't just the orgy scene and the strippers that made *Moses and Aaron* memorable. Hall had also introduced many masterly, theatrical touches. At one point Moses had to cast down his rod which then turned into a snake. This was achieved by a magnetic groove in the stage. When the rod was thrown down it broke into sections and was drawn along this groove, giving the appearance of wriggling, before coming back together again. Moses's leprous hand was another simple but effective piece of stagecraft. Forbes Robinson, who was singing Moses, had a glove, made up to look like a leprous hand, concealed inside his costume. At the moment Richard Lewis, as Aaron, sang,

'Behold the leprous hand of Moses,' Forbes was able to produce this revolting spectre. Simply by slipping off the glove out of view of the audience his hand was made clean again. All these little tricks looked marvellous from the front but they took time to work out. At one performance Richard forgot his words and was getting towards the leprous hand pages early. Forbes was wondering whether to get his glove on or not, his hand half-disappearing into his costume on several occasions before the diseased member finally came out correctly on cue. So many things could, and did, go wrong during rehearsals that Solti, ever the perfectionist, began to lose heart. And it was very difficult musically. But in the end a combination of the strippers, the orgy, Hall's production, and Solti's direction which was magnificent, brought it all together and the opera was a great success.

David Webster had always been keen on the idea of getting a permanent Director of Productions to run in harness with the Musical Director. He had tried in the very early days with Peter Brook, and had approached several other leading theatrical producers over the years. There's no doubt that he had also earmarked Peter Hall as a possibility, and when Solti finally departed and Colin Davis took over as Musical Director it was announced that Peter Hall would also be appointed Director of Productions. Quite why the scheme fell through, I'm not sure, but there were rumours that Hall realised he might have more problems with opera singers in getting what he wanted than with actors.

The 1965–66 season found me very busy, with performances of Fafner and Hunding in *The Ring*, Bartolo in *Le Nozze di Figaro*, Ferrando in *Il Trovatore*, Varlaam in *Boris Godunov*, and my first performances of Bottom in *A Midsummer Night's Dream*. I was now well established internationally, especially as Ochs, and during the middle of this hectic period I received a call from the Stuttgart Opera to enquire whether I could possibly fly out the next day and sing a performance for them that night. I obtained permission from Covent Garden and the next morning drove to Heathrow to catch the Stuttgart plane. While sitting in the departure lounge reading a paper, a headline caught my eye: 'English bass flies out to save performance.' I read it with interest. It was about me. I was reminded of the time when Marie Collier took over the role of Tosca at short notice from Maria Callas at Covent Garden. One newspaper reported that an 'Essex housewife' had left her washing up to rush to the Opera House to save the performance. I reflected that if I could keep all my engagements secret until the last minute and then announce I was rushing off to sing in a dire emergency,

I would receive all the free publicity I could wish for.

Singing Octavian again in Stuttgart was the delightful Sena Jurinac. She was so superlative in the role that I could not imagine her playing any other part in the opera. (And yet six months later we began rehearsals together at Covent Garden for a new production of *Rosenkavalier* in which she made her debut as the Marschallin. She was so good in that role that it was equally difficult for me to remember that she had ever played the other part.) Ruth-Margret Pütz sang Sophie (she was the Constanze once with me in Nice) and the whole performance came together as if it had been rehearsed for a month, as can sometimes happen in an emergency.

I had been delighted when I heard that there was to be a new production of *Rosenkavalier* at Covent Garden, to be produced by Visconti, and that I would be singing Ochs. We certainly needed a new production, and after the marvellous job Visconti had done on *Don Carlos*, I was looking forward immensely to renewing our acquaintance. It did not turn out to be quite as rewarding as I had anticipated. Although we did not know it at the time, he had had great reservations about having accepted the job. 'I don't know this opera,' he had told a colleague, 'I'm doubtful about taking it on.' In the event he largely allowed us to get on and do as we wished. Several times he would stop the rehearsals and ask me to repeat a bit of business, not because he wanted to correct something or make a suggestion, but simply because he had found it funny and wanted to see it again. He told one reporter who interviewed him about the production that I had been doing my part for so long that he knew it would be superfluous to interfere with any of my stage business!

The first time I realised there might be problems was when I went for my initial costume fitting. I tried on my first act costume and found it to be extremely heavy and magnificent. I asked wardrobe if it could be lightened in some way but was told that it would be most unlikely since Visconti wanted everything to look absolutely correct and would not be likely to agree to any cutting down. I then realised that what I was trying on was an imposing court costume. I enquired whether it was, in fact, supposed to be for Act I and was told that it was. I went to Visconti and explained that according to the text I was supposed to be in travelling clothes in Act I. 'That doesn't matter,' Visconti replied, 'it is a beautiful costume.' I agreed that it was very beautiful, but, I went on, 'I have to apologise to the Marschallin for being in travelling clothes.' Visconti thought for a moment. 'You think that matters?' he asked. 'I most certainly do,' I replied, beginning to wilt already because of the weight of the material. Visconti pulled out a sketch pad, did a rough drawing and showed it to me. 'Like that?' he asked. I nodded, and my costume was changed. I was, however, unable to get rid of the fur stole with which he had lumbered me.

When we eventually gathered at the London Opera Centre to begin the staging, we were shown the models of the sets. The first thing that struck us was the enormous bed that dominated the scene in Act I. To our amazement Visconti completely ignored the bed, arranging the two lovers on the rug in front of the fire. The bed, he explained, was merely a symbol. 'No one makes love in a bed nowadays,' he said. When someone asked what would happen to it, he replied that he would 'fade it out', and sure enough when we eventually moved on to the stage, the bed magically disappeared out of sight into the wings at the appropriate moment, drawn off by stage-hands.

We received our next shock when we saw the actual set. It was draped in heavy velvet curtains. They looked magnificent but they soaked up the sound and made it very difficult for us to hear ourselves. Jurinac and I discovered that the further downstage we got, the better the acoustics, and so each time we had a line, we inched our chairs forward until we were both sitting in front of the line of drapes. One critic paid me the compliment of writing that he felt that neither Jurinac nor Josephine Veasey, the Octavian, were in particularly resonant voice and he wasn't sure if it was the scenery that was responsible; when I came on and was also not resonant, he *knew* it was the scenery.

There were other problems with the staging and the sets, but if I am giving the impression that Visconti did nothing for the production, that would be wrong. He came into his own in the crowd scenes, moving the large chorus with consummate ease and always paying attention to the placing of the singers so that the sound would be right. The musical side of the production was in the hands of Solti. After his disparaging remarks about my Ochs in 1960 I was determined to show him how much I had improved and I made a special effort to re-study the music. He still managed to find the occasional place where I could be faulted. Solti's method was simple and direct. If a singer made a mistake, he would point it out. If the mistake occurred a second time, he would repeat the process more forcibly. If you were unwise enough to make it a third time, he would be likely to draw blood. Once one had performed a role to Solti's requirements, one could be confident that it had been learned accurately.

The musical sessions were hard but rewarding, and with Sena Jurinac, Josephine Veasey, Joan Carlyle as Sophie and Ronald Lewis as Faninal, the ensemble was ideally balanced. Musically and histrionically the first night was a great success. There was a certain amount of criticism of the sets, and the famous bed came in for its fair share of comment, but the audience left us in no doubt that, as far as they were concerned, the evening had been enjoyable. Solti, moreover, expressed his complete satisfaction with the way we had sung the music. Praise indeed.

Just a final comment on those costumes. A few weeks before the first night I had had my annual medical check-up, and my doctor informed me I should lose some weight since, he said, I followed a sedentary occupation. I was peeved, to put it mildly, and invited him to see *Rosenkavalier*. After the performance he came to my dressing room, where I was slumped in a chair like a man who has just gone fifteen rounds with Muhammad Ali. I asked him to take my costumes from their peg and bring them over to me. He tried but couldn't lift them. To his credit, he got the point immediately. 'Did I say *sedentary* occupation?' he asked humbly.

The year after the Visconti production opened at Covent Garden, Solti was invited to record *Rosenkavalier* for Decca. His opinion of me as Ochs had altered so dramatically that he asked me to sing the role for him in the recording. Although no contracts were signed, he went ahead with his plans even adjusting his recording schedule so that I could fulfil a contract to sing in *The Ring* in Buenos Aires towards the end of 1967. When I returned from Buenos Aires my agent John Coast phoned to say that something was happening with the recording and I should be prepared to be dropped from it. Within days he was on the phone again to tell me it was definite that I was no longer required. I had heard nothing directly from Solti. Some days later we were rehearsing a revival of the Visconti production when he asked to have a word with me during the coffee break. I went to see him. 'Mike,' he said, 'I have some bad news. Unfortunately it is not possible to have you in the *Rosenkavalier* recording. You know, some things are not quite suitable.' He was rather vague, but I think he was trying to give me the impression that maybe the part was not quite right for me vocally, something I cannot believe since he knew my voice and my work well, and had already told me and others that he thought I was the best Ochs in the world at that time. 'But,' he continued, 'I will make it up to you.' He waited for my reaction. I sat there, quietly sipping my coffee. 'You

137

are a gentleman,' he said finally. 'You are not angry.'

'I may be angry', I replied, 'but I'm not showing it.'

'I will make it up to you,' he repeated. 'We will do a recording of some other opera. I promise.' I then told him I had known already through my agent but had to have the satisffaction of hearing him tell me personally. I went to tell John Coast that Solti had finally broken the news but had promised me another recording. Coast was sceptical and we had a five pound bet, but with a time limit of two years, that I would make that other recording. I paid over my five pounds! I'm not sure why the recording of *Rosenkavalier* didn't happen for me, but I think it may have had something to do with the fact that it was being done in Vienna. Solti was already taking an English Octavian with him (it was originally to be Josephine Veasey but she was unable to obtain the release from an existing contract. Yvonne Minton eventually made the recording), and someone may have pointed out to him that whereas she would just have been acceptable, an English Ochs in Vienna was a completely different matter. Since Solti was already contracted to make several recordings with the Vienna Philharmonic, he could have decided not to jeopardise his own relationship with them, and so out I went. Perhaps it was this same business reasoning that led him not to engage Kenneth Macdonald, whom Solti always said was the finest exponent of the Italian tenor role he had ever heard, but to choose Luciano Pavarotti instead.

During the period between the end of the original Visconti production of *Rosenkavalier* and the 1968 revival at which Solti broke the news that I would not be taking part in his recording, I sang Ochs in Berlin, Brussels and Wiesbaden, while at Covent Garden I appeared in *Don Carlos*, *Le Nozze di Figaro*, the *Ring* (in which I kept up my record of always taking over a role I had been given to understudy, taking over at short notice as Hagen from Gottlob Frick when he injured his ankle), and as Count Waldner, Rocco, Kecal and Daland.

The climax of the 1966–67 season at Covent Garden was a Gala Performance in front of the Queen Mother. The programme consisted of Solti conducting Act II of *Der Rosenkavalier*; Joan Sutherland singing the mad scene from *Lucia*, and the first scene of Act IV of *Don Carlos*, with Christoff, Ward, Carlyle, Bumbry, Glossop and Edgar Evans, conducted by Ted Downes. It was a fantastic evening but it was also tinged with sadness, for it was to be Ronald Lewis's last appearance at the Opera House. We did not know at that time but Ronald, who had sung Faninal in every single performance of *Rosen-*

kavalier at the Garden since 1949, was already very ill and had keyed himself up just for that performance. Though thin and drawn, he sang as well as ever. A few months later he was dead. The first performance of *Rosenkavalier* following his tragic loss was a strange one, for without him it hardly seemed like a Garden performance at all.

Chapter 12 Vocal Troubles

As soon as Solti told me officially at the beginning of 1968 that he no longer wanted me for his recording of *Rosenkavalier*, I was determined to show him just what he was missing. I threw myself into the revival of *Rosenkavalier* with as much enthusiasm as possible. Lisa Della Casa was singing the Marschallin, and I will never forget the look on her face when she saw that enormous Visconti bed for the first time and was then told that the love-making would take place on the rug in front of the fire. She turned to her husband, who was standing at the side of the stage, shrugged her shoulders and with a 'So what?' reclined gracefully on the floor. Her scenes with Yvonne Minton, who was making her debut as Octavian, went very smoothly, and Yvonne enjoyed a well-deserved success, as did Gwynn Griffiths in the part of Faninal. Although it was a little unreal to be appearing in *Rosenkavalier* at the Garden without Ronald Lewis in the role, Gwynn gave an effective and fussy characterisation, played with a great sense of humour, and I felt that we were very lucky to have found such a fine replacement.

Elizabeth Robson was a delightful Sophie. She was most anxious that our scenes together should work well and asked me repeatedly during the rehearsals to correct her if she failed to react properly. I took her at her word, and she quickly remembered everything I told her, everything, that is, except for one thing. During the Act II exchanges between Ochs and Sophie, Ochs's remarks grow steadily more risqué until Octavian, in exasperation, smashes his glass on the floor. Betty seemed to have a blind spot at this point. I kept telling her that she had to recoil in horror at the suggestions I was making, but for some reason she never would. She would stand listening to my awful little speeches with an expression of mild interest on her face. I decided to make her react. During our next rehearsal together, while no one was watching, I undid the belt of my trousers and then played the scene with my left hand in my pocket holding them up. At the moment when I needed that reaction, I took my hand out of my pocket and let the trousers slip. I caught them before they had gone too far, pulled them up and did up my belt. I got my reaction all right. Betty screamed and stared at me in horrified disbelief. No one else had seen what had happened and when, at the end of the scene, they asked Betty what the matter was and why she had suddenly screamed, they refused to believe her explanation. From then on I always got a marvellous look of horror from her at just the right place.

The revival went extremely well and I felt I had proved my point with Solti. At about the same time as he had first approached me about singing Ochs on his recording, I had also been engaged to sing Claggart on the recording of *Billy Budd*, with Britten himself conducting. The fact that I was Britten's personal choice in the role went some way towards alleviating the disappointment I felt over *Rosenkavalier*, and the recording, made early in 1968, helped prevent my dwelling too much on the loss of Ochs. My rejection, however, hit me a lot harder than I was prepared to admit.

The recording of *Budd* was an enjoyable affair, with the minimum of retakes and splicings in. For once I was able to leave the recording studio without feeling that something had been missed out and that I would be recalled later to dub in five bars from the middle of Act II or whatever. Very often recordings are made like films, with scenes done out of chronological order and with takes repeated *ad nauseam*, all in the pursuit of perfection and, at the finish, one has no feeling of having given a performance at all. This is hardly surprising since the finished recording is simply a simulation of a performance. The splicing in of notes or phrases for a valid reason such as musical error or the poor intonation of either the singer or some section of the orchestra, is, I feel, acceptable, for much valuable time is saved and it can hardly be expected that a complete scene should be repeated endlessly until, by some miracle, everything comes exactly right. What I do find disturbing, however, is the practice of one singer dubbing in notes for another, and of singers who were not even present in the studio at the time of the recording dubbing in whole sections. I once had to travel to Walthamstow Town Hall to dub in the Ghost of Ninus in *Semiramide*, and it took about an hour to record successfully two pages of music while listening to the pre-recorded orchestra and the other voices on a set of headphones. Practically all the orchestration supporting Ninus is written tremolando and my voice had to move from note to note precisely in time with the pre-recording. It was extremely difficult and gave me no feeling of having participated in the opera.

Then, of course, there is the situation in which a singer who finds a part extremely difficult to bring off successfully in a live performance, is empowered, by means of frequent breaks for rest and refreshment, plus a little technical tinkering, to record a highly satisfactory performance, and, moreover, be praised for it by the reviewers as if it were live! All in all I prefer a recording (and here I also include recordings for radio broadcasts) to be made in the correct order and to encompass, whenever possible, a complete act at a time. Provided there is not a complete disaster, a feeling of live performance is produced, and this, surely, is what the listener wants. Erich Kleiber, I believe, recorded his famous *Rosenkavalier* straight through, an act at a time, without artificial inserts and including the usual crop of minor mishaps along the way. That did nothing to prevent its being the best *Rosenkavalier* recording of all. The danger with the 'perfect' recording is that it is unreal and so hones the expectations of some members of the audience, who have already heard the performance on record at home, that there is often a feeling of let-down when the same artists are heard live in the theatre. A live performance is exciting because people are performing it, because there is effort going into it, because you can hear the tiredness that has to be conquered, and because there is the glorious uncertainty over whether climactic moments will come off. Few recorded performances can ever match the thrill of the live performance. Perhaps that is why pirate recordings of live performances are so much in demand.

The 1968–69 season at Covent Garden opened with the traditional Ring cycle under Solti. On the first night of *Das Rheingold* I was in my dressing room, laughing and joking with Kurt Boehme, who was singing Fasolt to my Fafner, when I suddenly realised that we would soon be on and that I had better warm up. I went out into the corridor and tried a scale. It wouldn't come. I cleared my throat and tried again. This time I managed to get through the scale without the tone cracking but my voice sounded as though it had had a cheese-cloth thrown over it. There was no time for me to go down to my 'studio' in the basement and before I could attempt any further exercises the call came for us to go down to the stage. All the way there I was trying to get my voice in shape but I knew something was wrong, that I had not warmed up sufficiently.

The first phrase Fafner has to sing is right in the middle of the voice, but I felt very nervous and apprehensive. Boehme delivered his cue line and I began to sing. Even to me my voice sounded hoarse, and the words came and went as if I had no control over them at all. Solti, in the pit, looked up and pointed to his throat, asking by his gesture if I was all

142

right, while Theo Adam, Josephine Veasey and everybody on stage stared at me questioningly. It was a terrible moment made worse by the fact that it persisted throughout the evening. Vocally it was one of the worst performances I have ever given.

The following night I sang in *Die Walküre* and to my almost hysterical relief my voice was strong and clear. I thanked heaven that my mystery illness, whatever it may have been, had been of such short duration. But then, a week later, came *Siegfried* in which I sang the off-stage role of Fafner the Dragon through a microphone. During the dress rehearsal I again found I was having difficulties with the vocal line; my voice was not coming out clearly. Solti, with whom I had worked so often, automatically assumed there was something wrong with the amplifier. 'Damned electronics!' he kept muttering. After about four goes, during which my sound did not improve, he began to suspect that maybe the trouble was mine. 'Mike,' he called out, 'just come on stage. Let's see if it's possible we maybe do this from the stage.' A strange thing then happened. As I walked out on stage, all the tension disappeared. I sang nine or ten bars in my usual voice before Solti stopped me. 'Thank you, Mike,' he said, convinced now that it was the amplification system. 'Go back.' And so I retreated to the wings and immediately started to sing badly again. For the actual performance I warmed up with plenty of time to go and felt in good voice, but when the moment came for me to sing I found I was incapable of producing a full, steady tone and had to resort to all sorts of technical tricks to cover my deficiency.

Eight days later I was singing Hagen in *Götterdämmerung* and I was in a state of panic. Hagen is a long, exacting role, requiring strong, resonant tone to cut through the orchestral texture, a tone I felt I was incapable of producing in my present state. How I staggered through the first two acts I will never know. It was not until about the fifth word of my first phrase that my voice became audible and throughout those two acts my voice came and went as it pleased, as if it had a mind of its own. For some unaccountable reason, it found itself for the third act and sounded fine. Clearly there was something very wrong.

The next day I went to see Joan Ingpen to tell her I didn't think I could possibly sing in the second cycle, and I also went to see a throat specialist. Joan persuaded me at least to attempt the second cycle, while the specialist examined me and told me that, as far as he could see, there was absolutely nothing wrong with me. I did not find this very reassuring for I knew that, whatever he said, I was not singing properly and there had to be a reason.

My nightmare continued during the second cycle, and after the second *Siegfried* I went back to Joan and told her I would have to withdraw from Hagen in *Götterdämmerung*. She was sympathetic and agreed to try and find a replacement for me. Later that day she phoned to say that she had managed to engage Karl Ridderbusch and that I should stay at home for as long as I needed for my voice to recover. I decided to do nothing more strenuous than read a book while resting my voice for a few days in the hope that whatever was wrong would right itself.

Unfortunately, the German agent had misread Joan's telex. On the afternoon of the performance of *Götterdämmerung* from which I had withdrawn, Ridderbusch had gone to the Opera House. 'What time,' he had asked Joe Ketley, the stage door keeper, 'does *Die Walküre* start?' 'It starts at six,' Joe had replied, 'but not tonight. Tonight it's *Götterdämmerung*.' 'What!' exclaimed Ridderbusch, 'I've come to sing Hunding.' 'Not in this bloody opera you haven't,' retorted Joe. Not only had the wires become crossed, but to make matters worse, Ridderbusch had at that time not finished studying Hagen.

I had decided to go for a walk that afternoon when John Tooley, Webster's assistant, phoned and asked to speak to me. Vera, who couldn't think of anything else to say, told him I had gone to see my doctor. John had asked for my doctor's number so that he could call me there but Vera said she was expecting me home at any moment. Five minutes later the phone rang again. It was John once more, asking if I was back and, if not, could he please call me at my doctor's? Vera managed to put him off a second time. Shortly afterwards I arrived home. 'I don't know what's been happening at the Garden,' Vera said, 'but will you phone John at once?'

'I don't want to go into details now,' said John, when I got through to him, 'but do you think you can possibly get through Hagen tonight? I'll make an announcement before the start, but, if you don't sing, we'll have to cancel the performance.' Reluctant though I was, I really had no choice and left home immediately. Knowing that I was saving the performance and that an announcement had been made helped me to relax, but I still had vocal problems. I began all right but by the time I got to Hagen's *Wacht*, my voice was 'sticking' on the vowel sounds, especially on the 'e's'. As the *Wacht* starts on three 'e' vowels it meant, in effect, that the first three notes of the aria were completely missing. Had it not been for Ted Downes in the pit, who sacrificed his own interpretation to nurse me through, I don't think I could have finished the opera. And yet once again that strange thing happened: in Act III, by which time one might expect a singer to be sounding tired, my voice had come back and I was singing better than at any other time during the evening. As I came off Maurits Sillem congratulated me. 'That was the most marvellous bit of pacing I have ever heard,' he said. 'Thanks very much,' I croaked, my voice having by then gone completely.

The next day Webster himself phoned to thank me for taking part in the performance and told me to take off as much time as I needed to recover. And so Vera and I went away for a few days' holiday, during which I hardly spoke, resting my voice as much as possible. Then, tentatively at first, later with growing confidence, I began to vocalise. My voice had returned from wherever it had been. I could do anything with it. I could sing loudly, sing softly, sing legato or sing staccato. I rang Joan Ingpen to tell her I was fully recovered and ready to begin work again, and she straightaway put me into a performance of *Aida* a few days later to sing Ramphis.

I arrived at the theatre full of high spirits and thankful that my ordeal was over. I warmed up in the dressing room, joked with Charles Craig who was singing Radames, and felt in fine form. But, when the first scene began and I sang my first word, 'Si', I knew that my voice had retreated behind its blanket. I was so upset that I went to see Ted Downes in the interval and asked to be replaced for the remainder of the opera. He ordered me to finish the evening, which I did, but only just. I was in despair. I knew I had not been suffering from a cold, a throat specialist had said he could find nothing wrong, and yet I seemed to be incapable of producing the voice I knew I possessed. I phoned Joan Ingpen and again told her how I felt, that I would have to resign from the company, that my career was over. She gave me the phone number of Alfred Alexander, the eminent throat specialist, and an hour and a half later I was in his rooms in Harley Street. Alexander questioned me closely about my medical history, concentrating on any past vocal problems, and then began his physical examination. He soon established that my cords were red and asked me to remind him how long my vocal troubles had persisted. He nodded, and began to look at the space at the back of my nose, asking me to make certain muscular movements to facilitate his examination. 'There he is!' he cried suddenly. He withdrew his mirror from my mouth and smiled. 'My dear Mr. Langdon,' he said, 'you have a small polyp at the back of the right nostril. It's causing a post nasal drip, and I'm sure that's the cause of

145

your trouble.' Having discovered the polyp, Alexander did not wait but after administering a local anaesthetic, immediately cut it out, an operation which was more unpleasant than painful.

I went back home and rested for a week or so before I dared to try out my voice. When I did at last risk it, it seemed to be back to normal, but I could not help thinking of the many times before that I had vocalised satisfactorily only to fail in performance. This time, however, I felt it was different and gradually my confidence began to return. A couple of weeks later rehearsals started for another series of *Rosenkavalier*. I was surrounded by big voices – Tatiana Troyanos, Lisa Della Casa and Betty Robson – and I felt a strong compulsion to vocalise at every available opportunity to convince myself that my voice was still there and that I could hold my own. The result was that my voice began to roughen and tire, and I became convinced that my trouble was returning. I confided my fears to Alexander who explained what was happening to me physically and that any vocal problems I now had were entirely in my mind and had nothing at all to do with my larynx. I remained unconvinced and asked him if he would mind coming to a rehearsal. He agreed happily. Knowing that he was there, I lost my apprehension and sang well. 'What's the problem?' he asked afterwards. 'You sang beautifully.'

I was delighted when I discovered that Alexander had acquired tickets for the first night and I made him promise to visit my dressing room between acts to tell me how he thought it was going. The performance went well and his presence gave me such confidence that I asked him if he would mind attending all the subsequent performances as my guest. He agreed, but on one condition, that he did not have to sit in the house but could watch from the wings where, he said, he would be able to observe me from close quarters. And so he was able to keep an eye on me vocally and also, being of Viennese extraction, keep a check on my accent.

It was not just from Alexander that I needed reassurance at this time. Much as one may rant and rave about the critics, one believes them implicitly when they write nice things, and I was very pleased that, without exception, they all thought I had sung well. Friends also came in for their share of questioning about how they thought my voice was sounding, and Vera must have been completely fed up with being asked constantly if she could detect any flaws in my tone.

After the final performance of the series, I went with some friends to a nearby restaurant where the tables were separated by partitions. The people at the table next to us were in the middle of a discussion about the performance. They went through the artists one by one, starting with Della Casa, moving on to Troyanos, then Robson, followed by the minor members of the cast. Having exhausted their comments on the singers they moved on to the orchestra and the conductor. I could barely contain myself. It would have been preferable to hear my performance slated rather than to be ignored completely. Just when I felt I could stand it no longer one of their party poked his head over the partition. 'We discussed your performance on the way to the restaurant, Mr. Langdon,' he chortled, 'and we all agreed that you are a very fine Ochs.'

The performances of *Rosenkavalier* were followed by *Rigoletto* in which I sang Sparafucile without any problems, and I then left for Seattle to sing four performances of Ochs with Crespin as the Marschallin and Regina Sarfaty as Octavian. I was delighted to find that Howard Fried, an old friend from San Francisco, was singing Valzacchi, and the rehearsals, under conductor George Schick, went much as all rehearsals of *Rosenkavalier* do involving a team of artists who have worked together before, with a great deal of reminiscing and leg-pulling as well as hard work. If things in Seattle went well artistically, they certainly weren't going well at the box office. It was the first time *Rosenkavalier* had been performed in the city and tickets were not selling very quickly. Consequently we all spent a lot of time giving radio and television interviews and attending luncheons organised in our honour, trying to drum up interest. At one such luncheon I was engaged in earnest conversation by a bright-eyed elderly gentleman and thought I should weigh in with some hard-sell for the opera. He told me he had never been to any opera let alone *Der Rosenkavalier* but if it was, as I claimed, worth seeing, would I tell him the plot? I began by saying that it opened with a love scene between the Marschallin, a beautiful woman in early middle-age, and Octavian, a youth of seventeen. 'Jeez!' muttered my companion, 'that's sensational. This is real adult stuff, eh?' I tried my best to quell his lascivious enthusiasm but everything I said seemed to excite him even more and when I got to the bit about Octavian, who is sung by a girl acting the part of a boy, dressing up as a girl to pretend to be a girl, he suddenly held up his hand. 'That's enough, son,' he shouted. 'Don't spoil it for me. This I gotta see.' Whether he told all his non-operagoing friends that there was a dirty show on at the opera, I don't know, but all four performances were subsequently sold out.

I returned to Covent Garden to perform Rocco in *Fidelio* under Klemperer, then went to Geneva for Osmin before heading back to London for two further performances of *Aida*. Although I had had to cancel some performances of Ochs in Stuttgart when I was suffering my vocal troubles, now that I was back to normal my diary was again filling up.

The first new production of the 1969/70 season at Covent Garden was of Berlioz's *Les Troyens*. Sung in English, this opened in September under the baton of Colin Davis with Anja Silja, Jon Vickers, Peter Glossop, Ryland Davies and Josephine Veasey in the cast. I was singing the High Priest, Narbal. During the first scene change on the opening night, which was immediately before the scene with my big aria, I spotted Sir David Webster backstage. It was always an event to see him there and I had stood, waiting for him to approach me and perhaps enquire about my health. Instead he just drifted past without a word. I immediately began to wonder what was wrong. My main scene began. I had had a long wait of something like twenty minutes in the preceding scene, during which I had just to gaze out at the audience with nothing whatever to sing, and I had begun to grow nervous. The longer I stood, the more I became convinced that the following scene, my scene, would not go well. Sure enough, when I began to sing the same thing that had happened during the *Ring* happened again: my voice sounded thin and dry, as though it was coming through a layer of cloth.

Interspersed with the performances of *Les Troyens* were several performances of *Un Ballo in Maschera*, in which the same thing also started to occur. It was, however, completely unpredictable. On some evenings I would warm up and know I was in good voice, only to find that once I got on stage my real voice had retreated. On other occasions I would be convinced that something would go wrong, only to find that I was in perfect voice throughout the performance. It was the fact that I seemed to have no control over what I was doing that I found so depressing.

A month later I opened as Don Basilio in a revival of *Il Barbiere di Siviglia*. The first night went well but as I was driving up to the theatre for the second performance I suddenly found myself on the wrong road. It took me a minute or two to get my bearings and to realise that the road was familiar; I was heading away from London and back towards home. Where I had made my mistake I do not know, but it showed the mental state I was in. When I reached the opera house I went to see Fernando Corena who was singing Bartolo and explained that I was feeling lousy and he should not be surprised by anything that happened that night, especially during our first scene together when Basilio sings the 'La Calunnia' aria. Corena told me not to worry. 'I am a colleague,' he said, 'I will help you through.' Just as our scene began, even as I drew breath for my first line of recitative, I felt the tension run out of me as if someone had pulled out a plug. My aria just rolled out. I had probably never sung it better. Afterwards Corena was furious with me. He thought I had been deliberately playing around and I had a difficult job persuading him that right up until the moment I sang my first note, I had been feeling bad and was convinced I would not sing well.

It was then that I finally accepted that my vocal troubles were mental and that what had started a year earlier with the physical problem of that offending polyp, had now become psychosomatic. Every singer I have ever spoken to about this has admitted or volunteered that at some time during their career they have gone through a period of vocal instability when they have begun to question their ability to do a job which up until that time they have taken for granted, that there has been a point when their voice, for no apparent reason, has not functioned as they would wish. All singers know that during the course of a performance they will get one or two notes which are not as good as the rest. This happens all the time but usually you just accept it and get on with the job. It is, after all, the whole performance on which you are judged, not a couple of notes. But in the state I was in, I was listening for something to go wrong, and the moment it did a chain-reaction set in, my confidence was affected and I began to sing badly.

Most of the time my voice functioned quite normally and then, for no obvious reason it would sound as if someone had given me a completely different, inferior set of equipment. This invariably seemed to happen in those roles when I was on stage with nothing to do for some time, when my mind could start to worry about all the things that could go wrong. When it came to the larger roles in which I was kept busy continuously, I did not have time to think of the problems and consequently sang quite naturally. This was fortunate because I was much in demand abroad especially to sing Ochs. In December 1970, I flew to Stuttgart to sing under Carlos Kleiber, and two months later to Monte Carlo. Josephine Veasey had been booked to sing Octavian but fell ill at the last moment and Regina Sarfaty was engaged in her place. On the day of the dress rehearsal Crespin, who was singing the Marschallin, was unable to take part, while Sarfaty had caught a heavy cold, and I found myself having to sing the opening act on my own, the missing voices being supplied by George Sebastian in the pit. It was a strange experience, and stranger things were to follow. During that act, the man engaged to sing the Italian tenor, who was not at all suited to the role and who had been having problems with it throughout the rehearsals, suddenly began to sing in a pure, high voice which was obviously going to encompass the aria without any difficulty. From my position on the opposite side of the stage I looked across at him in surprise. He seemed astonished by the sound he was making and then I realised why: his mouth movements were not synchronising with the words. Someone was obviously dubbing for him. Sebastian, too, knew something was amiss, especially when the singer came to the high C flat. He pushed the orchestra along as usual, to spare the singer what had always been, until then, a poor note, only to hear the note ringing out loud, clear and sustained. The note continued and was left behind as the orchestra forged on.

Sebastian rapped on the rostrum. 'Will whoever is singing step forward?' he demanded. To everyone's amazement and amusement, the on-stage flautist, who had been busy going through the motions of accompanying the song, stepped forward. 'I was singing,' he told Sebastian, 'and it is usual at this point for the maestro to follow the singer.'

'But you are not *supposed* to be the singer,' roared Sebastian, albeit with an expression which suggested he wished the man *had* been. 'Stand back and let the other man continue.' The rehearsal continued as advertised. It turned out that the man playing the flute, a retired singer, had become so distraught at hearing the aria murdered at every rehearsal that he had been unable to stop himself singing it properly. The real Italian tenor had been so surprised by this extra voice that he had promptly begun to mime.

After the Monte Carlo performances I returned to London for a few days before flying out to Marseilles for further performances. While at home I had received a message from Alexander Gibson, Musical Director of Scottish Opera, asking if I could sing two performances of Ochs in Aberdeen. A late change of dates had meant that Noel Mangin, who was scheduled to do the performances, was no longer available and if I could not help out, they might have to cancel them. Two problems stood in the way of my accepting. The first was that the opera was being sung in English and I knew it only in German; the second was that I was already engaged to sing Sarastro in the Welsh National Opera's *Magic*

Flute at Llandudno on one of the dates. Gibson countered my first objection by saying that he was quite happy for me to sing the part in German with the rest of the cast singing in English, and that over the question of dates he would speak to James Lockhart, the Musical Director of Welsh National Opera, to see if it was possible to get them rearranged. He promised to phone me back within a couple of days. By the time I left for Marseilles I had not heard from him and so assumed it was no longer on.

When I got back to London at the end of February, I found that my dates had been juggled and I was down to sing Ochs in Aberdeen. I decided to try and learn at least part of my role in English. In the event this was more difficult than I had imagined. I was very busy singing at Covent Garden, playing Osmin at the Coliseum for the Sadler's Wells Company and preparing for Welsh National Opera's production of *The Magic Flute*, and I had little time to spare for Ochs. I arrived in Aberdeen on the morning of the performance and went straight to the theatre for costume fittings and to run through the part with the orchestra. There was an added task, since Scottish Opera had decided to play the opera in its entirety and it was the first time I had sung the part without cuts of any kind since my work in Vienna with Jerger.

As sometimes happens when a performance of *Rosenkavalier* is given at short notice, the evening went perfectly. Helga Dernesch sang the Marschallin, Janet Baker sang Octavian and Elizabeth Harwood sang Sophie, and although I had never worked before with any of them on the opera, they seemed to read my mind as they went along, fitting in with everything I did. The first act had never gone better and Alexander Gibson in the pit conducted as if we had been working together for a month. I must admit, however, that I was pleased when the act was over for I had found myself occasionally scrambling for my words. I had not had time to learn more than that act in English and from then on I reverted to German. The only person who had any problem was Helga Dernesch who comes from Vienna. She found herself singing a Viennese role in English opposite an Englishman singing his role in Viennese, and kept wanting to slip back into the original! She told me later it was an experience she had no wish to repeat.

The second performance in Aberdeen was my 96th in the role, and as I flew out of Scotland on my way to Llandudno to sing Sarastro, I was left to reflect that but for a strike by the chorus of the Paris Opera I would have been giving my hundredth performance there in the following November for I had signed to sing nineteen performances in Paris during their 1971–72 season. The management had refused to give in to the demands of the chorus and in place of *Der Rosenkavalier* had decided to mount performances of *Die Walküre*, which does not require a chorus. Both Régine Crespin and I had agreed to sing in *Die Walküre* instead of singing the Marschallin and Ochs.

Rehearsals in Paris began in September and I was immediately conscious of the fact that my vocal troubles had not gone away. I knew I sounded second-rate, not the sort of singer the Paris Opera would have engaged to come in from abroad. On the recommendation of Crespin I went to see a specialist in Paris but like his colleagues in England he could find nothing wrong with me, and I returned to the opera house feeling very dejected. My tone had still not improved by the first night and I gave a very mediocre performance. I sang a further two performances without any improvement and then went to see the director of the house, Bernard Lefort, who had been my agent in France. Bernard was very sympathetic and realising that I was having problems he agreed to let me cancel the next performance so that I could return to London for treatment. The specialist sent me straight to hospital where I was given a detailed examination by laryngoscope under a general anaesthetic, and the tissues minutely examined. As I came out of the anaesthetic the specialist was bending over me. 'Are you all right, Mr. Langdon?' he was saying. 'Do you understand what I am saying?' I closed my eyes again and tried to pretend I was not there for I knew he was about to tell me I had cancer. 'Do you understand what I am saying?' he repeated. I opened my eyes. 'Yes,' I replied weakly. 'What is it?' 'We've examined everything down there,' he told me, 'and there's absolutely nothing wrong. It's as clean as a whistle.'

After a couple of days' rest I flew back to Paris very relieved and sang another very mediocre performance, getting, for the first and only time in my life, the bird. It was a most unnerving experience. I promptly cancelled my remaining performances and returned to London feeling suicidal. I was due to begin rehearsals for a further series of *Rosenkavalier* at Covent Garden, under Josef Krips, and I had no idea whether I would be able to go through with them. I didn't know which way to turn, where to go to for help. On the advice of Joan Ingpen, who had never ceased to help and encourage me, I went to see a psychiatrist who gave me exercises to help me get rid of tension, but even that failed to work. My crisis was in my mind and it was only myself who could eventually do anything about it. This I managed in a rather strange way.

Our cat was terrified of me; every time I went into the garden, if it saw me, it would run away. One day I saw it playing on the lawn and somehow, in my paranoic state, convinced myself that it was a spiritual manifestation of my voice. If I could get it to come to me, something it had never done, I knew it would be my voice returning. If, on the other hand, it ran away, my career would be finished. I went out into the garden and knelt on the lawn, calling softly to it, afraid to move a muscle in case I frightened it. It looked at me and then gradually began to edge closer until at last I was able to put my hand out and stroke it. It rubbed itself against my leg, stepped back, gave me a long look and then ran off. But I didn't care. My voice had come back to me and I knew that I would not have any more problems vocally.

The rehearsals for *Der Rosenkavalier* began at the end of October. The cast was exceptional: Jurinac as the Marschallin, Brigitte Fassbaender as Octavian and Lucia Popp as Sophie; and I felt that they were the most important performances I had ever done, partly because I knew I had not been singing well and partly because Josef Krips was conducting. As far as I was concerned Krips was to Strauss what Klemperer was to Beethoven, and I was keen that he should be impressed.

News had already got back to Covent Garden that I had not been singing well in Paris and that I had had to cancel some performances, and everyone there was worried as to how my voice would stand up to the role of Ochs. Our first rehearsal was with Krips in Room 45 and we went straight through Act I without a break. After a cup of coffee, we went into Act II, and Krips realised immediately that the singer engaged for Faninal had not prepared the cuts that he, Krips, had approved. He took the man to task. 'With a cast like this,' he said, indicating with a sweep of his arm, Jurinac, Popp, Fassbaender and myself, 'you must know your work'. Even though it was at the expense of another artist, his comment gave me an enormous lift. 'Not only am I accepted,' I thought, 'he thinks I'm bloody good.' The next day Derek Hammond-Stroud arrived to take over the part of Faninal and proved to be absolutely tremendous in the role.

The entire rehearsal period was a joy. The first time I made my exit in Act I I dropped onto a beautiful bottom C and saw Krips turn and speak to one of the repetiteurs. 'He said,' I was told afterwards, 'that that's the first authentic bottom C he's heard for many years.' Krips's confidence in me helped boost my own and I knew that my vocal problems really were behind me. When it came to the actual performance Krips was again one of those conductors who mirrored what was going on on stage, acknowledging our work with a smile, a nod of the head or a gesture.

After the third performance there was a change of cast with Tatiana Troyanos coming in for Fassbaender. Her first performance, on 24th November, was my 100th in the role. After the performance I was presented with champagne and Krips invited me to join him for supper, an invitation I had to decline for I had already asked several friends to the performance and was taking them out. To my delight I found that we were all in the same restaurant. From his table, Krips saluted me, and then he and his wife came over and I proudly introduced them round the table. 'This,' he said to everyone, putting his arm round my shoulder, 'is my favourite Ochs.' It was a treasured comment during a very special series of performances.

Chapter 13 New Brooms at The Garden

During the latter part of the time when I had been wrapped up in my vocal problems, there had been major changes taking place at Covent Garden. On 30th June 1970, a gala had been held, in front of the Queen Mother, to mark the retirement, after twenty-four years at the head of the company, of Sir David Webster. The fanfare that opened the proceedings had been especially composed by Benjamin Britten and was conducted by Solti. I took part in two scenes from *Falstaff* and sang Osmin's third act aria from *Entführung*, while other singers and conductors who had been associated with the House during Webster's reign also went through their party pieces. At the close of the evening, with the stage crowded with artists who had taken part, Webster came on and made a speech of thanks and farewell; it was a moving and emotional experience.

Most of the singers were sad to see Webster go. We had got used to the idiosyncratic way in which he governed us from Mount Olympus on high, and although he was very rarely seen in the theatre itself, we had never been in any doubt as to whose hand it was steering the ship through often very stormy waters. Webster possessed the supreme virtue of all top administrators, the ability to gather round him a highly talented team. Not only did he do that, he was prepared to let them get on with their jobs, to delegate. Naturally he took full responsibility for what happened in 'his' house, but he was never a man to interfere with what was going on unless he really had to. Some people never came to terms with his autocratic style of management, disliking the fact that he was so rarely in evidence, but I felt it was the way a large company ought to be run. I do not think the head of a large organisation should be too readily available or accessible, and, indeed, whenever you went to see Webster it automatically became a special occasion. If you wanted to speak to him, you put in a request to his secretary and would then be told when would be convenient. If he said three o'clock on Tuesday, you were there, and you knew you had possibly ten minutes before he would be off to see the Prime Minister or some equally important personage. You made use of every minute in his presence for, as far as we were concerned, he was the fount of all wisdom. A meeting with Webster, even after I had been with the company for twenty years, was always a formal affair. The only times I ever knew him relax momentarily were those when I met him away from the opera house.

Webster certainly had favourites, and it was unfortunate for me, in my early career, that I was not one of them. Our relationship went through three distinct phases. At first he had not liked me. There was, I felt, a certain amount of the snob about Webster, and he did not approve of the idea of a chorister becoming a principal. After I had given my first unsuccessful principal's audition, he had turned to Douglas Robinson and remarked, 'Not for *this* House, I think.' His attitude meant that I had had to work half as hard again to prove myself, to convince him that he had been wrong. That he did eventually put me on a principal's contract shows, I think, that he was a big enough man to admit that, in my case at least, he had made a mistake. I'm quite sure that had I joined Covent Garden directly as a principal my career would have blossomed long before it did. The second phase of our relationship was while I was on my initial principal's contract. Webster was quite happy to go along with it, and with my later lack of progress, until after I had made good with the Grand Inquisitor and Kecal, and then he went out of his way to help me. When John Coast was negotiating my contract at that time Webster had agreed to the fee John was asking; 'I feel Langdon's been held back long enough,' was his comment (to which John was sorely tempted to reply, 'And who's been holding him back?') Finally, after my first Baron Ochs, he was sold on me, even going against Solti's advice and casting me in the role again. From that moment on he did all he could to help and promote my career at home and internationally.

The only major criticism I would make of Webster was over his handling of Rankl, which I felt was disgraceful, showing a ruthless, almost bitchy streak. But apart from that I always found him to be a scrupulously fair man. I have no doubt that he was the right man to be running the company. He had started with nothing; he left behind him one of the finest opera companies in the world, a company stamped with his personality.

In July, the month after his Farewell Gala, he was given a luncheon at the Savoy by the Friends of Covent Garden. After a superb speech by his friend and colleague Sir Frederick Ashton, we all sat back to be entertained and amused by Webster, a man known for his brilliant after-dinner speaking. After a few words he broke down and began to cry. It was a very emotional moment and everybody there felt for him. I never saw him again after that occasion but I believe he went downhill rapidly and he died eventually in May 1971. His death, while it came as a shock, was not entirely unexpected. Everybody, Webster himself included, seemed to accept that with his retirement from Covent Garden, his useful life was over.

A death that affected me in a more immediate manner was that of my great friend and colleague Kenneth Macdonald, some seven months earlier. Ken had not accompanied the company to Berlin in April 1970, ostensibly because of an attack of influenza. Only when we returned to London did we realise that he was a very sick man. I visited him in hospital a few weeks after our return, and he was dreadfully thin, having been put on a starvation diet to lose weight and facilitate the doctors' examinations. He had not lost his sense of humour. 'Mike,' he groaned, 'I'm so hungry that I look forward to the barium meal tests!' He eventually returned to active singing, but never again looked well, and finally had a heart attack during rehearsal at the London Opera Centre on October 7th 1970 and was rushed to hospital. I knew nothing of this, being busy rehearsing for a concert at the Festival Hall on that day. When I came off stage after the concert that night it was to find John Tooley waiting for me. He drew me aside and said, 'Michael, I have some bad news for you, but didn't want to tell you until after the concert'. 'I know,' I replied, 'Ken's dead, isn't he?'

It was John Tooley, of course, who succeeded Sir David Webster as General Administrator. His appointment came as something of a surprise to many of us. He had been with the company for fifteen years, and it is not unusual in such cases for the second-in-command to be over-looked while a new man is brought in from outside. Immediately there was a tremendous change in the style of running Covent Garden. If Webster left his office and appeared in the house, people noticed he was there with some surprise. It caused comment, and a few questioning remarks about what the purpose of his visit might be. John, on the other hand, seemed to be everywhere. You would meet him at the stage door, the next minute he would be backstage, and then you would meet him on the stairs going up to the rehearsal rooms. It was as if there were at least three John Tooleys loose in the house. And then there was the difference in the manner of address. Very few singers (and I was not one of them) would have dreamed of calling Webster 'David', but we had all grown up with John and knew him by his first name. I am old-fashioned enough to believe that one ought to be more formal with the head of an opera house, and for some considerable time after his appointment, I felt self-conscious calling him John in public, although he encouraged it. It was disorientating for some of us and took some time to get used to. To be perfectly fair, though, there was little he could have done about it, even had he wanted to: he could hardly have put a notice on the board saying that he was now going to be known as *Mr*. Tooley.

The second major change came a year after Webster's retirement, at the end of the 1970–71 season, when Solti, after ten years in the job, resigned his post as Musical Director. During his time he had helped turn Covent Garden into one of the major international houses, he had built up a tremendous ensemble and was largely responsible for a great many British singers, myself included, securing international engagements. But much as Solti had added to Covent Garden's stature, so Covent Garden had added to his. He left us as one of the leading conductors in the world.

How to follow him? It was a question for which there was no easy answer. Solti had been the third foreign conductor appointed to the post of Musical Director, and it is doubtful whether the powers-that-be would have permitted another foreigner to take over. But even if it had been agreed, who was there in the world who could have followed Solti? Who could have kept the sense of excitement, of achievement, going? In the event the Board decided to appoint the first British Musical Director since the Company had been re-formed, and the choice fell on Colin Davis.

Davis was no Solti, but how could he have been? He had held the post of Musical Director at Sadler's Wells for six years, from 1959 until 1965, and had gained a reputation for his interpretation of Mozart and Berlioz in particular, but thereafter, apart from the occasional foray into opera, his most recent work had been in the symphonic field with the BBC Symphony Orchestra of which he was Principal Conductor. Although he was known internationally it was not primarily as an operatic conductor. He did not have Solti's experience, nor did he have Solti's knowledge of the repertoire; indeed, he announced that amongst the operas he did not particularly like were those of Strauss, which constituted an important chunk of the repertoire. It was particularly disappointing for me. I had hoped that I would have the opportunity to sing Ochs under his direction. I have the impression that if Colin had ever felt the urge to conduct *Rosenkavalier* he would have made a fine job of it. His musicality could not be questioned and he possessed a

158

certain flamboyancy of expression, especially when striving for effect during rehearsal, that would have been well-suited to much of Strauss's own larger-than-life descriptive powers. On one occasion during a *Marriage of Figaro* rehearsal, he asked Heather Begg to sing a phrase during the Act II sextet, 'like a great wave swelling to its crest.' Heather, without changing her expression, said immediately, 'Like an opening chrysanthemum?' 'No,' replied Colin; 'Like a wave swelling ... ' etc. 'What I mean,' explained Heather, '"Like an opening chrysanthemum" is what you told me to do last time. Look, I've written it in my score.' She later confided in me that it was the one time she was able to answer Colin back with any authority.

Colin, too, wanted to be known by his first name; to be on familiar terms with everyone. This double-barrelled conversion to total informality by the two top men put quite a number of us off balance, especially those who had been associated with the House for many years. With John and Colin in charge, and in evidence everywhere, the atmosphere within the House became very relaxed; perhaps too relaxed.

There was one other departure at this time which was to have an equally important effect upon the company: Joan Ingpen, the Controller of Opera Planning, left in July 1971. The role of casting director, which is what Joan did, is a vital one in any opera house. In conjunction with the musical director he or she will help decide which operas should be put on, and most importantly from the singers' point of view, which artists should play which roles. A few of the top-line conductors might be allowed to pick their own casts, but the majority would be given a production complete with all the parts already allocated. Joan's great strengths were that she knew the repertory inside out, and also knew the singers at her disposal. She knew what they could and could not do. She was also extremely fair and straightforward, never leaving you in any doubt about what was happening. If you were doing a part, she told you. If you were not doing a part, she told you. And if you really wanted to know why, she would tell you that as well: that you weren't good enough, that it didn't suit you, or that she preferred to cast someone else. Joan was never one to hedge. She was not replaced immediately. Instead James Gibson, the chief of the music staff, took over her job on a temporary basis that lasted for two years until the appointment of Helga Schmidt.

Many companies can withstand the effects of a single change at the top without any noticeable alteration in its operations, but the departure of Ingpen, Webster and Solti, all within a year, proved to be too much of an upheaval, even for Covent Garden. I don't think any of us expected the company to do more than mark time for a while. In the event it went downhill while John, and Colin in particular, were struggling to establish themselves and put their own imprint on the Royal Opera House.

The arrival of Colin Davis as Musical Director had pleased me. I had already worked with him at the Garden in *The Flying Dutchman*, *Fidelio*, and *The Marriage of Figaro*, and shortly before his appointment was announced had sung King Marke for him in a BBC recording of *Tristan und Isolde* during which he had been extremely complimentary about my work. We had always had an excellent relationship, and I had high hopes for the continuation of my career under his tenure. I had, however, reckoned without my poor performance as Narbal in *The Trojans*, which Colin had conducted, and in which my vocal problems had returned, and the news that had filtered back from Paris. I am sure these events affected the thinking within the House, for although I was fully recovered by the time of the Krips *Rosenkavaliers* and sang as well as at any other time in my career, one of the first things that happened afterwards was that James Gibson, who had by then taken over from Joan Ingpen, asked to see me. He told me how delighted everyone had been with my performances and then said that I would not be doing the next series. Apart from one series when I had been absent in San Francisco, I had been cast as Ochs at every single Covent Garden performance of *Der Rosenkavalier* for the past eleven years and it was, they felt, time to ring the changes, to show the public that there were other singers who should be heard in the role. I appreciated their point of view but was far from happy with their timing. The more Gibson stressed that the decision had nothing to do with my recent performances, the more I felt that it had been taken prior to the Krips *Rosenkavaliers*. I was not unduly worried. The next series was not scheduled for another couple of years in any case, and in the meantime I had plenty of work to keep me occupied. Not all of it was booked well in advance. When I was at home with my family on Boxing Day, I received a phone call from Solti. Before he had given me a chance to answer his enquiry as to whether I had had a good Christmas, he asked if I would like to go to Tel Aviv the following day to sing a performance of Osmin. The way he asked left me with no option but to say I would be delighted. He wanted to know how much I would ask for the performance. I was uncertain and also unable to get hold of my agent,

160

and so Solti said he would act on my behalf. Shortly afterwards he phoned back. 'Your agent Solti, here,' he said, and then proceeded to tell me he had obtained a more than satisfactory fee for me.

The next day I flew out to Tel Aviv. On the way the plane put down in Vienna and a crowd of Jewish refugees from Russia climbed on board. As we crossed the Israeli coast, the pilot made an announcement in Hebrew, whereupon the refugees began spontaneously to sing a chant, half of lament for the homeland they had left behind, half of rejoicing that they had reached their promised land. It was a most moving experience. I sang the performance the following evening, with Beverly Sills as Constanze, and flew home the next day.

After a short break, I began rehearsals of Osmin for the Sadler's Wells Company at the Coliseum, and then started an intensive period of work with performances of *The Flying Dutchman* at the Garden, *Rosenkavalier* in Stuttgart, Osmin at the Coliseum, and *Saul and David* in Copenhagen, all within the one month. The next two months continued in similar vein with more performances of *Flying Dutchman* and the Grand Inquisitor in *Don Carlos* at the Garden, interspersed with a Sadler's Wells tour of *Seraglio* and a BBC radio production of Shostakovitch's *The Nose*, before, in June, I returned to Paris to complete the remainder of the *Walküres* which had replaced the cancelled *Rosenkavaliers*.

Being back in the Paris Opera where I had experienced such an unhappy time the previous year, and singing in the same role and production from which I had been forced to withdraw, naturally made me nervous. And the first night was a special occasion since it marked Hotter's farewell performance in the role of Wotan. Although I had nothing like the problems I suffered before, I was aware that I did not sing as well as I would have liked. I had, however, devised a way of counteracting my nerves. One of the first things that happens when a singer is nervous is that the mouth and throat dry out, and a singer with a dry throat cannot sing well. My solution was to drink pints of water just before going on stage so that no matter how nervous I felt, my vocal cords would remain well-lubricated. This worked, but brought with it another problem. Since my nerves only seemed to appear in those roles in which I was required to stand around for long periods without singing, I found that with so much liquid on board, I became desperate to go to the toilet. Frequently I would reach the end of a scene and only just make it to the loo in time.

It was while waiting for the elevator in the Paris Opera House during

161

one of the later *Walküre* performances that I found myself standing next to an elegantly dressed gentleman of slim build, who seemed somehow familiar to me. As we went up in the lift together he suddenly said 'Mike, you don't recognise me, do you?' I suddenly realised that he was my old friend Ernst Kozub, with whom I had sung so many times at the Garden. I hurriedly complimented him on his new 'streamlined' appearance, but he stopped me and told me that he was ill and was doubtful whether he would be able to complete the performances of Siegmund for which he had been engaged. He did, in fact, get through them, although with only about two thirds of his former voice, and was 'given the bird' as he took his curtain call at the last performance. He came off, as near to crying as Ernst would ever get, and said with a shrug, 'What can one do? They don't know!' A couple of months later Josephine Veasey rang me to tell me that he had died.

It was a good thing that those remaining seven performances of *Die Walküre* all went off satisfactorily, for, under the circumstances, I could hardly have afforded to cancel them. Christine, our elder daughter, was due to get married on the 29th July, and I needed the money to pay for her reception. I arrived back from Paris four days before the wedding, having left most of the arrangements to Vera, and promptly began rehearsals for a television recording of *The Gondoliers*. I did, however, manage to take the Saturday off in order to lead Christine up the aisle. During the reception I was having a quiet drink with Diane, our younger daughter, when she casually mentioned that she, too, was planning to get married. I enquired as to when this happy event might take place, wondering how long I would have to save up for another reception, when she replied, 'Is five weeks all right?' I managed to negotiate two extra weeks' grace, and just seven weeks later her wedding also took place.

Leaving the arrangements once more to Vera I had headed north to Glasgow to begin work on a new Scottish Opera production of *Don Pasquale*. The previous year, when I had flown up to Aberdeen to take over Ochs at short notice, Peter Hemmings, Scottish Opera's General Administrator, had taken me on one side and asked me if there was any particular role I had always wanted to play. Without hesitation I had replied, Don Pasquale. Peter had looked pleased. 'How would you like to do it with us if we mount it for you?' he had asked. I was naturally delighted by the idea and told him so. Some time later I found out that it was an opera he had been thinking of putting on anyway, and the happy coincidence of my wanting to appear in it had confirmed his decision.

162

The opera was up-dated and given in fairly modern dress and I played Pasquale as a sort of Capo, with trousers that were a little too short, displaying a bit of sock, with my braces showing and a straw hat tilted back from my face. One might well have imagined that I had made my money from dubious sources not unconnected with the Mafia, as I sat in my canvas chair, reading my paper and issuing orders. It was an approach that worked beautifully. The cast – Sheila Armstrong, Alexander Oliver, Thomas Hemsley and myself – and Peter Ebert, the producer, worked extremely well together and after just over two weeks of rehearsal everything seemed to have fallen miraculously into place. As so we spent the remaining time until the first night with only the occasional call to reassure ourselves that we had not forgotten anything.

During those rehearsals, the first scenes had almost produced themselves, and Peter Ebert remarked that what we needed, to end my dismissal of Ernesto with a bang, was some sort of gimmick. I lightheartedly suggested that I should ride round and round the stage on a bicycle. The next day I found myself being taken to a Glasgow health club and made to choose an exercise bicycle. The scene ended with me, having put Ernesto firmly in his place, and keen, now that I was to marry the young Norina, to get myself in trim, taking off my cardigan, lighting a cigar and then unveiling this mysterious object (which had been on stage throughout, covered with a cloth), to reveal my exercise bicycle. I sang the closing duet while pedalling. As I pedalled faster, I would sing a little faster and Alexander Gibson brought the orchestra along with us. It made a very funny and effective ending which invariably brought the house down.

While we were preparing for the opening night, Scottish Opera had been going through one of those periodic financial crises which grip opera companies all too often. Although our production of *Don Pasquale* was never seriously threatened, it did look as though part or all of the tour scheduled for it after Glasgow might have to be cancelled. However, a public appeal raised the enormous sum of £60,000 in a little over a week, and our tour, and Scottish Opera's other projects, went ahead as planned.

In between the end of the first series of *Don Pasquale* and my returning to Scotland for a second series in March 1973, I sang the Commendatore in Wales and Ochs in Geneva, in which I sang opposite Elisabeth Söderström's Marschallin for the first time. Marschallins must be aristocratic, of course, but Söderström, in the first act, brought an extra dimension to the character – a sense of fun. I had never before been so conscious of the *participation* of the Marschallin in all the humorous by-play. Making her debut as Octavian in the production was Anne Howells, another singer who had first appeared with me as Annina and then later as Octavian. She, too, was excellent. When I got back to Covent Garden and was asked how the performances had gone, and what, in particular, I thought of Anne Howells, I sang her praises. I also mentioned that if ever the Garden wanted a conductor with the real Viennese touch they should look no further than Theodor Gus-chlbauer, our conductor in Geneva. I was thanked for my recommendations and told that they would be kept in mind. To my knowledge Guschlbauer has never appeared at Covent Garden, while Anne Howells has certainly never sung Octavian there. Why she hasn't is an absolute mystery to me for she is a first rate Octavian of international stature.

Several times, in fact, I was asked for my opinion of artists with whom I had just been working abroad, and not one of those I praised subsequently appeared at Covent Garden. I can only assume such enquiries were made out of politeness and as a way of making conversation, and were not intended to be taken seriously even by me. Time and time again I have found within opera an attitude that singers do not really know what it is all about, that they happen to be blessed with an ability to make the sounds that are needed to put an opera on, but are incapable of thinking. One producer actually said to me, when I queried the way he wanted me to play a scene, 'Don't bother to think, dear boy. Leave that to us.' Producers are constantly coming up with ideas that any singer of average intelligence could tell him will not work, and yet if that singer dares mention it, he is immediately labelled as 'difficult'. There is a special group of superstar singers who are listened to, but that is more to humour them, to prevent them walking out, than from any genuine desire to hear if they have something constructive to offer. Singers, generally, are not highly regarded in the intelligence stakes.

But if my opinions on singers were not being considered, what was I to make of the fact that my own career at Covent Garden seemed to be going into a decline? From the end of May 1972, when I had appeared in *The Flying Dutchman*, until the April of 1973, when I sang Angelotti in *Tosca*, a period of almost one full year, I had appeared in the house only once, and that was for a single performance of *Rigoletto* when Joseph Rouleau, who was singing Sparafucile, was indisposed. During the whole of the 1972–73 season I had been cast only as Angelotti and as

164

the First Journeyman in *Wozzeck*, and yet I was in my second century of performances as an international Baron Ochs. Admittedly most of my work took me abroad or away from Covent Garden, but that was only because Covent Garden, which had first call on my services, had no use for me. If it had not been for my outside commitments, I would have been having a very thin time of it artistically. During the 1973–74 season I appeared as Quince in *A Midsummer Night's Dream*, as Varlaam in *Boris*, as Sparafucile, as the 2nd Soldier in *Salome*, and then, at the very end of the season, as Pistol in a revival of *Falstaff*. This was the first time since his appointment three years earlier that I had worked with Colin Davis, a fact which led me to the conclusion that I was far from indispensable to his plans. When rehearsals for the first scene of *Falstaff* began, with Tito Gobbi, Robert Bowman, John Lanigan and myself, our combined ages, if my reckoning is correct, was at least 215 years, and our combined experience formidable. I got the strong impression that Colin did not relish working with such experienced singers. Only after he realised that we were out to enjoy ourselves and the rehearsals had gone well did he begin to relax.

The 1974–75 season followed a similar pattern. At Covent Garden I was given only Varlaam, the Doctor in *Wozzeck*, and Pistol to sing, while elsewhere I appeared in Scottish Opera's *Lucia di Lammermoor*, a revival of their *Rosenkavalier*, Welsh National Opera's *Flying Dutchman*, Houston's *Der Rosenkavalier* (in which Frederica von Stade made her debut as Octavian), and the world premiere of a new opera commissioned by Scottish Opera, *Hermiston*, which opened at the Edinburgh Festival on 27th August 1975, conducted by Alexander Gibson. I had been given the leading role of Lord Hermiston and during the opera's composition, Robin Orr, the composer, had approached me to say that since it was such an important part, he naturally wanted it to be in the best part of my voice. This is, of course, every singer's dream, to have a role written especially for him. I told Orr that being a deep bass I would relish plenty of low notes down to E flat and D. When I finally received the score, I was astonished. *Hermiston* must be one of the few operas, if not the only one, in which the bass begins on a bottom E and stays consistently in the lower and middle reaches of the voice for pages on end. On about the third performance, after I had grown tired of growling around, I put the opening lines up a minor third, beginning my first phrase on a G. Afterwards Robin Orr came round to my dressing room to say that he thought the whole scene had gone much better. I'm still not sure if he realised what I had done!

It was strange how I had spent most of my career disliking travelling, preferring to remain at Covent Garden so that I could be close to my home and family, and now, at an age when most people begin to think of settling down, I was actually looking forward to going away, to appearing with those companies where the work for me was so much more interesting than at Covent Garden. The high hopes I had entertained for myself when Colin Davis had become Musical Director were certainly not being realised. It was quite clear to me that those of us who were over fifty were gradually being phased out. I was not the only person to sense this. David Ward had said to me, in his typically blunt way, soon after Colin's appointment, 'You realise they'll soon be bloody farming us out, don't you?' And he was right. David was farmed out even before I was. At least I still had Ochs to cling to. Nobody had come up to supersede me, but I have the very definite feeling that had there been someone who could have taken over as Ochs from me in 1971 my days at the Garden would have been numbered even earlier.

If the management's attitude towards me had altered after the changeovers in 1970 and 1971, then so too had my own attitude towards Covent Garden. During the sixties everything that happened in the House seemed to me to be of supreme importance and I had taken an interest in every production, whether I was involved in it or not. If other artists were having success, the company was having success, and that reflected on me as a member of the company. But after Solti's departure so much excitement went out of the House that I soon felt no longer a part of the company. I was being given a mixture of not very interesting roles and those I had sung many times over the years; casting was unpredictable; the productions were far from memorable; and I tended to look upon my appearances there more as a guest artist. Working at Covent Garden had become just a job.

Chapter 14 Changing Careers

My interest in singing underwent a resurgence during the 1975–76 season, which opened for me in November with performances of *Der Rosenkavalier* under Silvio Varviso. These were to be my last appearances as Ochs at Covent Garden and, indeed, to date the opera has not been performed in the house since. (The last scheduled series was cancelled.) This was followed in January by Bartolo in *Figaro*, and then two months later by Simone in *Gianni Schicchi* and Bottom in *A Midsummer Night's Dream*. This sudden and surprising spate of interesting work came about, I think, because of a mistake. Just before the season had started, when the only dates in my diary were for *Der Rosenkavalier*, I had been called into Helga Schmidt's office and was asked if I would be free to undertake these other roles. It was obvious that some sort of miscalculation had occurred and they had found themselves short of a bass.

But then in the middle of these enjoyable roles (especially Bottom, a part I relished doing) I found myself cast as Pirro in the production of *I Lombardi* brought in from the Hungarian State Opera, Budapest.

Not knowing *Lombardi*, and in the context of my other roles that season, I had assumed that Pirro would at least be interesting. It is, in fact, a very small part, and to have to sing it in the same season that I was appearing in leading roles only reinforced my suspicion that nothing had really changed.

Immediately after *I Lombardi*, we began rehearsals for *We Come To The River*, a new opera especially commissioned from Henze. I had been cast as the Doctor. Although I had previously sung in modern operas and had not always been bowled over by them at first, I had always come to find some merit in them eventually. This never happened with *We Come To The River*. It was a series of experimental scenes, involving fifty-eight artists, and containing, I believe, a garbled political message which none of us were able to fathom. To me it was not an opera at all. Nor did I find the music worth any serious consideration.

Henze produced the work himself. During rehearsals of the madhouse scene he explained that he wanted the cast, dressed in white shifts, to float around like white cotton-wool clouds on a fine English summer day. 'I want you to float around without any meaning, without any direction, because you are all mad,' Henze said. He had just reached the middle of his piece on looking like white cotton-wool clouds when he caught sight of Frank Olegario, the black singer. Henze stopped in mid-sentence. 'Don't you worry about me, boss,' said Frank. 'I'll just be that great big black thunder cloud.'

My first entrance was made through the auditorium and I had to be in position in the pit bar before the opera began. I was dressed in Edwardian clothes, with very pale make-up, shadowed eyes and a rather bloodless mien. Latecomers would congregate in this bar and stare at me in disbelief. I heard one lady whisper to her escort, 'Look at that man at the end – he's wearing make-up!' When the time arrived for me to make my entrance, I finished my gin and tonic, smiled at her and said, 'Excuse me, I have to go and sing.'

During my first encounter with the General, I had to tell him that he was going blind as the result of an old war wound. Henze told me that every word was very important, and so, in rehearsal, I spat them out to make them clear. When it came to the time to put the scene on stage with the other scenes that were being played simultaneously, I discovered that in the action going on behind me, Gillian Knight, playing the part of a prostitute, was busily servicing a soldier on the edge of a table. I stopped singing and asked Henze what was going on. 'That is the other scene that's being played,' he replied. 'But,' I said, 'you told me that every word I sing must come across and yet you provide the ultimate distraction to take away from what I am saying.' 'Don't worry,' said Henze. 'We'll take the lights down on that particular scene.' 'That will only make it worse,' I complained. 'All I will hear is the money going into the slots while they get their opera glasses out to see if it's really true.' Henze had no answer to that and I, like most of the cast, just gave up and did what I was told. It was impossible to take seriously. In the final scene, to amuse my colleagues, I would sing my last phrase to a different sequence of notes every evening. No one ever noticed. And when Robert Tear arrived one evening with the news that they were letting the audience in free, not one of us was too surprised. 'But,' said Bob, having got us to swallow the bait, 'they're having to pay to get out.'

As far as I was concerned the whole production was a waste of time and effort, and I'm sure I was not alone in feeling this. When the ladies

21. On stage at Covent Garden
during a Friends of Covent
Garden Christmas
Evening, 1972.

22. Gazing over the Danube at Budapest
during my engagement at the State Opera in 1964.

23. The cast of *The Magic Flute* at the Budapest State Opera, 1964.
I was Sarastro, György Melis (front) sang Papageno.

24. Celebrating the birth of Solti's daughter in a Berlin restaurant
    while on tour with the Covent Garden company in 1970.
    Also at the table are Donald McIntyre and Ava June.

25. Members of the cast of Strauss's *The Silent Woman*, Covent Garden, 1961.
    Left to right, David Ward, me, Joseph Ward, David Kelly, Ronald Lewis.

26. Meeting the Queen Mother after a gala performance of *Die Fledermaus* in which I played Colonel Frank. Sir John Tooley watches. This was to be my final appearance at Covent Garden before my retirement from singing.

27. With Sir Geraint Evans at a Savoy luncheon given in his honour by the Friends of Covent Garden to celebrate his 25th anniversary with the company, 14 February 1973.

28. The cartoon by Coia which Scottish
Opera presented to me to mark my
retirement, 4 January 1979. Also in the
picture, left to right, Sir Alexander
Gibson, Sir Patrick Thomas (the then
Chairman of Scottish Opera)
and Peter Ebert.

29. Vera with the girls, Christine (left)
and Diane (right).

30. Outside Buckingham Palace with
(l to r) Diane, Vera and Christine
after receiving my CBE in 1973.

of the cast had to exit through the auditorium, talking ad lib amongst themselves as instructed in the score, they would say things like 'Money back at the box office' as they made their way up the aisles. I felt particularly sorry for Norman Welsby, who played the General, for he put so much work into his fine performance for such little return. We all had to work extremely hard to put on a very complicated and difficult piece with the virtual certainty that it would never be performed at the Royal Opera House again.

If I was disillusioned with the way my career was going at Covent Garden, *We Come To The River* did nothing to help cheer me up. This was not opera as I knew it, but it did seem to be symptomatic of the direction in which certain people were trying to push opera, and I wanted no part in it. At the end of the season I flew off to Cleveland to take part in two performances of *Fidelio* at the Blossom Festival, and I realised more and more that this sort of trip, which previously I had not enjoyed leaving home for, was the work that I was most looking forward to, the work that meant something and gave me pleasure.

I returned from Cleveland looking forward to going down to Cardiff to take over the role of Osmin in their new production of *Il Seraglio*, in which Suzanne Murphy as Constanze made her debut with the Welsh National Opera. After the way the Covent Garden season had ended I felt I was ready for the fun of Osmin. I had, however, been so out of touch with things Welsh that I had not heard about the fire in WNO's workshops which had damaged most of the *Seraglio* scenery beyond repair, and did not know we would be working in a hotch-potch, jury-rigged production. This created its own difficulties. In Osmin's first scene he sings the famous aria 'When a maiden takes your fancy' while plucking figs from a tree. I was very put out when I saw the new improvised set, for the fig tree was represented by bunches of figs hanging just below the level of the proscenium arch. There was no sign of a branch. In order to reach them I had been given a ladder made of rough, thick wood, on which the rungs had been lashed across the uprights at intervals of about three feet. Since I was wearing a great false belly, wide loose-fitting pantaloons and curly-toed shoes, I found it extremely difficult to negotiate these rungs. And at the same time I had to carry a basket and sing an aria. I was also expected to drag this massive ladder on by myself and place it precisely on two marks so that when I eventually attained the altitude of the figs they would not be out of my reach. This was the 'fun' I had been looking forward to. That first scene was so exhausting physically that in later performances I insisted on having a slave to drag on and place the ladder for me. It may have ruined my entrance but at least it helped me save my energy for the actual ascent and delivery of my first aria.

Michael Geliot, who produced *Seraglio*, is an extremely intelligent man, but sometimes gives the impression that he is the *only* intelligent man, often going into great detail explaining points which need only a few words to get across. My conception of Osmin did not agree exactly with his and I felt the tension beginning to build up. I was reluctant to try out unfamiliar business, not because I was not open to suggestions or thought my interpretation was the only possible one (there is no such thing as the 'definitive' performance), but because I was uneasy with it; I could not make it work for the character. If an artist feels uncomfortable about something he is asked to do, the audience will sense his unease and become uneasy themselves. Geliot, however, can be very persuasive and despite my experience I fell into an elementary trap, adjusting my performance to include things with which I was not at all convinced. The result, as far as I was concerned, was a routine performance without any of the flair or excitement I was accustomed to expect.

To crown everything I broke the rule I had imposed in about 1970 (after I had been written off by one critic as not being able to sing high enough and by another as not being able to sing low enough) of never reading reviews. I bought a paper the following morning to see what had been thought of the improvised production and found that everyone except me had received very good notices. The critic felt that I was not well suited to the role and that I needed more experience. I read these comments just before Vera and I left Cardiff to visit my relatives in the Midlands, and for the first twelve miles or so of our journey I sat with my eyes fixed firmly on the road ahead, saying nothing. Vera sat waiting for the inevitable explosion. When it came, liberally larded with expletives and comments about fashion writers doubling as music critics, she heard me out and then told me to calm down, that it wasn't worth being upset by the remarks of an uninformed critic who obviously knew little about the opera and even less about me. I refused to be consoled so easily and throughout the journey continued to fulminate on how the fun had gone out of singing and how little point I felt there was in continuing.

For the first time I began to voice the thoughts that had been crowding in on me with increasing regularity. Just where was I heading? I was now fifty-six, the end of my big, international career had

170

to be in sight, and I had lost almost all of my old zest at being a member of the Royal Opera House, Covent Garden. Although I had sung a number of leading roles in the previous season at the Garden I had also had to contend with Pirro and *We Come To The River*, and the new season which was just about to start was as pathetically uninteresting. I was scheduled to sing only Angelotti in *Tosca* and Orestes' Tutor in *Elektra*, until at the very end of the season I had been given my only rewarding role, Count Waldner in *Arabella*. It was as if the clock had been turned back twenty years to the Kubelik era. Additional proof of my waning value to Covent Garden was furnished when my contracted salary, for the first and only time in my career, was considerably reduced. At least under Kubelik it had stayed the same. Another pointer of the direction things were going came in the experience of a close friend and colleague, who happened to be about my own age. He was summoned for an interview and asked, quite bluntly, where he thought his career was going. One way or the other it did seem that the old guard, those of us over fifty, were scheduled for the chop. We would either be phased out quickly, or, by being assigned only small roles at infrequent intervals, be persuaded that the time had come for us to depart of our own accord. The Covent Garden management was, of course, behaving in a very logical and businesslike manner, for no international house can continue to flourish unless it has a transfusion of new blood into the ensemble. It is a difficult and often distressing duty to have to get rid of older singers in order to make way for new talent, but my ego told me that, as far as I was concerned, they were putting me out to grass several seasons too soon.

The fact had to be faced that my career at Covent Garden was almost over, and that the only interesting and rewarding work I was being offered was outside the company. One such engagement took me to the Wexford Festival to play Falstaff in Nicolai's *The Merry Wives of Windsor*. It was a role with the most beautiful music and I had always wanted to sing it, though until I began to study the score I had not realised just how short the part is when compared with Verdi's Falstaff. I was determined to look right, but for a man of six feet three to look fat, he has to wear a great deal of padding, and I felt I would never be able to put on enough foam rubber to make the role anything other than an ordeal. I therefore devised a false stomach which had two curved pieces of metal that sat on the tops of my thighs and was held on by straps around my back. This left a large gap between my own stomach and the false one which I thought would make me extremely comfort-

171

able. I would look enormous and yet not have to carry a lot of weight. I had, however, forgotten the string vest principle, that the way to keep warm is to create a layer of hot air between the inside of your clothing and your skin, and the more I exerted myself, the more super-heated the air in this hollow stomach became, until I felt like a chicken in an oven. It was most uncomfortable. When the moment came for me to be bundled into the basket I had to grab hold of my neckpiece and pull it away from myself so that I wasn't throttled. I could also feel the framework of my false stomach buckling. This too created a problem, for during the performance it moved so much that when the time came for me to go to the toilet, I could not align myself with the aperture provided for that purpose.

At one performance, just before the magical forest scene, I was in the loo trying frantically to locate my member, which I couldn't see or find beneath my false stomach, and align it with the opening of my costume, when there came a tap on the door. 'Mr. Langdon,' came the voice of one of the wardrobe ladies, 'you're on stage.' 'I'm not, you know,' I replied, 'I'm trying to have a pee.' 'What's the matter then?' she asked solicitously. I explained my predicament. 'I can't find it; I can't get my hand inside my costume.' 'I'll come and help you,' she said in all innocence. There was no time to accept her kind offer and I had to abandon my gropings and rush back on stage. All the running and jumping about in Windsor Forest that night was most uncomfortable!

Had things been going swimmingly at Covent Garden, as I had expected them to when Colin Davis became Musical Director, I would have been perfectly content to sing myself through to the end of my career there and then retire. But as things were, I had become so disillusioned that I felt that I had to make some sort of decision without delay. One night, in November 1976, after Vera and I had gone to bed, I lay with my hands cupped behind my head and stared up into the darkness. After about half-an-hour spent weighing up the pros and cons, I finally reached the decision that I had been moving towards longer than perhaps even I had realised. 'Are you asleep?' I asked Vera. 'Not any more,' she sighed. I told her that I had decided to complete all my outstanding engagements, which would take me into January 1979, and then retire from the operatic stage. 'Good,' she said. 'Now go to sleep and we'll talk about it in the morning.'

In the morning I knew that my decision was right. I wrote to John Coast and told him, explaining my reasons. He replied that he felt I had made a wise choice if only because too many singers do not know when to make the break. Now that the uncertainty was over, my body felt relaxed and my mind clear. The only question that remained was what I would do instead. I did not wish simply to retire and sit back for I felt I was still able to offer the operatic world something, though in what capacity I was not sure. There are really only two things an opera singer can do when he retires, unless he has an alternative trade, and they are to teach singing or to produce opera. I have always wanted to produce. Having seen the results of some producers' efforts I reasoned that I could do a much better job myself, and at least I start with an understanding of the music and of singers that a great many producers do not possess. However these are qualities most managements seem to think are hardly necessary, and, in any case, one has to be invited to produce, and I knew the chances of my receiving an invitation were remote. That left teaching. Not all successful opera singers make good teachers; indeed, there are singers who go through their whole lives without really knowing how they make the noise they do. Frank Mullings, the famous pre-war tenor, is reputed to have said that the resonance came up his right side, under his armpit and somehow got into his head through the right side of his neck before coming out through his mouth. That happened to work for him but is hardly the way to teach raw beginners. It doesn't matter what mental picture you conjure up in order to place your voice, provided it produces the best sound you are capable of making, and teachers who use hard and fast methods with every single student are on the wrong track. Every person is an individual, and as a teacher you have to find out how best they can produce their voice. I felt I had the ability to do this. In 1972 I had given my first lecture at the London Opera Centre, with, I was told, great success, and had followed this with a series of Master Classes at the Guildhall School of Music and Drama.

In November that year I received a letter from the office of Edward Heath, the Prime Minister, inviting me to accept the CBE. This award, for my services to music, thrilled me greatly and I was deluged with congratulatory telegrams when it was announced in the New Year's Honours List. I was invested by the Queen on 6th March 1973, and the ceremony was watched proudly by my wife and daughters.

I now embarked on a further series of Master Classes at the Guildhall and in September 1973 was made an Hon. GSM, an honour I deeply appreciated. It seemed to be 'Honours Time' for me, and I was encouraged to continue with my lecturing and master-classing. My only problem was that I became increasingly bored when working with what I can only describe as 'no hopers'. I have never understood how professional teachers of voice or deportment can bring themselves to slog away hour after hour with people who have little or nothing to give in return. However, by 1976 I reasoned that as we had moved from Sutton to Brighton, I might be able to persuade a sufficient number of promising young singers to take a trip to the sea and at the same time take a lesson with Langdon.

I found a reasonable studio on the top floor of a music shop in Western Road, Brighton, and arranged terms with the manager, explaining that it might be some time before I would be using it on a regular basis. A short time afterwards, having a hefty piece of singing to practice and not wanting to give our new neighbours a breakdown similar to the one I had given our neighbour in Sutton during my interminable bellowings as Ochs, I rang the music shop to enquire about the studio's availability. I kept getting the number unobtainable sound and so decided to walk round to the shop itself. I found that a disgruntled employee had burnt it down the previous day. With no other suitable studio space available anywhere in Brighton it was obvious that someone somewhere was trying to tell me something.

Vera now came up with an alternative suggestion. Why not move up to her home town of Norwich, after I had completed my singing engagements, and teach there? It seemed a sensible idea, so the next time we visited Norwich I placed an advertisement in the local paper stating that I intended to move to the area and would be prepared to take on a number of selected students. Whether I was too vague about exactly when I intended to make my move, or whether prospective pupils were put off by the 'selected students', I do not know, but I received only seven replies (six, if you count as one the two identical letters from the same person posted on different days). The only reply which showed any real enthusiasm was from a lady who had much admired my performance as Claggart in the television version of *Billy Budd*. Her letter left me in no doubt that it was 'the way I had used my whip' that she found most exciting and she added, in underlined capitals, that she would 'pay most highly for my services'. Vera felt a move to Norwich might not be the answer.

One person who did find the lady's offer amusing was Kiri Te Kanawa with whom I appeared soon afterwards in *Arabella*. She had so enjoyed the story when I told her that I toyed with the idea of appearing at the dress rehearsal of the Act II ballroom scene with a riding crop in my hand, but knowing Kiri's propensity for uninhibited laughter when the mood takes her, decided the risk of bringing the rehearsal to a complete standstill was too great.

In February 1977 an advertisement had appeared in the magazine *Opera* inviting applications for the post of Director of the National Opera Studio which was being set up to replace the London Opera Centre. The Centre had been providing advanced operatic training for some fourteen or fifteen years, but it was felt by an Arts Council Committee of Enquiry into the state of operatic training in Britain that much of its work was now being duplicated in music colleges and academies. What was required in its place, it was suggested, was a Studio where young professionals, further advanced than students, could be given specialist training to prepare them for entry into one of the major companies. Harold Rosenthal, the editor of *Opera*, phoned to tell me about the advertisement and suggested that I ought to put in for the job. I duly sent off my application and received an acknowledgement by return.

I must here correct a misapprehension. In a profile of me in his magazine in December 1975, Harold Rosenthal had concluded his article with the following words: 'I would like to suggest that the time has already come for this seasoned and knowledgeable artist to be invited to pass on some of the wealth of his experience to the younger generation of singers; or better still to play an important part in the administration of one or other of our musical institutions that help train potential operatic artists.' Several of my professional colleagues have been under the illusion that Rosenthal wrote those words knowing that everything had been fixed for me to be offered the job of Director at the National Opera Studio as soon as the organisation was ready to be set up. Nothing could be further from the truth. Indeed, the last person to expect to get the job was me. A few weeks after I had replied to the advertisement I was sent a copy of the Committee of Enquiry's report and an application form on which I had to list my places of education, my musical education, my musical degrees, previous positions held, and so on. As I read through it, I realised that after putting my name and address at the top, all I could add would be 'Joined Covent Garden chorus 1948, became a Principal 1951, have sung internationally and am still at Covent Garden.' It looked very thin on such a long, important document. I then turned to the Arts Council report and read what sort of person they wanted as Director. 'Basically, his function will be administrative ... He must have a knowledge of music and opera, but also be able to move easily and persuasively in several different worlds: to deal with local authorities and grant-giving bodies as well as with opera house managements and music college principals, with teachers of music and drama as well as with young singers. He will have to travel a good deal and frequently visit performances . . . It has been suggested to us that the post should be filled by a very distinguished retired opera singer or conductor, whose genius and prestige would bring to the Studio a special quality. Despite the obvious attraction of such a proposal, we are doubtful whether such a personality would fit the functions now described.' There seemed little point in even attempting to fill in the form. I wrote back very respectfully and said that having read more closely what they wanted, I had to admit that I was not their man and that I was withdrawing my application.

Another attempt to provide a career to follow my retirement had foundered and I must admit I felt very disappointed. I still felt that I had something to offer opera and yet I had no opportunity to show what I could do. But then a few days before the final performance of *Arabella* I was sent for by Helga Schmidt who, without any preliminaries, asked me if I would like to take over the position of Company Manager. My first reaction was to ask whether it would mean I would have to be in the house every night. Helga said that it would not. I had no idea of just what the job would entail, but Helga assured me that whatever attributes were required, I possessed them all in abundance. Although it was obvious to me that the decision had been taken to phase me out as a singer, I was flattered and relieved that the management still seemed anxious to find me a place within the organisation; that somebody wanted me. And when both John Tooley and Colin Davis later told me that they would have the utmost confidence in me should I decide to accept the offer, I was quite moved. There, for the time being, the matter rested.

As the 1977–78 season began I knew that my decision to quit singing was the right one. Outside the house I was singing in *Arabella* in Houston (with Kiri again in the title role), as Osmin in Miami and a clutch of *Rosenkavaliers* in Scotland, but at Covent Garden I had been cast only as Pantheus in *The Trojans* at the start of the season and been asked to understudy Bartolo in *The Marriage of Figaro*, otherwise I had nothing scheduled for eight months, until mid-June, when I was to sing Pistol in a revival of *Falstaff*.

Rehearsals for *The Trojans* began at the end of August 1977, about one month after the idea of my becoming Company Manager had first been mooted. I had given the matter much thought and had more than

176

half convinced myself that, once I had discovered what was required of me, I would be able to do the job quite well. The only disturbing aspect was that no one had said any more about it. *The Trojans* opened eventually after a certain amount of industrial dispute, and after the third or fourth performance I was in my dressing room washing off when John Tooley put his head round the door. 'We haven't forgotten about the Company Manager's job, Michael,' he said, 'but something else has come up. Will you be at home tomorrow?' I said that I would and asked why. 'Expect a phone call,' was all he would reply.

The next day Sir Hugh Willatt phoned and said he would like to talk to me about the National Opera Studio. We arranged to meet at the Garrick Club for lunch on the 4th of October. We had a most enjoyable meal and, in true British fashion, got to the dessert before Sir Hugh suddenly asked, 'What do you think about the National Opera Studio? Do you think it's a good idea?' I replied that I thought it was an excellent idea. 'Would you be prepared to help us?' Sir Hugh went on. In that Arts Council report there had been a paragraph to the effect that the Studio would be hoping to persuade distinguished singers to give regular master classes, and I naturally thought this was what he meant. 'Of course,' I said, 'I would be delighted to give lectures or master classes.' 'No, no, no,' said Sir Hugh, 'would you be interested in being Director, in setting the thing up?' I was quite overwhelmed and said that nothing would please me more, but I reminded him that, having read the Arts Council report, I had felt that I was hardly the man they were looking for and had actually withdrawn my application. Sir Hugh replied that there had been a slight shift of emphasis as far as the top jobs were concerned and that the Board of Management would like to interview me and assess my suitability for the post of Director.

Towards the end of the same week I received a call arranging a date for me to meet the Board of the Studio at Covent Garden on 11th October, three days before I was due to depart for Houston. When the time came, I walked into the room and sat down. No one said a word to me. Realising that I was expected to start, I began to expound my ideas on how a Studio should be set up and the sort of work it should attempt to do. I went on for some length. A few questions were asked including a very pertinent one from Lord Harewood. 'You use this word "professional" a lot, Mike,' he said. 'Does it have some mystic significance for you?' 'It does for the singer,' I replied, 'because it means that moment when he realises that people are willing to pay to hear him sing; when he realises he has the talent to make a career out of what may until then have been a hobby. I think we have to engender this professional attitude in our trainees.' I was relieved that this explanation seemed to be well-received.

I was then asked to leave the room, returning some ten minutes later, for Sir Hugh Willatt, as Chairman of the Board, to invite me to become the Studio Director. I went home to break the news to Vera with a new thought to impart to my future students: 'Do not abandon hope all ye who are not heavily laden with degrees.' I flew to Houston a very happy man.

In the excitement of first being offered the post of Company Manager and then actually being appointed Director of the National Opera Studio, I had almost forgotten that Helga Schmidt, shortly after the start of the season, had asked me to look at the part of Colonel Frank in *Die Fledermaus*. A quick glance had been sufficient to tell me that it is a highish baritone role totally unsuitable for me. Helga countered this with the comment that it didn't matter; it was, after all, 'operetta'. I failed totally to grasp what she meant. Never having sung operetta I was under the impression that a composer wrote a sequence of notes with the expectation that whoever took the part would sing them. Reluctantly I turned the part down for I found the character of Frank just the sort of role I enjoyed playing.

When I was in Houston I received a call from Helga asking me to reconsider my decision and repeating that it was, after all, operetta. Although Kiri, who was to sing Rosalinde in the production, urged me to accept – 'Look, Mikey,' she said, 'if they are so keen on you, take it on and then let *them* work out the musical problems' – I again said I could not do it. Only when a score, rewritten to make the part suitable for my voice, arrived by express post at my hotel did I call Helga and say I would do it. An added bonus for me was that, having already signed my contract for the season (at the same modest rate as the previous one), Covent Garden now had to pay me performance fees as well to appear as a guest artist! Some time after our production had opened, Australian Opera decided that they too would do *Die Fledermaus*, and cast a bass as Frank. The poor man tried valiantly to encompass the higher reaches of the score but eventually had to turn it down. 'What do you mean, you can't do it?' was all he got from the management; 'Langdon sings it, and *he's* a bloody bass.' It was only later that they learnt of the transpositions.

During rehearsals for *Fledermaus* we had the utmost difficulty in persuading Leopold Lindtberg, the producer, to let us have a run at the

178

scenes. He kept interrupting every few bars, and we were all getting rather desperate. Only after a near-revolution did he permit us to go through without stopping, thereby finding out where the 'thin' spots lay. No one except the cast will ever know the desperation with which we clung to the old theatrical saying, 'It will be all right on the night.' It *was* all right, and not just for the audience in the house but for the millions around the world who watched it live on television. It was estimated that in Britain alone it was seen by more people than had visited Covent Garden since it had re-opened after the war. Only near the end of the evening, probably because of the sheer relief that it had gone so well and was nearly over, did disaster almost strike. Benjamin Luxon as Falke was supposed to say to me, 'After all, she did go to the ball in his wife's dress.' Instead he began, 'After all, she did go to the dress . . . ' and for one timeless moment it seemed that he was about to complete his Spoonerism ' . . . in his wife's balls.' Ben, however, as unflappable as ever, paused and began again: 'As I intended to say . . . ' The audience roared with delight. That night was one of those magical occasions when even mistakes seemed to enhance the performance.

Die Fledermaus ended its run on 17th January 1978. The following day I took up my appointment as Director of the National Opera Studio.

Chapter 15 Singers of the Future

Not long after I had taken up my job at the National Opera Studio, I was up a ladder at home, painting a ceiling, when John Coast phoned to ask if I would like to go to Vienna to sing some performances of *Rosenkavalier*. I told John I would think about it and call him back. It was a very attractive offer but as I carried on painting I found myself beginning, just as I had many years earlier when I had had to decide whether to leave the Garden and go to Düsseldorf, to think of all the reasons why I did not want to accept. I rang John and told him that I would be far too busy with the National Opera Studio and that I would not have the time to spare to brush up my Viennese accent. Even as I was speaking to him I knew that my decision was right.

Saying that I was too busy with the Studio was not just an excuse. At that stage there were no staff, no premises, no students, no programme, nothing, except the Board and me, and a commitment to open in September. The first appointment to be made after me was that of Gerald Macdonald as Administrator, a recommendation from our chairman Sir Hugh Willatt. As with all Sir Hugh's advice, it could not be faulted. Gerry had been a regional director for the Arts Council and General Manager of the Royal Philharmonic Orchestra, and during the early sixties had been approached about becoming Director of the London Opera Centre. He had decided not to proceed with this because David Webster, as General Administrator of the Royal Opera House, would have been in overall charge of the building and Gerry would have had to work in close harness with him. As Gerry himself put it: 'I had always been used to getting up early but I felt that I would never be up early enough to win an argument with DW should the occasion arise!' Gerry's knowledge and experience were invaluable to me, and without his help I could never have hoped to set up the National Opera Studio.

In true British fashion we had both been appointed without any buildings in which to carry out our work, and our first task together was to search London for suitable premises. Ideally we wanted to be located in the West End, close to the opera houses and the theatres from where we would need to draw our outside professional help. We looked at the building in John Carpenter Street vacated by the Guildhall School when they moved into the Barbican, but found that although it had been empty only a few months it was already in a bad state and would have taken more money than we could possibly have afforded to put even the small number of rooms we needed into shape. We realised eventually that the only possible way of setting up the Studio in time would be for us to utilise existing facilities and premises. Our search took us to Morley College in Lambeth. I had been hoping to acquire a separate building or area which would have its own identity and a door marked 'National Opera Studio', beyond which everything would belong to us, but it was not to be. Morley's rooms were dotted about the building, but at least they gave us the space we needed in which to work, and I felt that it was important for the Studio to begin functioning and show very early on what we were capable of doing.

I still had several singing engagements to complete, before my official retirement, in Miami, in Scotland and at Covent Garden, and these had to be fitted in with my work trying to set up the Studio. While I was in Scotland singing Ochs, I contracted a viral infection which, although I could still sing, left me very short of breath and very tired, particularly when I got back to London and began the rounds of musical colleges, explaining to them what we were doing and inviting them to recommend singers for audition. We had decided that the ideal number of trainees (we prefer to call them trainees since they have completed their musical studies by the time they get to us and are really young professionals) would be twelve voices and three repetiteurs. We wanted the twelve best young voices we could find, even if that meant twelve sopranos or twelve mezzos. In practice, of course, we have always managed a mixed number, although in the first three years of the Studio's operation we managed to recruit only one bass.

Now came two more important appointments at the Studio. Martin Isepp, the internationally-known teacher and accompanist, agreed to become Head of Music, and Isobel Flinn left the Royal Northern College of Music to assist him and take over whenever his work took him away for any appreciable period. Both of them possess a comprehensive knowledge of voices and of repertoire, and if the secret of success is to have the right people around you, I was already well on the way. Together with Celia Harding, who became my personal assistant and who seemed to know everyone in all the operatic administrations, we now had lines of communication open on first name terms to all the professional people needed to start the Studio successfully.

Auditions took place during June and we heard well over 200 singers during the all-day sessions. Several of my evenings that month were spent at the Garden appearing as Pistol in *Falstaff*. It was all extremely tiring. Eventually we found the people we were after and the Studio opened its doors officially on the 23rd October 1978, three weeks later than we had intended. It had taken much longer than anyone expected to set up but I felt it was better to open late rather than postpone for a year, for I wanted to get it off the ground while interest was high and not risk any lessening of enthusiasm if unproductive months slipped by.

The main object of the Studio is to give young singers a chance to work in opera under professional conditions, and to try and give them some idea of what life as a professional opera singer will be like. At a preliminary meeting we discover which roles people are interested in performing and then work out a programme of scenes from the relevant operas for them to work on. We try to give each trainee enough time to prepare a role fully, coaching them through the entire role musically from start to finish, and picking out key scenes to be rehearsed and performed on stage, supported by their colleagues. They in turn will then support their colleagues while they are doing *their* main piece, and so everybody gets used to singing major roles and also to appearing as a supporting artist. If we run short of voices when casting, then my preference is to bring in professional artists from outside. When we did a scene from *Falstaff*, under the direction of Tito Gobbi, in which all the ladies were from the Studio, all the men, with the exception of Ford, were from the Covent Garden cast – John Lanigan, Frank Egerton and myself. This kind of mix, when it can be managed, makes trainees realise just what is needed to perform opera far more than any number of lectures or in-house rehearsals. The main difference I have discovered between the talented young singer and the experienced professional is in the amount of inner energy that the experienced singer brings to his work. Inexperienced singers often sing beautifully but without that inner tension, that 'presence' that experienced singers bring to their performance. Perhaps the very first aspect of opera that I try to bring home to them is that singing it is not a genteel job in which you lean one elbow on a piano and sing 'Home Sweet Home'. Opera is hard, heavy, strenuous and sweaty, and you have to be proud, not embarrassed, to sweat. Whenever we take them to a rehearsal at Covent Garden or at the Coliseum, and manage to get them close enough to the action, they are invariably astonished by the tremendous effort and energy that world-famous singers put into their performances. To watch a man like Domingo, for example, at close quarters is to realise that he is a dynamo who gives everything, and when the curtain comes down he will be as exhausted as a boxer or a footballer at the end of the match.

Some idea of just how tiring a performance can be, and just how much an artist gives, is demonstrated by something Kirsten Flagstad once told Thomas Hemsley. After singing Brünnhilde she liked to have breakfast in bed the following morning. She had always given so much vocally that when she phoned down to Room Service to place her order, she had never failed to be called 'Sir'.

A well-trained voice, no matter how tired, will always recover quickly. It is, however, vital that it should be warmed up properly in exactly the same way a sportsman exercises his muscles before going onto the pitch. Indeed the Italians actually speak of 'moving' the voice. During the performances of *The Bartered Bride* in which I sang Kecal, I was unable to find a parking space for my car one night, and was so delayed that I had to go on cold without warming up. The part of Kecal begins on a succession of high D naturals and I could hear that my voice sounded hard and dry. I literally sang myself in during the first act. The audience must have thought I was not in very good voice but, as the evening progressed, my voice warmed up and by the time it came to the second act I was fine. This is why it is so much easier to sing a large role than a small one. You can have a lousy first act but as long as you deliver in the second everyone will remember a marvellous performance. If on the other hand you are singing the Gaoler in *Tosca* and you fail to get out your first two phrases, that is it; the part is over, and the audience will say that it is obvious why you are not being given a larger role.

No two singers warm up in the same way. Some will just do exercises, others will sing through their lines, and the time taken to do either will vary enormously from singer to singer. A member of the audience standing in the corridor outside the principals' dressing rooms before a performance, and hearing some of the sounds that issue forth, could well be forgiven for dashing straight to the box office and demanding his money back. What happens on the stage, of course, is completely different.

On the day I was appointed to the Studio, Lord Harewood told me that he hoped I would be a 'track-suit manager', and that is what I try to be. After the initial, intensive musical preparation, I take the trainees on to the rehearsal stage and tell them, without any prompting from me, to get on and act out the scenes they have been allocated. The results are very informative. Some may already have some experience, others none at all. Some may show an immediate aptitude for the stage, while others may find it difficult to do much more than stand and sing. But there is one thing that they all have in common – a voice of operatic potential, and as long as they have that there is something rewarding to work on.

During our first term I was given carte blanche to engage whomever I wanted to help me teach them how to use the stage. I have seen many producers, working with experienced singers, who would say what they wanted and how they wanted it but then leave the singer to take it from there. They had neither the time nor the inclination to lead a youngster by the hand and tell them when to turn, when to move, when to stop. That aspect of the singer's art was *our* job. And so initially, as teachers, I went for those people who would know and understand the singer's problems, and that meant singers who could themselves act, people like Tito Gobbi, Regina Resnik and Graziella Sciutti. While watching them at work with our trainees, I noticed that they all had one gesture in common: a finger pointing up at the back of the room, reminding the youngsters where the audience is sitting.

One would expect an inexperienced singer to be conscious above all things, of the audience, and to adopt a somewhat formal stance with only the occasional foray into an attempt to act out a part. Almost the exact opposite is true. Thrown on to the stage to play, say, a duet, they will be so eager to 'act' that they will play it for themselves. They have to be reminded constantly that they are singing into the wings and that the audience, which has paid to see them, will be cupping their hands to their ears in frustration. It is difficult to make them realise that they are being trained to perform in a very large theatre holding upwards of two or three thousand people, and that their voices, whenever possible, must be directed within the bounds of the proscenium arch. In such a house and on a very large stage, they must also be taught that the full area must be used as much as possible, and that even in a love duet it is not necessary, or desirable, to get into close proximity too soon. A most moving duet can be performed with the singers a considerable distance apart – moving into a close embrace only at a suitably climactic moment in the music. In a play this would probably look ridiculous; in opera, it can be most effective.

The object is to teach our young singers to move into positions from which they can sing out into the auditorium in a most natural manner,

184

but at the same time, to encourage them to seize every opportunity to show their profile or back to the audience, as when, for example, they are listening to other artists or performing lightly accompanied recitative. This not only enables their colleagues to direct *their* voices out front, but also gives variety to their own stage movements, so that the audience will not be tempted to remark, as they depart for their interval refreshment, 'We've only seen the front of him so far'. It is for this reason that we take them to watch rehearsals in the main opera houses whenever possible, for to observe experienced singers making good singing 'angles' for each other is a wonderful lesson for them. This is preliminary work, but is not true production, of course; it is basic stage geography. Only after it has become second nature can detailed work on the interpretation of a part commence.

One of the main reasons why I distrust some producers who come to opera from the straight theatre is because they do not seem prepared to accept that this basic stage geography is necessary and that an aria, if it is to be heard to best advantage, has to be sung out to the front. There are no such restrictions in straight theatre. Ordinary theatres are generally much smaller than opera houses and the sound travels much more easily, and actors do not have an orchestra to ride over. The straight producer has carte blanche to interpret a piece as he wishes, but in opera, if he does not understand the acoustical problems of singing, he will not understand that singers, no matter how 'big' their voices, need to be singing in the direction of the audience whenever possible and be spared worrying 'business'.

An example of this occurred when Birgit Nilsson took over as Isolde in Peter Hall's Covent Garden production of *Tristan*. While singing the Liebestod, a difficult enough piece even for a singer of Nilsson's calibre, she was required to spread her cloak and walk *round* the dead body of Tristan, played by a ketchup-coated Jess Thomas. There had been no time to rehearse this move, and on the darkened set on the first night, Birgit misjudged the size of Jess and stumbled over his feet, almost falling flat on her face, just as she came to the words 'Höchste Lust'. Had she fallen it would have been a complete disaster. As she had also been asked, in the Act II love duet, to lie on top of Tristan, and then to have the process reversed (a direction she refused to carry out because she found she could not get enough breath to sing) she could hardly be blamed for putting the music first and declining to repeat her risky walk. She was much criticised, of course, at subsequent performances for 'ruining the production'.

185

I have always thought it self-evident that music is the main ingredient in any performance of opera. This, I know, is a view that is not shared universally and there are people in the profession who think that opera is nothing more than a play with music added. Most of these people happen to be producers who began their careers in straight theatre. Dr. Jonathan Miller, who has established a reputation as a producer of opera, was quoted in the magazine *Classical Music* as saying, 'My commitment is first of all to the language ... we make ourselves understood and we communicate with words, *not music* [my italics]. We do not sing notes to each other, we speak words, the cutting edge of the human mind is linguistic. No specific thought is expressed through notes or a sequence of notes. There is no dictionary which gives the meaning of a sequence of notes.' He went on to say that he dislikes critics who say 'it is in the music'. I find it hard to understand why Dr. Miller produces opera if he really believes what he says. Can it be that when he comes to produce *Tosca*, he will so concentrate on the words that he will fail to read anything into that magnificent and terrible sequence of chords that announce the entrance of Scarpia in the first act? Would that particular 'sequence of notes' have nothing to say to him? They tell me more about the character of Scarpia than a page of programme notes.

Miller concludes his observations with the comment, 'My only ambition with any opera production is to have the audience leave the theatre not *quite* sure whether it was an opera or a play they had seen.' No person trained in the musical tradition of opera could have made such a statement or have said that there is 'no dictionary which gives the meaning of a sequence of notes'. If what Miller was really trying to say was that he dislikes the operatic performance that concentrates on the music to the almost total exclusion of all else, in which one rarely hears the words because the singers are too busy making tone, and the acting is rudimentary, then I would agree with him. But to have expressed himself as he did, Miller demonstrates to me that he lacks that vital quality which every great producer needs – a feel for the music. Without it, no producer, however brilliant intellectually, can hope to bring forth a masterpiece.

To produce opera well a producer must know what the music is 'saying' at any given moment. The late Carl Ebert, one of the greatest of all opera producers, used to sit in at orchestral rehearsals with his friend Berthold Goldschmidt by his side making sure he missed nothing, noting everything down in his score. Consequently Ebert never did anything on stage that went against the music. This was one of the principal reasons he was so successful, for if the sound and the action match, if the thoughts and emotions expressed in the pit are reflected on the stage, then the production is halfway towards being successful already. If they do not, then no amount of fantastic costume designing, stunning sets or clever lighting will save the day.

Opera must, of course, be a visual as well as an aural experience, but while the eye should be pleased there are occasions when a choice has to be made between stage business which can only be brought off at the expense of the music, and a musical effect which can only be realised if the singer does something the producer would prefer him not to do. This situation arises in almost every traditional opera, and in my opinion the music must always come first. It is then that the differences occur between producer and conductor, or producer and singer. The non-musical producer will have a mental picture of what he wants to happen, and woe betide the singer who says, 'I can't do that. I need to breathe here,' or the conductor who says, 'If you have him looking off into the wings at that point he will not be able to pick up my beat.' It is at times like this that famous producers from the straight theatre have been known to break down and cry, 'My God, do we really *need* all this terrible music?'

It is both opera's strength, and its weakness, that it is illogical. It needs to be done extremely well if it is to transport its audience into a world of make-believe. Done badly, it can be just ridiculous. A singer is often required to repeat a line three, four or more times; he is often required to die from a bullet wound, a stab wound, or from tuberculosis (a particularly popular death for heroines this one), and as he or she is dying, will invariably be asked to sing louder than any mortal in his supposed condition would find possible. Two male singers can meet and swear eternal friendship within a matter of minutes; while a male and female singer can meet and take even less time to swear undying love. That is opera. Take away the music (that infernal music) and what is left? It is certainly not a play. The only way in which these situations, which seem so ridiculous on paper, can take hold of the emotions is because the music communicates on a deeper level than mere words. A repeated line is given different colouring or increased intensity with each repetition, while the dying heroine has the orchestra in support, reinforcing her emotions and *demanding* that the voice give more than would be possible in real life or even in the straight theatre. At moments like this the audience should be so immersed in the action that their disbelief is suspended. The emotions should be questioned no more than a cinema-goer would ask if there really *is* an orchestra behind the wainscoting as the girl goes upstairs towards the man with an open razor in a Hitchcock thriller.

To return to Jonathan Miller. Of course words are important and every effort should be made to get them across, but it is a sad fact of operatic life that this is not always possible. There are times when it is best for the singer to accept that the orchestra is in the driving seat and the voice must become one of the instruments in an overall sound. Such moments do not mean the scene loses impact because the words can't be heard clearly. It is precisely at those moments, when the orchestra is at its most overwhelming, that the orchestra is doing the 'speaking'. This is very often during the great ensembles when there may be four or five different sets of words being sung, and opposing factions may be making diametrically opposed statements. Where should the listener direct his attention in such cases, even if every single voice is enunciating clearly? The answer must be to the overall sound, for the orchestra is doing all the descriptive work and the voices are simply part of the process.

It is also impossible sometimes during duets and even arias to convey the words to the audience, particularly if there is an enormously difficult vocal line to be sustained in the very highest part of the vocal register. If, in such cases, a singer finds that the words have to take second place to the preservation of well-produced tone, he should not feel apologetic about it. If, in order to get every single word across clearly, he is compelled to make an unsatisfactory sound at odds with the rest of his voice, then clarity of diction must be sacrificed; the music must have priority.

I hope I have not given the impression that I consider producers as a species fail to understand the singer's problems and are unsympathetic to them. It is just that grand opera does seem to attract more than its fair share of people who are rather hazy as to what opera is all about, and who are learning as they go along, with varying degrees of success. The strange thing is that managements around the world actually seem to be more delighted to acquire a producer the less he has had to do with opera. I feel that it is part of my duty at the National Opera Studio to warn trainees against some types of producer they will eventually come across when they enter the profession.

On the other hand, there are very many really fine producers, many of whom I have had the privilege of working with over the years. Luchino Visconti knew what he was about and he used the music. He gave the singer credit for having thought about his part, generally allowing a scene to go through without interruption. When he did stop proceedings he would discuss the scene in great detail, not making changes for the sake of change, which made those he insisted on all the more important. Most important of all, Visconti always worked in harness with his conductor, never insisting on stage business that would interfere with the flow of the music. Franco Zeffirelli, too, can turn his hand to anything theatrical or cinematic, and also understands the special requirements of opera, as did Herbert Graf with whom I worked in Geneva. Graf knew every note of the score and was always looking for ways to use the music. He was one of those men who claimed you could find all the answers you needed in the music, and as far as *Der Rosenkavalier* is concerned, he was right, for Strauss, if you know where to look, has said everything.

Closer to home, producers like Colin Graham, John Cox and John Copley all have this same love and understanding of the music. Copley, like Graf, knows every note of every singer's part in any work he produces; but unlike Graf he is also capable of singing them. This can sometimes be a little disconcerting for he sings much better than any producer has a right to! Like Zeffirelli, John is a great experimenter and one must expect the preparation of scenes to be measured in days or even weeks rather than hours. At the end of it all you invariably play the part better than you did before and that, after all, is the true test for a successful producer.

These few names are by no means the only ones I consider to be good and successful producers of opera, but what they, and the others I haven't mentioned, have in common is a knowledge and love of the music which helps shape their productions, because they know that without music there is, quite simply, no opera.

If I feel it is my duty to warn the trainees against certain types of producer, I also feel I have to warn them against a certain type of designer. All too often during my career I have been asked to wear costumes of incredible weight, with accoutrements that frequently obscured my hearing and vision, none of which helped my performance. Perhaps the worst case for complaining I ever had was in 1953, when I sang Fafner in *Rheingold* for the first time. The performance was conducted by Fritz Stiedry, and my brother giant was played by Frederick Dalberg. We had heard on the grapevine that something special had been planned for us, and it had. The designer had given us revolting rubber heads to wear, and long rubber arms and hands, coloured a sickly grey-green and covered with coarse hair matted with congealed slime.

We saw them for the first time when we arrived at Covent Garden for the dress rehearsal. Fred gazed at them as they lay on the table and then proceeded to undress in grim silence. I followed his example. Having stripped off to his underpants Fred picked up his rubber head and tried it on. The back came down to the nape of his neck while the front part covered his face to a point just below the nose. His mouth was completely hidden by hanging hair, and his own ears were encased in large rubber ones. The effect was, as it was supposed to be, hideous.

Fred tried a few notes up and down the scale, carefully removed the head and called for the dresser. 'Scissors,' he commanded. 'But, Mr. Dalberg,' replied the dresser, his voice trembling, 'hadn't we better speak to somebody first?' 'Scissors,' repeated Fred. The dresser and I watched in horror as Fred took the scissors and began to cut away the front portion of the head just below the eyebrows. He then cut off the ears and, having completed the operation, put the head back on, looked at himself in the mirror, tried a few notes and pronounced himself satisfied. He then filled in the missing pieces with hair, spirit-gum and make-up. Much as he urged me to follow his example, I was still too much of a new boy to dare alter anything without permission and I wore the full contraption. People said after the rehearsal that my voice had seemed to lack its usual resonance but I failed to associate it with the fact that my hearing was impaired and my head encased in rubber; I thought everything had gone rather well.

In the dressing room before the first night Fred again tried to make me alter my head. 'Must have your nose and ears free, my lad,' he advised. But I was still too timid. How I wished later I had possessed the necessary courage. As I turned to sing my first line to him, I found myself singing in pitch darkness. I continued to sing of course (the cardinal rule in opera is to keep going no matter what happens), even though I was delivering my lines into a wall of rubber. My own head had turned inside the false one and I was singing out of my right ear! Worse was to follow. Having completed my phrase, I tried to turn back only to find that my nose was caught in my right ear and as I turned to the front, the rubber head suddenly veered over my left shoulder at an alarming angle. The natural thing to have done would have been to reach up and straighten the rubber head, but I was wearing my long, rubber arms with false hands, in to which our clubs had been glued because we had no chance of gripping them. I was due to sing again and I was still in complete darkness. Fred was aware of what was happening. 'Turn your head to the right, Mike,' he whispered, 'or the audience will think you've broken your bloody neck.' 'I can't see Stiedry,' I wailed. 'I'll tap you on the shoulder in time,' answered Fred, raising his left arm and proceeding to hit me. How we would have got through the entire scene I do not know, but Providence came to my rescue. My nose suddenly disengaged itself from my right ear, and I was able slowly to turn my face front until I could see out of the eyeholes in the mask. When we got back to our dressing room, Fred silently handed me the scissors.

Not every designer comes up with such outlandish designs but many do require singers to wear hats, cowls, large upstanding collars, heavy wigs, and so on, all of which interfere with hearing and prevent you placing your voice properly. Footwear, too, can also have its problems. In another performance of *Rheingold* I was required to wear a pair of built-up boots on a steeply sloping set. The inevitable happened: while making my final exit on the second performance, I stumbled, lost control of my feet and fell down some six or eight steps. I was lucky. I got away with just a bad shaking. A number of years later Gwynne Howell, again during a performance of *Rheingold*, injured himself so badly while trying to negotiate some steps in a similar type of built-up boot that he had his ankle in plaster for six weeks. The few extra inches of height gained by wearing such contraptions is definitely not worth it, and yet it happens all over the world almost every time *Rheingold* is performed. It is essential to have comfortable footwear, especially if you are singing a long role, and yet shoes or boots are often the last items of a costume to be considered. When Birgit Nilsson was asked by an aspiring soprano what advice she would give to anyone wanting to sing Isolde, Birgit replied, 'Make sure that you are wearing a comfortable pair of shoes, my dear.'

The greatest bugbear of all for the singer is the weight of the costumes. Men almost invariably come off worst in this because they often have to wear costumes made from the heaviest material which button up to the neck, have sleeves that come down to the wrist, complete with gloves, and also have to wear beards, moustaches, hats, fur collars and cloaks. In all there is probably about nine square inches of skin exposed from which the body heat is supposed to escape. It is no wonder that many singers have to be poured out of their costumes at the end of a performance. Whilst accepting that designers love elaborate and flamboyant creations dearly, I have always been puzzled by their insistence on using the heaviest materials. Many of the world's opera houses are vast places in which everything gains by being a little larger than life, including the costumes, but *heavier* than life? With the synthetic materials now available – lightweight and authentic-looking from the front row of the stalls – why not use them? Why insist on real velvet, real leather, real metal, even real chain-mail, when substitutes are available at a fraction of their weight, not to mention cost? I have never been given a satisfactory explanation.

The only time I was ever on the carpet in front of Webster was over a difference of opinion concerning a costume. I had taken over from Joseph Rouleau as Ramphis in *Aida*. It was a sweltering summer evening as I changed into my costume and I remarked that although it was heavy and I was already starting to perspire, I did not think it was unmanageable. As I was about to go down to the stage, Leon, my dresser, stopped me. 'We have to put on your cloak, Mr. Langdon,' he murmured. The cloak in question was made from quilted material, was about ten feet long, and required two dressers to lift it onto my shoulders. Not only was it heavy, I found it almost impossible to move in. When I attempted to turn no amount of kicking would flip it in the new direction. For one of the few times in my career I lost my temper. 'I will not wear this bloody thing!' I roared. Stella Chitty, the stage manager, did her best to try and persuade me but I was adamant. If I wore the cloak, I told her, I would probably pass out; if I didn't wear it, I could possibly complete the performance. I was exaggerating, of course, but I felt it was a matter of principle. I did, however, make one concession: I carried a staff of office that had not been included in the original design. And on I went.

A few days later I was summoned to appear before Webster to explain why I had refused to wear the cloak. He listened quizzically as I gave my reasons, then asked why I had not complained at my first fitting. I pointed out that Joseph Rouleau had sung in the first series and that I had been away at the time of the fitting. 'All right, Langdon,' Webster said eventually, 'I am prepared to accept your reasons, especially as no one has written in to complain of your being improperly dressed, but I have some advice for you.' I waited expectantly. 'I believe you are singing the part of Narbal in *The Trojans* next season?' I nodded that I was. 'And Mr. Narbal is a High Priest like Mr. Ramphis, if I remember correctly?' I nodded again. 'Then my dear fellow,' he went on, 'go without delay and have a word with the designer. Try to persuade him to reduce the weight of your costume if possible. Explain your propensity for fainting when the weather is hot. You see, the man who designed the *Aida* costumes is also designing for *The Trojans*.' I took his advice and went to see Nicholas Georgiadis at the earliest opportunity. He was extremely understanding and dispensed with several layers from his original design, and also found some beautifully lightweight material for my robe. The finished costume looked magnificent and I was certainly the most comfortable singer on the stage when we came to perform the opera. In fact it was probably just the sort of thing a High Priest in that part of the world *would* have worn. So it *can* be done.

It is obviously very difficult, if not impossible, for young singers to complain about the costumes they are asked to wear. If they did, they would probably lose their contract. There are, however, ways of getting round some of the problems which I try to pass on to them. The first thing they have to learn is never to criticise. They must say during a first fitting whether the costume is comfortable but they must never criticise. If a cloak is too long and can't be shortened because the designer says it would ruin his effect, the singer must not make a fuss and refuse to go on stage. Only star names can get away with that. The young singer must go on, do his best to manage the cloak, but if it gets entangled round his feet, ensure that the damaging effect is seen, and preferably fall over. Before he has a chance to get up, there will be someone there with a pair of scissors cutting off a couple of inches. Similarly, if a hat or wig obscures the hearing, it is important not to try and compensate for the fact that you can't hear yourself properly. Instead, sing flat if you must and then, when the conductor speaks to you about it, make a great show of removing the offending headgear before being able to hear him properly. If he doesn't take the point first time round, put the hat back on and then sing flat again. The art of getting a costume changed is to demonstrate the problems it causes, not to argue about it.

There is another hazard today's opera singer has to cope with, and this is the increasing use of mechanical sets. Fortunately my experience of these was limited, but I have been told horrifying tales by artists who could not get back on stage because they were caught in the air on a piece of failed equipment, and of things moving on and off at the wrong time because something had gone wrong with the mechanics. And they can sometimes make a very distracting hum or vibration, neither of which helps the singer pitch his notes or hear the orchestra. One of the few occasions on which I had to work on a mechanical set was in *The*

Dutchman at the Garden, designed by Sean Kenny. The central piece of his design was a huge slab mounted on pistons driven by a motor and controlled by a board in the prompt corner. This slab could be tilted backwards or forwards, or from side to side, or a combination of both, and very precise musical cues were worked out for its movements. In the first scene, the slab represented the deck of Daland's ship, while in the next, suitably tilted, it represented the floor of Daland's house, complete with spinning wheels anchored against the slope. It is fair to say it looked nothing at all like either! It also malfunctioned regularly and we never knew what to expect it to do next. Perhaps the worst mishap was at the end of the first scene after the great male chorus. The wheel would be swung to the left and the whole slab would swing that way as the ship supposedly got under way. We, naturally, all braced our right legs against the swing. On this particular night the man on the control board pressed the wrong button, the ship swung right instead of left, and the entire crew fell over.

In pointing out these possible pitfalls to our trainees I do not feel I am undermining the authority of certain producers and designers; I am simply looking to the singers' interests. I bless the tips given to me in my own early days by older singers like Frederick Dalberg and David Tree. Most singers are intelligent enough to adapt advice to their own needs and, ultimately, to their own betterment. Of the thirty-six singers who passed through the Studio during its first three years of operation, twenty-six have achieved their first objective – a successful entry into the profession. Of these, twelve have landed contracts with companies (two in Germany), while the other fourteen have either decided or were compelled by circumstances (mainly the scarcity of money for new contracts) to embark on a freelance career. Some of these freelance singers will be heard of internationally one day, I am sure, although to mention names would be invidious. Of the remaining ten who, by our own standards I deem to have been unsuccessful, some may yet make the grade, given the luck to be 'liked by the right people at the right time'. In the Glyndebourne tour of autumn 1981, for instance, no less than nine principal parts in two of the operas being staged were taken by Studio singers. Six of our repetiteurs have also made a successful start, including two with home-based companies and one as Head of Music in Nancy.

This record of success, somewhat to everyone's surprise at the Studio, is not generally known, however. This applies especially to some of our eminent music critics, who are obviously waiting for us to perform a full length opera, although the brief assigned to us by the Arts Council Working Party stipulates that we should prepare young professional singers, within the period of a one year course, for entry into one or other of the main Opera Companies in Great Britain. For reasons that should be self-evident the casting and performing of a complete opera within the allotted time is out of the question. Even if we felt that a full performance would be of benefit to our specialized operation, our policy of taking only the best voices, regardless of their particular range, makes the whole idea quite impossible.

At the beginning of January 1979, some two months after the first course had started at the Studio, I returned to Scotland to sing my final performances of Ochs. It was entirely coincidental that this role should have been my last, for it just happened to be the last firm engagement I had had in my diary on the night I had decided to retire. Strangely enough I did not feel very emotional during the performance on 4th January. I remember thinking, as I sang certain phrases, that it would be the last time I would be singing them in public, but I did not feel my life's work was over, rather that one phase of my career was ending and a new one was beginning At the end of the performance I was presented with a cartoon portrait by Emilio Coia of myself as Baron Ochs and given a reception. It was a memorable occasion, and after returning to my hotel I slept like a log – all the tension of impending performances behind me. Although Glasgow was completely snowbound and icy I startled my wife the next morning by dispensing with my undervest – retaining only my underpants. I donned a shirt and suit, pulled on my overcoat, and sallied forth without either hat or scarf! And so it has been since that day. No longer do I muffle up against a cool breeze for fear of catching cold, or rush for the Vitamin C at the slightest sign of a snuffle. Needless to say, I rarely, if ever, catch cold nowadays!

But it was not to be my last appearance as Ochs! Just over a year later Opera North had both their Ochses unavailable at the same time and I was asked to come out of singing retirement for two performances in Hull. What pleased me immensely was that I first picked up my score to check the part the day before leaving for Hull and that I did not even take it with me to the theatre. The performances, which were given in English while I sang in German, were most enjoyable, largely because they were so unexpected, and they proved to me that my reasons for retiring were the right ones. There is little virtue if you are, for instance, a footballer who can no longer run after the ball, in announcing that you intend to retire. I found in Hull that I was unimpaired vocally and physically, and that I was still singing well. I knew I had not given up because I could no longer sing.

Had I become the star of the summer seasons that I had wanted when I first embarked on my career as a singer, I would probably after four or five years have become so fed up that I would have dropped everything. I became an opera singer by accident but it was the happiest of accidents. It has taken me round the world, and it has encompassed everything, from extreme success to those periods when no one seemed to want to know me. Every singer becomes known for a certain type of role and I would perhaps have liked to have been better known as Philip in *Don Carlos*, as Fiesco in *Boccanegra* or as Boris, and yet at the same time I have to be realistic and admit that perhaps my particular voice would not have been as well suited to those roles. Christoff, after all, who was so effective in these roles, would not have been as successful as Ochs, Kecal or Osmin. You are fortunate if you discover early in your career what your strengths are and even more fortunate if you are permitted to demonstrate them. What stood me in good stead throughout my career was that people recognised in me, before I even knew it myself, a talent for amusing people. Above all things I am pleased that I became noted as the only non-German-speaking international exponent of the role of Ochs.

From the time my career began until I retired from active singing, I have seen a steady development in the prestige of the British singer abroad to the present position where they are welcomed anywhere in the world. For some reason there used to be the belief overseas that British singers could not sing, that the international British artist was a phenomenon. Whereas it was expected that the Italian peasant might develop into a world-famous tenor or baritone, no one ever thought the man working in a factory in Birmingham could possibly do the same thing. It was an attitude perpetuated by people like Sir Thomas Beecham who said that we 'eat the wrong sort of food' and 'don't get enough sunshine'. Now British singers can be heard wherever opera is performed in the world, and we have artists' agents coming to the National Opera Studio from abroad to hear our next generation of singers. I am proud to have been among those singers who helped carry the flag into far-off opera houses, and I am proud that I still have a part to play in making sure that British talent will continue to be heard on the stages of the world.

Index

rehearses with Solti, 1961 93; plays Pistol in *Falstaff* 94–6; plays Ochs in Hamburg 96, 97–8; plays Ochs in Berlin, 1962 104; plays in *Rosenkavalier* with Schwarzkopf 104–5, 108, 109–10, 113–14; commutes between Paris and Lausanne 105–6; plays San Francisco, 1962 108–11; strains tendon 110; plays Los Angeles and San Diego 111; plays in *Die Walküre* and *Falstaff*, Covent Garden, 1962 111; plays Ochs in Vienna 111–13; gives up counting method of keeping time 114–15; Covent Garden roles, 1963 115, 116, 118, 119; plays Sarastro and Ochs in Budapest 119–21; plays Ochs in Switzerland 121–5; refines characterisation of Ochs 121–3; single performance of Ochs at New York Met, 1964 125–7; has successful ankle operation 129, 130; problems with 'cuts' singing Ochs in Berlin 130–1; plays in *Arabella* at Covent Garden 131–2; plays in *Fidelio* in Marseilles 132; plays in *Moses and Aaron* at Covent Garden 133; engagements for 1965–6 season 134–5; plays Ochs in Stuttgart 134–5; plays in Visconti's *Rosenkavalier* at Covent Garden 135–7; has problems with costumes in *Rosenkavalier* 135–6, 137; fails to record *Rosenkavalier* with Solti 137–8, 140, 141; international appearances as Ochs 138; in Gala performance at Covent Garden, 1967 138; in Covent Garden revival of *Rosenkavalier*, 1968 140–1; plays Claggart in recording of *Billy Budd* 141; problems with voice, 1968–9 142–54 *passim*; programme for 1968–9 season at Covent Garden 142–7, 148; sings Ochs in Seattle 147; programme for 1969–70 season 148–54; sings Ochs in Monte Carlo 149–50; plays Ochs in Aberdeen 150–1; has voice problems at Paris Opera 152; cures voice problems

with help of cat 152–3; plays Baron Ochs for 100th time 154; engaged by Solti to play Osmin in Tel Aviv 160–1; busy programme in 1972 161; redeems reputation at Paris Opera 161–2; attends daughters' weddings 162; plays *Don Pasquale* for Scottish Opera, 1972–3 162–3; plays Ochs in Geneva 163–4; decline of Covent Garden career post-1972 164–6; programme for 1973–5 165–6; plays in *Hermiston* for Scottish Opera 165; programme for 1975–6 season at Covent Garden 167–9; sings last Ochs at Covent Garden 167; unhappy with *We Came To The River* 167–9; plays *Fidelio* in Cleveland 169; plays Osmin in Cardiff 169–70; disillusioned about Covent Garden career 170–1; plays Nicolai's Falstaff at Wexford 171–2; problem of padding for Falstaff 171–2; decides to retire from stage in 1979 172–3; decides to teach 172–4; awarded CBE 173; gives classes at Guildhall School 173; question of directorship of National Opera Studio 175–8; offered job of Company Manager at Covent Garden 176; accepts directorship of National Opera Studio 178, 179; programme for 1977–8 season 176–7, 178–9; plays in *Die Fledermaus* at Covent Garden, 1978 178–9; engaged on establishing National Opera Studio 180–2; work at National Opera Studio 183–5; defends Studio from criticism, 1981 195; sings final performance of Ochs 196

on 'conversations' on stage 48–9
on energy of opera singer 182–3
on importance of music in opera 186–8
on importance of warming up 183
on mechanical sets 193–4
on opera producers 185–7, 188–9
on parts for basses 95
on problems posed by costume designers 189–93